CHARLES S. PEIRCE
THE ESSENTIAL WRITINGS

Charles S. Peirce
The Essential Writings

Edited by Edward C. Moore

Preface by Richard Robin

GREAT BOOKS IN PHILOSOPHY

 Prometheus Books

59 John Glenn Drive
Amherst, New York 14228-2197

Published 1998 by Prometheus Books

Charles S. Peirce: The Essential Writings. Copyright © 1972, 1988 by the estate of Edward C. Moore. Preface © 1998 by Richard Robin. All rights reserved. No part of this publication may be reproduced, stored in a retrieval system, or transmitted in any form or by any means, electronic, mechanical, photocopying, re- cording, or otherwise, without prior written permission of the publisher, except in the case of brief quotations embodied in critical articles and reviews. Inquiries should be addressed to Prometheus Books, 59 John Glenn Drive, Amherst, New York 14228–2197, 716–691–0133. FAX: 716–691–0137. WWW.PROMETHEUSBOOKS.COM.

02 01 00 99 98 5 4 3 2 1

Library of Congress Cataloging-in-Publication Data

Peirce, Charles S. (Charles Sanders), 1839–1914.
 [Selections. 1998]
 Charles S. Peirce : the essential writings / edited by
Edward C. Moore ; preface by Richard Robin.
   p.   cm.
 Originally published: New York : Harper & Row, 1972.
 Includes bibliographical references.
 ISBN 1–57392–256–0 (alk. paper)
 1. Philosophy. I. Moore, Edward C. (Edward Carter),
1917–   . II. Title.
B945.P41M66   1998
191—dc21   98–47538
                                              CIP

Printed in the United States of America on acid-free paper

Additional Titles on Metaphysics and Epistemology in Prometheus's Great Books in Philosophy Series

Aristotle
De Anima

Aristotle
The Metaphysics

George Berkeley
Three Dialogues Between Hylas and Philonous

René Descartes
Discourse on Method and
The Meditations

John Dewey
How We Think

John Dewey
The Influence of Darwin on Philosophy and Other Essays

Epicurus
*The Essential Epicurus:
Letters, Principal Doctrines,
Vatican Sayings, and Fragments*

Sidney Hook
The Quest for Being

David Hume
*An Enquiry Concerning
Human Understanding*

David Hume
Treatise of Human Nature

William James
The Meaning of Truth

William James
Pragmatism

Immanuel Kant
Critique of Practical Reason

Immanuel Kant
Critique of Pure Reason

Gottfried Wilhelm Leibniz
Discourse on Metaphysics and
The Monadology

John Locke
*An Essay Concerning
Human Understanding*

Plato
The Euthyphro, Apology, Crito,
and *Phaedo*

Bertrand Russell
The Problems of Philosophy

George Santayana
The Life of Reason

Sextus Empiricus
Outlines of Pyrrhonism

See the back of this volume for a complete list of titles in Prometheus's Great Books in Philosophy and Great Minds series.

CHARLES SANDERS PEIRCE was born in Cambridge, Massachusetts, on September 10, 1839. He graduated from Harvard in 1859 and earned a degree from Harvard's Lawrence Scientific school in 1863. A philosopher, mathematician, and logician, until 1891 Peirce was associated with the United States Coast and Geodetic Survey, an organization concerned with measurements of the earth's geographical features. Peirce's work on gravity determinations gained him international acclaim, and he was elected to the American Academy of Arts and Sciences, the National Academy of Sciences, and the London Mathematical Society. From 1888 until his death, Peirce lived on an isolated farm near Milford, Pennsylvania, conducting research and writing papers.

Peirce has been called one of America's most original and versatile thinkers, although his accomplishments are far from well-known. The founder of the philosophical movement known as pragmatism (which he later called pragmaticism to distinguish it from popularized versions such as that of William James), Peirce argued that the truth of any assertion is to be evaluated from its practical consequences and its bearing on human interests. In other words, concepts are to be understood in terms of their practical implications.

Peirce's chief interest was logic, on which he lectured at Johns Hopkins University from 1879 to 1884 (he was creator of the algebra of logic), but he also cofounded the science of signs (semiotics), designed an electric switching-circuit computer, was the first modern psychologist in the United States, and an expert on the pronunciation of Elizabethan English.

Having resigned from the Coast and Geodetic Survey over disagreements regarding the methods and careful quality of his work (called procrastination by some), Pierce lived out his last years in poverty and illness, dying at his Pennsylvania farm on August 19, 1914.

Contents

Preface by Richard Robin   xi
Foreword   xv

Introduction   1

  I. Preface to an Unwritten Book, 1897–98   45

 II. Review of the Works of George Berkeley—1871   51

III. Questions Concerning Certain Faculties
      Claimed for Man   64
      (The Journal of Speculative Philosophy
      series of 1868)
        1. Questions Concerning Certain Faculties
          Claimed for Man   66
        2. Some Consequences of Four Incapacities   85

 IV. Illustrations of the Logic of Science   119
      (Part of the Popular Science Monthly
      series of 1877–78)
        1. The Fixation of Belief   120
        2. How to Make Our Ideas Clear   137

  V. A Guess at the Riddle   158
      (The Monist series of 1891–92)
        1. The Architecture of Theories   159

2. The Doctrine of Necessity Examined   174
3. The Law of Mind   190
4. Man's Glassy Essence   216
5. Evolutionary Love   237

VI. Pragmatism and Pragmaticism   261
     (Part of the Monist series of 1905)
     1. What Pragmatism Is   262
     2. Issues of Pragmatism   281

VII. Some Contributions to Baldwin's Dictionary—
     1902   300
     1. Pragmatism   300
     2. Uniformity   302
     3. Synechism   312

Suggestions for Further Reading   315

Suggestions for Future Reading (Post 1972)   319

Preface

Since 1972—the year Edward C. Moore's edited volume of *Charles S. Peirce: The Essential Writings* first appeared—much has transpired in the area of Peirce scholarship with the consequence of increasing dramatically Peirce's already well-established reputation as a philosopher of the first rank. Indisputably America's greatest philosopher he has broken through national boundaries and presently is regarded by many as one of the eminent philosophers ever, placed in the company of those who influenced him most—Aristotle, Leibniz, Kant and Hegel. Although Peirce died eighty-five years ago, he has become a living presence in the sense that his views have entered forcefully into contemporary debates on a score of questions, epistemological and metaphysical, ranging from questions concerning meaning and truth, sign theory, and ontological commitment to highly speculative questions of a cosmological and religious kind.

To appreciate how much Peirce's worldwide stock has grown, one needs only to note the numerous translations of significant portions of his work. It now can be said that there are Peirce scholars all over the map. Indeed two international congresses devoted to Peirce were held. The Bicentennial Congress in the Netherlands was a prelude to the week-long Sesquicentennial Harvard Congress which included some 450 scholars, representing 26 countries, all actively engaged. That engagement yielded several collections of papers. The plenary papers were published under the title of *Peirce and Contemporary Thought* (K. L. Ketner editor). Papers on mathematics and formal logic appeared under the title of *Studies in the Logic of Charles Sanders Peirce* (N. Houser, D. Roberts, J. Van Evra editors). Semeiotic, its theory and practice, is the subject of *Peirce's Doctrine of Signs* (V. Colapietro and T. Olshewsky editors); epistemology of *Living Doubt* (G. Debrock and M. Hulswit editors). *Charles S. Peirce and the Philosophy of Science* and *From Time and Chance to Consciousness* contain papers on the broad dimensions of science and on metaphysical underpinnings and speculation respectively. Both were edited by E. Moore, the latter in collaboration with me. The fallout included *Peirce and Law* (R. Kevelson editor). The Sesquicentennial was a fitting celebration and tribute to Peirce's legacy as philosopher, logician, scientist.

These compilations are a relatively small sample of the writing that deal in one fashion or another with Peirce, which is to say that much has been added to what was known about Peirce prior to 1972. Even so much of the essentials remains the same. The editor of the *Essential Writings* chose his texts shrewdly for their inherent interest and suspected longevity. They are from different periods of Peirce's life and cover representative subject matter. Taken together, the texts reveal the systematic character of Peirce's thought and its comprehensiveness. Moore is at pains to reinforce this in his lengthy introduction, written in a straightforwardly clear style, admirably suited for its purpose. His discussion of the nominalist/realist controversy, imperative for coming to terms with Peirce, is again a model of exposition.

Of course, the problem with clarity in the face of enormous complexity is that it may settle nothing, thereby creating openings for disagreement. Disagreement is nothing to fear any more than the complexity of Peirce's thought that gives rise to it. That complexity is what makes Peirce exciting to rad and rewarding when fully understood.

Texts other than those comprising *Essential Writings* inevitably came to mind, undoubtedly texts Moore himself must have considered and set aside because of space limitations. The only change in *Essential Writings* that was made was mandated by the need to update the original "Suggestions for Future Reading." One addition, the first full scale biography of Peirce, deserves special recognition. Joseph Brent's biography, recently revised and enlarged, offers a balanced and sympathetic portrait of Peirce which treats him as the tragic figure he actually was. Born with genius-like gifts into the most favorable of social circumstances, Peirce was programmed for success. Yet his life was a downward spiral. There is a story here asking to be told.

Foreword

Charles S. Peirce published no book in philosophy. He published a great many articles and he left unpublished an even larger amount of manuscript material. Although he tried to organize his material into book form, he never successfully did so. He described himself as "a mere table of contents . . . a very snarl of twine." To seek to present the thought of Peirce in one volume is, therefore, to seek to accomplish something he himself found to be a matter of great difficulty.

In the absence of published books by Peirce, a natural focus is on his published articles. This choice has several advantages. First of all, these articles represent materials that Peirce himself saw as properly complete for publication. A second advantage is that such material can be presented chronologically. Chronology is one of the major problems that students of Peirce's work need to deal with constantly. Peirce had an active writing career extending over fifty years. To ignore changes and developments in his philosophy during this time span is to omit a factor of real importance and leads to interpretations of Peirce as having been contradictory and inconsistent.

A final advantage of working primarily from Peirce's published articles in philosophy is that he tended to concentrate them into four major groups, each with a somewhat different emphasis and each spaced at different periods in his working life. The first series of three articles appeared in *The Journal of Speculative Philosophy* in 1868. They dealt with "Questions Concerning Certain Faculties Claimed for Man," and state Peirce's basic epistemology. The present collection includes two of the three articles in this series in their complete form. The second series consisted of five articles in *The Popular Science Monthly* for 1877–78. The first two are included here. They describe Peirce's early pragmatism and his notion of the nature of scientific inquiry. The third series appeared in *The Monist* in 1891–93. Borrowing a title from a proposed book of Peirce's, I have called them "A Guess at the Riddle." They contain Peirce's basic metaphysics and are included completely. The final series on Peirce's later pragmatism appeared in *The Monist* in 1905–06, and included three articles of which the first two are reproduced here.

To introduce this material, I have provided an early (1871) book review of Berkeley, in which Peirce states his doctrine of scholastic realism, and have concluded with some of the entries he prepared for Baldwin's *Dictionary.*

While these selections will not be a substitute for the full collection of Peirce papers, they will provide the interested reader with a basic grasp of Peirce's fundamental philosophy. Hopefully, the reader may feel encouraged to look beyond them into the total work of the finest philosopher the United States has yet produced.

—EDWARD C. MOORE
State University of New York at Binghamton

Editorial Note

The *Collected Papers of Charles Sanders Peirce* have been published in eight volumes by Harvard University Press, 1931–58. References to the Peirce papers are customarily made by volume and paragraph, thus (5.585) is to be interpreted to mean volume V, paragraph 585 of the *Collected Papers*.

Introduction

Charles Sanders Peirce

I

Charles Sanders Peirce was born in Cambridge, Massachusetts in 1839 and died in Milford, Pennsylvania in 1914. In a recent assessment of Peirce as a philosopher, Ernest Nagel wrote that "there is a fair consensus among historians of ideas that Charles Sanders Peirce remains the most original, versatile, and comprehensive philosophical mind this country has yet produced."[1] Although Peirce published a wide variety of papers and reviews, he published only one book (*Photometric Researches*, Leipzig, 1878) and that was not in philosophy. In 1923, Morris R. Cohen edited a volume, collecting some of Peirce's published papers, under the title of *Chance, Love and Logic*, but it was not until Harvard University Press published volumes one through six of *The Collected Papers of Charles Sanders Peirce* in 1931 to 1936 under the editorship of Charles Hartshorne and Paul Weiss and volumes seven and eight in 1958 under the editorship of Arthur W. Burks that American philosophers began to be aware of the range and depth of Peirce's work.

Since the appearance of *The Collected Papers*, a considerable interest in the philosophy of Peirce has developed, both in this country and abroad. A wide range of book-length studies, an extensive group of articles, an association of Peirce scholars—The Charles S. Peirce Society—and a quarterly journal, *The Transactions of the Charles S. Peirce Society*, all evidence the growing recognitions of Peirce's importance.

---

[1] Ernest Nagel, *The Scientific American*, 200 (1959): 185.

Although Peirce is best known as the founder of the philosophical doctrine known as pragmatism—and had a considerable influence on William James and John Dewey—it is becoming increasingly clear that Peirce was first and foremost a scientist. The philosophical problems he was most interested in were those of the scientist. For this reason among others he belongs in the tradition of Aristotle. He was a precursor of philosophical scientists like William James, who was a physiologist; P. W. Bridgman, a physicist; and Michael Polanyi, a chemist.

Peirce's father, Benjamin Peirce (1809–90), was a distinguished professor of mathematics at Harvard University; Peirce himself received a bachelor of arts degree from Harvard in 1859, a master of arts in 1862, and a bachelor of science in chemistry in 1863. He worked as an assistant at the Harvard Observatory from 1869 to 1872 and made a series of astronomical observations there from 1872 to 1875. Solon I. Bailey says of these observations, which were the base of Peirce's book *Photometric Researches*, "The first attempt at the Harvard Observatory to determine the form of the Milky Way, or the galactic system, was made by Charles S. Peirce. . . . The investigation was of a pioneer nature, founded on scant data."[2]

Peirce was employed for over thirty years by the United States Coast and Geodetic Survey as a physicist.[3] He did significant work on the determination of the gravitational constant and ultimately left the Coast and Geodetic Survey in a dispute with his superiors about the reliability of the pendulum technique used for making such determinations. His position has only recently been vindicated and a whole series of subsequent observations are now considered questionable.[4]

Peirce made major contributions also in mathematics and logic. C. I. Lewis has remarked that, "The head and front of mathematical

[2]Solon I. Bailey, *The History and Work of Harvard Observatory, 1839–1927*, Harvard Observatory. Monograph No. 4 (New York: McGraw Hill, 1931), pp. 198–199.

[3]In 1963 the Coast and Geodetic Survey commissioned a survey ship, *Peirce CSS 28*, named after Charles Peirce. At that time the Director of the Coast and Geodetic Survey, Rear Admiral H. Arnold Karo, wrote me that, "In addition to being a logician and philosopher, Peirce made many important scientific and technical contributions to the Coast and Geodetic Survey during his thirty years of service in the bureau."

[4]Victor F. Lenzen, "An Unpublished Scientific Monograph by C. S. Peirce" in *The Transactions of the Charles S. Peirce Society*, 1969 V, no. 1, p. 5–24.

logic is found in the calculus of propositional functions as developed by Peirce and Schröeder. . . ."[5]

Peirce invented, almost from whole cloth, the study of signs. Ogden and Richards say that, "By far the most elaborate and determined attempt to give an account of signs and their meanings is that of the American logician C. S. Peirce, from whom William James took the idea and the term Pragmatism, and whose Algebra of Dyadic Relations was developed by Schröeder."[6] The range of Peirce's interests was such that he has been compared to Leibniz.

Nevertheless, Peirce received little recognition from American intellectuals during his lifetime. His personality traits were such that he often offended men of eminence. He taught for a few years at Johns Hopkins and gave a few public lectures at Cambridge, Massachusetts. Most of his income came from book reviews and from his work for the Coast and Geodetic Survey. In 1891 he inherited a house in Milford, Pennsylvania and lived there until his death in 1914. He died in the greatest poverty, unknown except to a few friends. Upon his death his wife sold his unpublished manuscripts to Harvard University. Difficulties in editing the cartons of manuscripts protracted the process of making the papers generally available to scholars. Only recently have all the papers been made available on microfilm through the Harvard University Microreproduction Service, and an annotated catalogue has been published so that American scholars can now study the Peirce papers carefully and fully.[7]

II

Perhaps because the material published in *The Collected Papers* dealt primarily with matters of philosophical concern, the first phase of Peirce studies was based on the belief that Peirce was primarily a philosopher who only incidentally made his living as a scientist. Largely due to the

[5] C. I. Lewis and H. L. Langford, *Symbolic Logic* (New York: The Century Company, 1932), p. 21.

[6] C. K. Ogden and I. A. Richards, *The Meaning of Meaning* (London: Routledge and Kegan Paul, Ltd., 1949), p. 279.

[7] Richard S. Robin, *An Annotated Catalogue of the Papers of Charles S. Peirce* (Amherst: The University of Massachusetts Press, 1967).

efforts of Victor Lenzen, American philosophers are coming to realize
that Peirce was first of all a scientist. His interest in philosophical
problems was that of a scientist. Max H. Fisch has written of Peirce that
in his own day "he was known and valued chiefly as a scientist, only
secondarily as a logician, and scarcely at all as a philosopher. Even his
work in philosophy and logic will not be understood until this fact
becomes the standing premise of Peircean studies."[8]

The present collection is intended to present the broad spectrum of
Peirce's thought. However, the focus of the selections is on those questions that Peirce regarded as basic: the nature of potentiality, the validity
of the process of scientific inquiry, and the problem of the definition of
concepts. These questions are basically metaphysical in nature and have
pervasive philosophical implications.

For Peirce these problems did not come from a background of previous philosophy but rather from his concerns in science. The problem of
the nature of potentiality came from his concern to understand the
notion of a scientific law. While this led him back into a study of the
views of earlier philosophers, and particularly of the medieval scholastics,
still the origins of his interest came from his scientific concerns not from
philosophy as such. He developed a detailed position about the nature
of potentiality in his "scholastic realism."

The problem of the validity of the process of scientific inquiry obviously came from his background in science. This problem was of great
interest to the nineteenth century which, as a result of the work of
Darwin, had a pervasive concern for articulating the methods of scientific inquiry and the methods of religious inquiry. Peirce's work here led
him to his view of scientists as a community of investigators and to his
definitions of truth and reality as the culmination of the work of such
a community.

Peirce's peculiar genius is perhaps nowhere more evident than in the
manner in which he came to formulate his theory of the definition of
concepts—his doctrine of pragmatism. He here picked up almost casu-

[8]Max H. Fisch, "A Draft of a Bibliography of Writings about C. S. Peirce," in Edward
C. Moore and Richard S. Robin, eds., *Studies in the Philosophy of Charles Sanders Peirce:
Second Series* (Amherst: The University of Massachusetts Press, 1964), p. 486.

ally the problem that was to be the chief concern of twentieth-century philosophy—the problem of an adequate theory of meaning—solved it as a scientist would solve it and as well as it would be solved for a hundred years—and dropped it into an article that lay ignored and forgotten for two decades after it was written. To call Peirce the father of pragmatism is something akin to calling Mendel the father of Darwinism. Peirce first stated his pragmatic doctrine in 1878 in the essay "How To Make Our Ideas Clear." No attention was paid to it until William James (1842–1910) referred to it in another connection in a popular lecture "Philosophical Conceptions and Practical Results" in 1898. James published this essay in 1904 and the movement known as pragmatism was launched. The uses to which James put the doctrine were alien to Peirce, and he spent the next decade trying to take credit for having originated the term but seeking to dissociate himself from James's version of it.

Finally, it should be noted that Peirce's work was not influenced greatly by previous philosophers, other than in his scholastic realism, nor by his contemporaries. Although he knew both Kant and Hegel he is not akin to either of them. He resembles Kant in using "categories" but they are not the categories of Kant. He resembles Hegel in his basic insistence upon the categories as being triadic, but Peirce's triad is not that of Hegel. Although he shared with Josiah Royce (1855–1916) the notion of community, the debt was from Royce to Peirce. Although he shared with William James the notion of pragmatism, the debt was from James to Peirce. Peirce was an authentic genius, who was at least fifty years ahead of his time. The problems he dealt with in the philosophy of science and in theory of meaning have been the chief preoccupation of philosophers of our day.

III

The writings of Peirce reveal two basic themes. He is most widely known for his epistemological position which he named pragmatism; or, in order to give a distinctive name to his own version of it, pragmaticism. Peirce's pragmatic theory of meaning has been favorably received by many philosophers of our day who tend toward a positivistic interpretation of philosophy. But Peirce also argued for a metaphysics which he called metaphysical or scholastic realism. This side of his thought has been neglected, in spite of the fact that Peirce himself said that "Before we treat of the evidences of pragmaticism, it will be needful to weigh the pros and cons of scholastic realism. For pragmaticism could scarcely have entered a head that was not already convinced that there are real generals" (5.503).

Peirce, therefore, did not think that his pragmatism was metaphysically neutral. He thought it was grounded in the metaphysics of scholastic realism. His pragmatism grew out of his interest in the controversy over the nature of universals. Bertrand Russell, in commenting on Peirce's interest in this problem, said, "I think Peirce was right in regarding the realist-nominalist controversy as one which is still undecided and which is as important now as at any other time."[9]

The realist-nominalist controversy is often interpreted as an issue revolving around the question of whether there are real Platonic entities. There is enough discussion of this question in the controversy to provide some grounds for this interpretation. But to accept this view is to make a shift in emphasis that leads to an important misunderstanding of the problem. Peirce's irritation with this version of the controversy led him to make a rather extreme statement. "The notion that the controversy between realism and nominalism had anything to do with Platonic ideas is a mere product of the imagination which the slightest examination of the books would suffice to disprove" (8.17). Although overstating the situation, this statement should at least serve to indicate that, for Peirce, the primary emphasis in the controversy was not on the problem of Platonic entities.

The crucial issue is this: All of our knowledge consists of concepts. These concepts are such that they may be predicated of different objects and hence they are universals. But objects in the external world appear to be particular determinate individuals. The question, then, is whether anything in the external world corresponds to our concepts of it. If all our knowledge is universal, and if all that exists is particular, then our concepts have no external analogue and are mere fictions; they do not

[9] In the foreword to James Feibleman, *An Introduction to Peirce's Philosophy* (New York: Harper, 1946), p. xv.

faithfully reveal the external world and cannot therefore be said to be real knowledge of it.

If one holds that the concepts in the mind correspond to something in the external world, then he thinks that the *concepts* are real, not fictional, and hence he is a realist. Of course, one way to be a realist is to argue that there are Platonic entities. But one who holds such a view is called a realist not because he believes there are real Platonic entities (although this is true, too) but because he believes that the universals in the mind are real, i.e., correspond to something in the external world. As Peirce says (1.27 n.1), some of the realists may have believed that there were real Platonic entities, but their realism (in the medieval sense) did not consist in *that*, but only in their believing that the mental entity was real, i.e., corresponded to an extra-mental entity. Obviously, to prove that the mental entities correspond to something outside of thought it is necessary to show that in some sense there are real extra-mental entities; but the important point for understanding the scholastic controversy or Peirce's realism is that realism does not consist primarily in holding that the *extra-mental* entities are real, but rather in holding that the *mental* entities are real because they correspond to something outside of the mind.

During the Middle Ages, four solutions to this problem were proposed: The first was extreme realism, or platonism, whose most famous proponent was John Scotus Eregina (c.810–c.877). According to this view there are universal entities existing in an extraphysical realm. The ideas in the mind correspond to these entities. The objects in the physical world reveal them. Thus there are universal entities both within and without the mind. Therefore, the mental entities are real.

At the opposite extreme from this view was nominalism such as that developed by Roscellinus (fl.1100). Nominalism models the idea on the thing. Since the thing is particular, the idea is particular. There are no general ideas because there are no general things. What are called general ideas, or concepts, are merely names, *nomina*, or even noises, *flatus vocis*. Thus there are no universal entities either within or without the mind. Therefore, universal entities are not real, in fact they are not even fictions, for there are no such things even within the mind.

A mediating view between these two extremes was a conceptualism such as that of Peter Abelard (1079–1142). On this view the mind experiences only particulars, but by a process of comparison attains generalized concepts. These mental entities are compounds of particular experiences. Thus, there are universal entities within the mind, but none outside the mind. Therefore, the mental entities are not real.

The fourth position with regard to this problem was called moderate realism. This position was in the current of the Aristotelian answer to the problem. Following a suggestion made by Avicenna (980–1037), the Mohammedan commentator on Aristotle, this position was developed in the works of Albert the Great (c.1193–1280), Thomas Aquinas (1225–74), and Duns Scotus (c. 1270–1308). As the moderate realists set the problem it was this: All knowledge is in terms of concepts. If these concepts correspond to something that is to be found in reality they are real and man's knowledge has a foundation in fact; if they do not correspond to anything in reality they are not real and man's knowledge is of mere figments of his own imagination.

The moderate realists rejected extreme realism, nominalism, and conceptualism. They rejected extreme realism because of the objections Aristotle made against Plato. They rejected nominalism because on that view knowledge of the sort we would call scientific knowledge was not possible.

Science, and knowledge generally, is of the nature of concepts or general formulae; but if, as the nominalists hold, man has no general ideas, only particular experiences and general names, and if there is nothing in reality corresponding to these general names, then the general names are names of mere fictions and all science is fictitious. From this point of view conceptualism is but a form of nominalism. The conceptualists do not go so far as to say that man has no general concepts, just names, but they hold that the concepts do not correspond to anything in reality. In man's mind there are concepts, in the world there are particulars; this being so, concepts are but fictions.

As their solution to the problem, the moderate realists argued that each external object has an essential nature, or an essence. This essence *qua* essence is neither universal nor particular; it just is. It is neutral. It cannot exist in a separate realm by itself, but it can exist either in an object or in a mind. When it exists in an object it appears as a particular; when it exists in a mind it appears as a universal; but in neither case is it either particular or universal in itself. The conceptual universal is the essence in one form, the external particular is the essence in another form, but since the essence is the same in both cases the universal has an external referent and therefore is real.

Because they adopted this solution to the problem these men were called *realists;* because they did not take the extreme view of platonism —that the universal existed out of any mind or any object—they were *moderate* realists.[10]

Even from this cursory examination of the controversy it is possible to see that the basic problem involved goes to the heart of contemporary discussions of theories of meaning. Man has certain ideas. If these ideas are meaningful (in the medieval terminology, real) they must ultimately refer to something in the external world. Any idea that does not refer to some external entity is meaningless (in medieval terminology, fictional). On this view anyone who argues that a given concept is real must be able to show the existing object to which it refers. If he cannot indicate such an object the concept is a fiction.

That Peirce saw the issue in this light may be seen from his statement of the medieval problem: "The question . . . is whether *man, horse,* and other names of natural classes, correspond with anything . . . independent of our thought" (8.12). The moderate realist position—that the referent of a concept is to be found in the experience of a specific object —provided the impetus for Peirce to develop his pragmatic position: The ultimate meaning of an idea is to be found in our experiences of specific objects.

The three basic concepts in Peirce's epistemology are what he calls firstness, secondness, and thirdness. These are terms that Peirce uses in a categorial rather than a substantive sense, and which therefore have

[10]In working out the details of the moderate realist position Scotus and Aquinas differed. Peirce accepted Scotus's final analysis and hence allied himself with the Scotistic wing of Aristotelian realism (5.77 n.1). Although the detailed issues here are of interest, we cannot examine them in the present brief sketch which is intended merely to show the affinities between the general moderate realist position and Peirce's pragmatism.

different referents in logic, metaphysics, epistemology, etc. He describes them variously as three modes of reality (6.342), three categories of being (1.417), or three universes of experience (5.455). As they appear in his epistemology they are closely analogous to some of the basic concepts of scholasticism. A firstness is an idea (6.455)—not an actual idea but only the potentiality of an actual idea. For this reason Peirce often calls it a possibility (1.25). It is not an hypostatization such as Plato's forms are, but neither is it an existent thought in some mind. One might argue that it is therefore a nothing. A firstness is between a mere nothing and an existent thing. The difference between a firstness and nothing is that it is possible for a firstness to become actual whereas nothing cannot. Nothing is defined by Peirce as the self-contradictory (6.352), so that that which is a possibility is not a nothing, i.e., is not self-contradictory. Because it is not, it is possible that it should become actual. In this way it is more than a nothing but less than an actual thought. A firstness is something that can enter a mind, but considered in its state as a pure firstness it is only the possibility of an idea, not an actual idea.

What Peirce is seeking to describe is a realm analogous to Platonic ideas (6.452) or unactualized scholastic essences (1.432, 6.337), although he is apparently striving to avoid hypostatizing either firsts or the realm of firstness. The similarity of firstness with the medieval view of unrealized essences may be seen by comparing firstness with Minges's statement of Scotus's opinion on unrealized essences.

> Scotus . . . does not attribute to the universals or abstract essences . . . an existence of their own, independent of the individual beings in which they are realized. . . . In the state of mere ideality or possibility before their realization, things have an essence, an ideal conceivable being, but not an actual one. . . .[11]

An example of a firstness would be the possibility of a simple sense experience—the possibility of a color sensation, such as "redness"; or the possibility of a pain sensation, such as "toothache." Peirce does not wish to do as Plato did and say that these possibilities exist as actualities. They exist only as possibilities of experiences that may become actualized.

A secondness is an actually existing object (1.419). Peirce analyzes an

[11]Parthenius Minges, "Duns Scotus," *Catholic Encyclopedia*, Vol. V (1909).

existent object into qualities and matter (1.527). The qualities are firstnesses which have become embodied (1.527). But as such they are still not actualized ideas; they only become actualized when they are experienced by some mind (1.422, 1.25). When a secondness is experienced, the qualities produce a percept in the mind. Peirce uses "percept" in a sense analogous to contemporary usage of sense-percept, sense-datum, or sense-image. The percept is the result of a psychological process of sensation that is subconscious in its operation (5.182). The percept appears in consciousness as a kind of image (5.115) or feeling (5.116).

A percept in Peirce's thought is the analogue of the scholastic first intention. A first intention is the first immediate "given," the inarticulate apprehension of an object prior to any conscious recognition of its nature. Both Peirce and the moderate realists subscribe to the Aristotelian doctrine of immediate perception. "The realist will hold that the very same objects which are immediately present in our minds in experience really exist just as they are experienced out of the mind; that is, he will maintain a doctrine of immediate perception" (8.16). The object is exactly as it is perceived, or the perception is exactly like the object. Because of this doctrine of immediate perception, first intentions are sometimes spoken of by the scholastics as though they were the object. Peirce also does this. "The percept is the reality" (5.568). Epistemologically, then, a secondness, a percept, and a first intention are equivalent terms.

A thirdness is a meaning, a general concept (1.339); it is Peirce's analogue of the scholastic second intention which is the abstracted concept—the "universal" idea "abstracted" from the percept. Peirce uses the term "generals" to describe these ideas. We would call them concepts. Peirce's metaphysical realism, then, consists in his view that the general concepts that go to make up meanings are real. That is, they have a real external counterpart in the percept—which is the equivalent in consciousness of a firstness present in the perceived object.

His position is that every thirdness (abstract concept) must refer to a secondness (sense-percept) to be meaningful (real), that is to say, that every idea must refer to some percept. In scholastic terminology his view consists in asserting that no second intention (abstracted concept) is meaningful except insofar as it refers to a first intention (sense experience). Stated in detail his position is as follows: A percept rises to consciousness as a concept by the application to the percept of attention, or "the power of abstraction" (5.295). "By the force of attention, an emphasis is put upon one of the objective elements of consciousness" (5.295). That is, the entire percept, as such, does not rise to consciousness, but attention, like a searchlight, plays over first one part of the percept and then another part, abstracting various elements from the percept and bringing them to the level of consciousness as concepts. Thus, in any judgment about a percept there are at least two abstracted concepts—the subject of the judgment and the predicate of the judgment.

As an example let us take the judgment: "This stove is black." On the basis of this judgment we make the abstraction of "blackness"; that is, we consider blackness in itself. This blackness as considered in itself is not a fiction; it is not a product of my imagination. It is real. It has an external counterpart, namely the blackness that is in the stove. All that is meant by saying that blackness is real is that there is something that has blackness in it, that is, something which is black. Since this is so, blackness is not a fiction but a reality. "It is perfectly true that all white things have whiteness in them, for that is only saying, in another form of words, that all white things are white; but since it is true that real things possess whiteness, whiteness is real" (8.14).

Furthermore, since it is also possible to abstract blackness from the perceptual judgment, "This chair is black," then blackness is found in both the stove and chair. But the fact that blackness is found in two different objects shows that blackness is indeterminate with regard to what it is predicated of. Since it is indeterminate as to what it may be predicated of, it is general. Hence, blackness is a real general.

A final point is that if blackness is found in two objects, it is not that the *same* blackness is found in both of them but that blackness *as* found in both of them is the same.

This was one of the points brought out in the controversy in reference to the nature of universals. As Sir William Hamilton says, not even the humanity of

Leibniz belongs to Newton, but a different humanity. It is only by abstraction, by an oversight, that two things can be said to have common characters (2.415).

Thus, to assert that all men are mortal does not assert that the same mortality belongs to all men; it asserts that the mortality that belongs to each man is similar to the mortality that belongs to each of his fellow men. It is only when we speak loosely and treat concepts as pure abstractions, or pure firstnesses with no reference to their exemplification, that we identify the mortality of A with that of B. When we express ourselves more rigorously, we cannot say that the mortality of A is identical with the mortality of B, but only that the mortality of A is similar to the mortality of B.

Two other examples taken from one of Peirce's early (1868) articles help to clarify his point. In speaking of triangularity, he said,

The nominalists, I suspect, confound together thinking a triangle without thinking that it is either equilateral, isosceles, or scalene, and thinking a triangle without thinking whether it is equilateral, isosceles, or scalene (5.301).

That is, the nominalists are right in holding that whenever we think of *a* triangle we must think of one that is equilateral or isosceles or scalene. But they are wrong in holding that this is all we can do. By abstraction we can abstract the general concept of triangularity from the percept of any particular triangle, and think of it without thinking *whether* it is equilateral, isosceles, or scalene.

This point is stated more fully in a second example referring to the general concept "man."

. . . scholastic realism is usually set down as a belief in metaphysical fictions. But, in fact, a realist is simply one who knows no more recondite reality than that which is represented in a true representation [i.e., a percept]. Since, therefore, the word "man" is true of something, that which "man" means is real. The nominalist must admit that man is truly applicable to something; but he believes that there is beneath this a thing in itself, an incognizable reality. His is the metaphysical figment. . . .[12] The great argument for nominalism is that there is no man unless there is some particular man. That, however, does not affect

[12]Peirce means here that the nominalist denies that the percept and the reality are identical. The nominalist introduces an unknowable thing-in-itself as the cause of the percept.

the realism of Scotus; for although there is no man of whom all further determination can be denied, yet there is a man, abstraction being made of all further determination (5.312).

Consider the general concept of man-ness as rational animality. This concept is real if there is something in the physical world that corresponds to it. The nominalists object that there is not. They say there is this man and that man, but there is no man-ness, no rational animality. The Scotists (and Peirce) answer: (1) You admit that there is a man; (2) any man has the following characteristics: (a) generic: animality, (b) specific: rationality, (c) other individuating and particularizing determinations that make him *this* man; and (3) but since *every* man exemplifies the generic and specific qualities, i.e., rational animality, there is something in the world that exemplifies rational-animality, and since a concept is real if it is exemplified in the physical world, this concept is a real concept. Although man-ness is not exemplified by itself without any particularizing determinations, it is exemplified in every man. To see it, all we need to do is to ignore the particularizing features. What is left is man-ness.

This is not conceptualism. For, according to conceptualism, we form an abstract concept by abstracting from a number of different objects, no one of which completely exemplifies the concept. Thus the concept of "chairness" would be obtained by examining a number of different chairs and abstracting one feature from this chair, another feature from that chair, another from a third, etc. By combining these ideas in our mind we formulate a conception of chairness that is not completely exemplified anywhere in the world and is therefore only a convenient fiction, a mnemonic aid for summarizing a group of experiences. According to the moderate realists, it is not necessary to experience a number of chairs to form the concept; it may be formed by experiencing only one chair.

It should now be clear why Peirce considered himself a Scotist. Scotus tells us that the species "man" is real because it may be found in any man by making a distinction between the species in any man and his other accidental characteristics. Peirce tells us that the species "man" is real because it may be found in any man by abstracting it from his accidental or particularizing characteristics. Obviously these two views come to much the same thing.

IV

With this statement of Peirce's metaphysical realism as a background, let us now examine his pragmatism and see what he meant when he said that "pragmatism could scarcely have entered a head that was not already convinced that there are real generals" (5.503).

In the broadest sense pragmatism is a theory of meaning. That is, it is a theory about how to state the meaning of terms or concepts or ideas.

If the meaning of a term is stated loosely or vaguely or poorly, misunderstandings will be the result. It is therefore important to have a method for determining the meaning of a term as precisely as possible. The title of the essay in which Peirce first stated the pragmatic doctrine was "How To Make Our Ideas Clear." In this essay he points out that a single unclear idea may lead us astray for a whole lifetime of work. Unclear ideas are like trying to follow a road on a foggy night—they lead us off the path, down dead ends, and off cliffs. An entire nation may be led astray for centuries by unclear ideas. It is, then, important to have clear ideas.

Peirce tells us that pragmatism "is a method for ascertaining the real meaning of any concept, doctrine, proposition, word, or other sign" (5.6). Now clearly, as a method, pragmatism may be used by different philosophers to study the meanings of different terms. Thus William James used it to study the meaning of the term "truth." It does not follow from this that pragmatism is James's theory of truth. Pragmatism is only a method which James used to state what he meant by truth—although he thought other people meant a similar thing. John Dewey (1859–1952) used pragmatism to explore the notion of "value," but it does not follow from this that pragmatism is a theory of value. Pragmatism is a method for ascertaining the meaning of terms. It is a slightly different method in the hands of Peirce and James and Dewey. Let us look first at Peirce's version.

In an effort to develop a theory of the meaning of ideas Peirce begins by examining ideas to see what types there are. He concludes that there are three types of ideas, which he states in terms of his three categories of firstness, secondness, and thirdness. He says that the idea of a firstness is an idea of something by itself, in no relation to anything else. Thus the idea of redness is a firstness—not the idea of any thing that is red but simply redness *qua* redness. The idea of a secondness involves two things; it is the idea of something acting upon something else, or the idea of being acted upon by something else, so that the idea of a secondness is an idea of an action; whereas the idea of a firstness is an idea of a perception. Finally, an idea of a thirdness is an idea that involves three things, where one of them represents another to a third. An example of this kind of an idea is a sign. A sign represents some object to some interpreter. Thus a red traffic light represents the action of stopping to some driver. These three types of ideas are not reducible to one another. Thus the idea of A acting on B is more than the idea of A plus the idea of B, so that a secondness is not reducible to firsts. Finally, Peirce concludes that all other types of ideas are reducible to these three.

Peirce calls these "the indecomposable concepts." They may be understood better by recalling that Peirce is a chemist. What he believes he has found here are types of ideas analogous to atoms in chemistry. Atoms cannot be reduced to other atoms, but any physical compound can be expressed as a combination of atoms. What Peirce proposes then is that just as chemistry expresses the nature of a physical compound by stating the atomic elements that go to make it up, that we seek to state the nature of a complex idea by enumerating the atomic ideas that go to make it up. The doctrine of pragmatism then emerges as a device for discovering the atomic ideas that constitute the explication of a complex idea.

As Peirce sees it, the chemist has a procedure for formalizing his statements by embodying them into a chemical formula. Pragmatism must also formalize its statements. In what form shall we put them?

Peirce observes that no theory of meaning can explicate the meaning of firsts and seconds. If a man does not know what redness is, we cannot tell him verbally. If he does not know what being acted upon—being stuck by a pin, for example—is, we cannot tell him. Firsts and seconds are what in contemporary terminology are called "brute givens"; they cannot be defined verbally. The only type of idea definable verbally is a thirdness, what Peirce calls an "intellectual concept." So pragmatism becomes a method for listing the firstnesses and secondnesses—the sense-experiences and the actions—involved in a thirdness: a concept.

Such a list, if simply stated in a random fashion, would not be as helpful as if it were ordered. Peirce observes that the sense-experiences and actions are related to one another—they do have an order. If we are trying to explicate our idea of an automobile, for example, we note it contains the idea of turning the key in the ignition and the idea of hearing the motor start. Now the idea of turning the key is an idea of acting on the key and is therefore a secondness, the idea of hearing the motor start is the idea of a sense-experience and is therefore a firstness. If I think about it I note that these ideas are related. They are related by my idea that if I turn on the key, then the motor will start—that is, if I act so as to produce this secondness, then I will experience that firstness. In this interpretation, that the firstnesses and secondnesses that go to make up concepts are related, Peirce discovers his form for expressing the meaning of the idea. He calls such a relation (If action A, then experience B) a *consequence*. A common misunderstanding of Peirce occurs here. He is not talking about consequents. He tells us that "In the language of logic 'consequence' does not mean that which follows, which is called the *consequent*, but means the fact that a consequent follows from an antecedent" (4.435 n.1). So that a consequence is not the antecedent (the action) nor the consequent (the experience) but the assertion that the consequent follows from the antecedent.

If we then list all the actions and all the sense-experiences associated with the idea of automobile so that they are ordered in terms of consequences, that list of consequences would contain the meaning of the idea of automobile.

Finally, Peirce calls these consequences "practical consequences" not because they come from practical experience but because they serve as a guide to future practice. Thus when I wish to start my car my practice is to turn the ignition key. In doing so my behavior is determined by my belief in the consequence that, if I turn the key, then I will have the experience of the car starting.

The list that we will make up to give us the meaning of an idea will be a list of the practical consequences of the idea—and so we come, at last, to a statement of the pragmatic maxim: "In order to ascertain the meaning of an intellectual conception one should consider what practical consequences might conceivably result by necessity from the truth of that conception; and the sum of these consequences will constitute the entire meaning of the conception" (5.9).

Because Peirce thought of this analysis as being concerned with the way in which our ideas guide our practice he called it "pragmatism."

There are three major interpretations that may be placed on the pragmatic method. In considering a practical consequence one might emphasize the antecedent or the consequent or the consequence, i.e., the relation between the two. Depending on where we place the emphasis we get either the pragmatism of John Dewey, or of William James, or of Charles Peirce.

Thus if we emphasize the antecedent, the action, if we think of ideas as basically modes of behavior, the result is the "instrumentalism" of John Dewey. This is a form of pragmatism that emphasizes the dynamic nature of ideas; their roles as a plan for action, for altering the world; as instruments for acting on things. If we emphasize the consequent, the particular experience that results from the action, we get the pragmatism of William James with its insistence upon explicating ideas in terms of where they take us in experience, where they lead to. If we emphasize the consequence, the relation between the antecedent and the consequent we have the pragmatism of Charles Peirce. For him this relation was always general: thus "If A, then B" does not refer to any particular A or B but prescribes a general relation between actions of the sort A and experiences of the sort B, which has held in the past, does hold now, and will hold in the future. It expresses what Peirce called a "would-be," the experiences that would be had if you acted in manner A. This emphasis on the general nature of meanings with their reference to the future was what Peirce insisted upon. The absence of it in William James's version, with its emphasis on the particular experiences in the present, was what led Peirce to develop the name "pragmaticism" for his own version.

V

We may now see why Peirce considered his pragmatism to be grounded in his metaphysical realism. Pragmatism is a method for defining concepts. But concepts are general, they are not particular. The concept of "automobile" applies to all automobiles, not only particular existing automobiles. A percept is particular, it is of only one automobile, but a concept is general. A great deal of our knowledge, and certainly all scientific knowledge, is general. Newton's law of gravitation applies to "all" physical objects. But if our knowledge is general and all that exists is particular—as the nominalists would have it—then our general concepts are of mere fictions and cannot be meaningfully defined. On the other hand, if real general objects exist then our concepts may be of them and hence may be "real" in medieval terminology. They are not simply memory aids; they define real general forces and real general objects.

If one is a nominalist and believes that there is no such thing as "triangularity" anywhere—that triangularity is only a fiction—then there is no place that he can look to see what triangularity really is. But if he is a realist and believes that triangularity may be found in any triangle, then he knows where to find triangularity and he knows how to define it—it may be defined as what one will experience when one examines any triangle. Therefore, if we list the possible experiences one might have of a triangle, these experiences will define triangularity.

Now how would we go about listing these experiences? We could just list possible experiences, but the list by itself might not suffice to enable the individual, for whose benefit the definition is being made, actually to obtain those precise experiences. The best approach would be to prescribe for him a certain action such that if he accomplishes it, he will then have the experience required. Such a prescription would be a plan or a guide for action. One who undertakes the action will have the requisite experience and will then know, by experience of it, the property being defined. Of course, such a plan for action would necessarily be complicated, but if it is sufficiently detailed so as actually to give a perceptual acquaintance with the property being defined, then it would serve as a definition. Peirce gives an example of this procedure:

> If you look into a textbook of chemistry for a definition of *lithium*, you may be told that it is that element whose atomic weight is 7 very nearly. But if the author has a more logical mind he will tell you that if you search among minerals that are vitreous, translucent, grey or white, very hard, brittle, and insoluble, for one which imparts a crimson tinge to an unluminous flame, this mineral being triturated with lime or witherite rats-bane, and then fused, can be partly dissolved in muriatic acid; and if this solution be evaporated, and the residue be extracted with sulphuric acid, and duly purified, it can be converted by ordinary methods into a chloride, which being obtained in the solid state, fused, and electrolyzed with half a dozen powerful cells, will yield a globule of a pinkish silvery metal that will float on gasolene; and the material of *that* is a specimen of lithium. The peculiarity of this definition—or rather this precept that is more serviceable than a definition—is that it tells you what the word lithium denotes by prescribing what you are to *do* in order to gain a perceptual acquaintance with the object of the word (2.330).

Thus on Peirce's view a concept may be defined by saying that: If you act in a certain manner, then you will have certain experiences, and the sum of the ideas resulting from these experiences constitutes the meaning of the concept being defined. This is Peirce's version of pragmatism.

> Now this sort of consideration; namely, that certain lines of conduct will entail certain kinds of inevitable experiences is what is called a "practical consideration." Hence is justified the maxim, belief in which constitutes pragmatism; namely,
>
> *In order to ascertain the meaning of an intellectual conception one should consider what practical consequences might conceivably result by necessity from the truth of that conception; and the sum of these consequences will constitute the entire meaning of the conception* (5.9).

Such a definition can only be accepted if one believes that concepts are real; that is, if one believes that the concepts have a real external counterpart. If one believes this, and wants to know where to look for this counterpart, then a pragmatic definition will give one a practical guide for actions that will result in an experience of the counterpart. But if one does not believe that concepts are real, then when one follows out the pragmatic definition one will not believe that what one experiences will be the external counterpart, or the referent of the concept, for one does not believe that the concept has any referent. In short, to accept pragmatism is to accept metaphysical realism with reference to concepts.

As Peirce says (1.27), the realist-nominalist controversy is a question to which only two answers are possible: yes and no. If one admits that concepts are general ideas and then asks, is there anything in reality that stands in a one-to-one relation to the concept, an affirmative answer is possible only on a realist position; a negative answer relegates concepts to the realm of fictions.

VI

It is not difficult to see how the pragmatic maxim would be applied in the case of comparatively simple objects such as an automobile. I can make my idea of an automobile clear by listing all of the ways in which I would act and all of the experiences I would expect from any object that I would call an automobile. If you and I disagree about what an automobile is, we can each make our own listing and by comparing them we can discover where we differ. If I have on my list a practical consequence that is lacking from yours, and if I assert that the consequence should be on the list and you deny it, we can put the matter to the test by going to an automobile and acting in the manner prescribed by the antecedent and observing whether we get the sense-experience prescribed in the consequent. If the experiment succeeds—if we obtain the sense-experience—then I have grounds for asserting that that consequence is part of what is meant by something being an automobile. If the experiment fails—if the sense-experience is not had—then you have grounds for denying that that consequence is part of what is meant by something being an automobile. Thus we have an experimentalist theory of meaning—which is what Peirce thought he was explicating when he developed pragmatism.

It is not so easy, however, to see how the pragmatic maxim would apply in dealing with abstract properties such as reality or truth. In the essay "How To Make Our Ideas Clear" Peirce applies the notion to develop a definition of reality. In the immediately preceding essay on "The Fixation of Belief," he argues that there are three characteristics that are desirable in that which we accept as a basis for fixing our beliefs: (1) it must control our thinking, our thinking must not control it; (2) it must be publicly observable; and (3) it must lead to a common opinion.

Peirce says that the scientific method seeks to fix beliefs in terms of these three characteristics by proposing "reality" as that which would fix belief—as opposed to earlier methods that had proposed authority as a way of fixing beliefs, or what is agreeable to reason or what is agreeable to personal taste.

In defining reality Peirce uses two definitions. In the first definition he says that "The real is that which is not whatever we happen to think it, but is unaffected by what we may think of it" (8.12). In the second definition he says, "The opinion which is fated to be ultimately agreed to by all who investigate is what we mean by the truth, and the object represented in this opinion is the real" (5.407).

According to the first definition, an object is not affected by my thinking of it (experiencing it); it remains unchanged by my experiencing it. Since my experiencing it does not change it, it will appear the same way to you if you subsequently experience it. Since it does not change from my experience to yours, a real object may be defined as an object that will appear the same to every observer. A second characteristic that follows from the first definition is that an object is real if its nature is independent of *how* I happen to think it to be. Compare this with the situation when a dramatist is creating a character for a play. The nature of the character is dependent on how the dramatist happens to think him to be. If he thinks of him as happy then he is happy; if sad, then sad. We call such a character a "fiction" not a reality because his nature depends on how he is thought to be. However, suppose that I think that Napoleon was stupid. An historian would properly object that Napoleon could not have been stupid and have accomplished what he did accomplish—so that Napoleon is a reality since his nature remains unaffected by how I happen to think him. We all recognize that a characteristic of reality is that "thinking does not make it so."

Suppose that by using these criteria we seek to find objects in the world that satisfy them, i.e., real objects. I undertake to examine one of these objects critically to see what its real features are. I make a careful study of it and find it to have five properties. I examine the object carefully, and I am convinced that it really has these five properties. But this is not adequate to satisfy our criteria. For we said that the real properties would appear the same to every man. Accordingly, I call in another observer. He studies the object and applies the same techniques that I have applied, but he is unable to find property y that I found. If he is a competent investigator and his results are verified by other investigators, I know that property y cannot be real, for the real is by definition what is knowable to any man. Since property y is not knowable to other observers it cannot really be present in the object but must be a subjective element that I introduced into the object by virtue of some idiosyncrasy in me, not in the object.

Of course, there may also be some property among the four remaining that is subjective and due to some idiosyncrasy in both observers. If so, they do not know the object as it really is. To find out if this is the case they must call in a third observer. But for all they know there may be some subjective idiosyncrasies common to all three observers. The only way they can check this is to call in a fourth observer. But it is easy to see that this will be an indefinitely long process involving a whole community of observers in the whole of time. The opinion to which this community ultimately comes will be considered by them to be the truth and the object they will certainly describe with no subjective elements in it—if they continue long enough—will be the real object.

But this is Peirce's second definition of reality. The opinion that is fated (certain) to be ultimately agreed to by all who investigate (the community of investigators) is what we mean by the truth, and the object represented in this opinion is the real.

This definition satisfies Peirce's statement as to what is required to attain fixed beliefs. It gives a method that controls our thinking rather than our thinking controlling it, it is public and it will lead, if carried far enough, to a common opinion.

Its disadvantages are that while it is self-corrective—subsequent investigators will correct idiosyncrasies introduced by earlier investigators—the method does not tell us at any one point in time that it has removed all subjective elements so that our knowledge is never absolute—it is always fallible—we can only say of it that it is the best we have. And of course there is no guarantee that by following the method we will ever find final answers to our question—we can only hope. Peirce says that "the assumption that man or the community (which may be wider than man) shall ever arrive at a state of information greater than some definite finite information, is entirely unsupported by reasons. There cannot be a scintilla of evidence to show that at some time all living beings shall not be annihilated at once, and that forever after there shall be throughout the universe any intelligence whatever. . . . The only assumption on which he can act rationally is the hope of success" (5.357).

Finally, we should note that this is a definition in accord with the pragmatic maxim, for it defines reality in terms of human experiences. If all competent observers—those who have divested themselves of all personal idiosyncrasies—perform identical experiments on a real object then they will observe identical results.

VII

As Peirce developed his scholastic realism in his later work he turned his attention to the notion of a scientific law. Here he asserted that a scientific law was a general idea in the mind that has a real counterpart in general forces operating in the physical world. Since these general forces control the future they are potential forces not just actual forces as the nominalist would have it—who sees a scientific law as simply a summary statement of actual events that have occurred in the past.

Peirce put it thus:

With overwhelming uniformity, in our past experience, direct and indirect; stones left free to fall have fallen. Thereupon two hypotheses only are open to us. Either 1. the uniformity with which those stones have fallen has been due to mere chance and affords no ground whatever, not the slightest, for any expectation that the next stone that shall be let go will fall; or 2. the uniformity with which stones have fallen has been due to some *active general principle;* in which case it would be a strange coincidence that it should cease to act at the moment my prediction was based upon it.

That position, gentlemen, will sustain criticism. It is irrefragable.

Of course, every sane man will adopt the latter hypothesis. If he could doubt it in the case of the stone—which he can't—and I may as well drop the stone once and for all—I told you so!—if anybody doubts this still, a thousand other such inductive predictions are getting verified every day, and he will have to suppose every one of them to be merely fortuitous in order reasonably to escape the conclusion that *general principles are really operative in nature.* That is the doctrine of scholastic realism (5.100–101).

The view that Peirce expresses as number one in this quotation is what he considered to be the nominalistic position on natural law. He states it elsewhere as the view "that the facts are, in themselves, entirely disconnected, and that it is the mind alone which unites them. One stone dropping to the earth has no real connection with another stone dropping to the earth" (6.99). This position with its insistence on particular events as being united only by the mind is what leads Peirce to identify it with medieval nominalism.

He stated his own realist position to be that "No collection of facts can constitute a law; for the law goes beyond any accomplished facts and determines how facts that *may be,* but all of which never can have happened, shall be characterized. There is no objection to saying that a law is a general fact, provided that it be understood that the general has an admixture of potentiality, so that no congeries of actions here and now can ever make a general fact" (1.420).

For the realist there are forces in the universe that provide for the actual regularity when the law is being instanced but that are a potentiality for regularity when it is not.

To account for laws and to explain their nature Peirce develops a philosophy of objective idealism. Because he sees no way for matter to give birth to mind, he takes mind as basic and sees matter as a form of mind. Since mind can take on habits, the material universe becomes "mind hidebound with habit" where the habits are laws of nature. He argues that habits are never precise so there is always an element of absolute chance in the universe—a doctrine he calls tychism. He says also that habits tend to spread and to connect with one another to make larger networks of habits—a doctrine he calls synechism—so that the universe is a process moving from complete tychism (chance) at the beginning to complete synechism (order) at the conclusion through the medium of habit-forming. He sees this evolution as a process proceeding through an inward principle of creative love which he calls agapasm.

The ultimate resolution of all the parts into a single continuum of love will be God. "Every reality then is a Self, and the selves are intimately connected, as if they formed a continuum. Each one is . . . a quasi-map of the entire field of selves, which organic aggregate is itself a Self, the Absolute Idea of Hegel. So far as a philosophical conception can be identified with God it is God."[13]

The universe is God's purpose working itself out in the world. "The universe is a vast representamen, a great symbol of God's purpose, working out its conclusions in living realities" (5.119). This purpose is to infuse everything with "that Reasonableness for the sake of which the Heavens and the Earth have been created" (2.122).

Although Peirce never developed these views in detail, it is clear that he did not feel that his scientific empiricism precluded metaphysics. The general view suggested here by Peirce foreshadows in many ways that which was to be developed in the first part of the twentieth century by other science-oriented philosophers—most notably in the work of Alfred North Whitehead.

Among his contemporaries Peirce made a significant impact on only two of them, Josiah Royce and William James. The publication of Royce's *The World and the Individual* (1899–1901) brought Royce into close contact with Peirce and his work. As a result of this, Royce stated in the Preface of his *The Problem of Christianity* (1913), "As to certain metaphysical opinions which are stated, in outline, in the second volume of this book, I now owe much more to our great and unduly neglected American logician, Mr. Charles Peirce, than I do to the common tradition of recent idealism. . . ."[14]

James and Peirce were friends at Harvard and continued to be close friends until the death of James. They exchanged many letters on

[13] *The Nation*, 75 (1902): 95.
[14] Josiah Royce, *The Problem of Christianity* (New York: Macmillan, 1913), I, p. xi.

philosophical problems and were close friends long before the pragmatic movement became of philosophical interest. In 1897, James dedicated his first book on philosophy, *The Will to Believe*, to Peirce with these words: "To My Old Friend, Charles Sanders Peirce, To whose philosophic comradeship in old times and to whose writings in more recent years I owe more incitement and help than I can express or repay." Peirce evidenced his reciprocation of this attachment in his later years when he used to sign his name as "Charles Santiago Sanders Peirce"— the "Santiago" being Spanish for "St James."

Although differences in age made for less direct association between Peirce and John Dewey, the influence of Peirce has been acknowledged by Dewey on a number of occasions. In his *Logic: The Theory of Inquiry*, for example, Dewey says, "The readers who are acquainted with the logical writings of Peirce will note my great indebtedness to him in the general position taken."

Much of Peirce's work in science, in mathematics, and in logic has now been superseded by the work of other investigators. But the problems that he posed concerning a theory of meaning, the processes of scientific inquiry, the nature of a scientific law, and how it can be envisioned as including generality and potentiality are still very much with us and have occupied a great part of the concern of philosophers of the twentieth century.

VIII

It will be useful to compare the position of Peirce with that of contemporary positivism. An examination of publications by positivists indicates that they are not completely satisfied with their own criterion of meaning.[15] Such an examination reveals a basic problem that positivists have been implicitly striving to solve; namely, the problem of the meaning of potentiality and the consequent difficulty of allowing propositions involving potentiality to be meaningful.

[15]E.g., the articles by R. Carnap and C. G. Hempel (as well as Bertrand Russell's more complete disavowal of positivism) in the *Revue Internationale de Philosophie*, vol. 4 (1950); H. Feigl's "Existential Hypotheses," in the *Philosophy of Science*, vol. 17 (1950) pp. 35–62; and A. J. Ayer's preface to the second edition of his *Language, Truth and Logic*.

In its earliest formulations—in the writings of Auguste Comte (1798–1857)—positivism was based upon an epistemological nominalism that says that we can have empirical knowledge only of the realm of sense-experience, and everything found in that realm is an actualized particular. Therefore, if we use the term "empirical knowledge" to apply only to those ideas that have a referent in sense-experience, we can have knowledge only of actualized particulars. If we claim to have a concept that does not denote either an actualized particular or, at best, a series of such particulars, we are referring to a fiction.

In its beginnings, in the writings of Comte, positivism had as its basic motivation the elimination of trans-empirical metaphysics. Proceeding from this motive Comte began with a strict adherence to the nominalistic principle. His original formulation advised us that a proposition was empirically meaningful only when it could actually be verified. Propositions for which the actual verification—or disverification—was at the moment impossible, were meaningless. From this position Comte attained his notorious assertion that propositions about the chemical constituents of the stars were meaningless—because at that time no technique had been developed for determining the truth or falsity of such propositions. Similarly, the proposition "On the other side of the moon there are St. Bernard dogs running around in circles with their tails in their mouths" was meaningless because of the impossibility in the foreseeable future of actually seeing the other side of the moon.

But it soon became evident that a strict adherence to this meaning criterion would not do. It ruled out too many propositions that obviously had a meaning, and it did not actually suffice even for the purposes of science. Unless an observer knew the meaning of a proposition before he was actually able to verify it, if he did develop a technique for dealing with the proposition, he would have no way of recognizing the verification, when it occurred, as referring to the proposition with which he was concerned. That is, unless one knew, in advance of the actual experience, what was meant by St. Bernard dogs running around on the other side of the moon, he would be unable to recognize the actual experience, if and when it occurred, as a verification of the proposition in question. From this consideration it follows that a proposition must have some meaning even before it can actually be verified.

Because of difficulties of this order, the logical positivists of the Vienna Circle relaxed the criterion to what has come to be known as the less rigorous formulation: A proposition is meaningful if it can, in principle, be verified. If in theory we know how to verify a proposition, that is, if we know what experience would, if actualized, prove or disprove it, then it is meaningful. This formulation may be seen, for example, in Rudolph Carnap's articles in 1936–37 on "Testability and Meaning."[16] In substituting confirmability for verifiability Carnap says, "When we call a sentence S confirmable, we do not mean that it is possible to arrive at a confirmation of S under circumstances as they actually exist. We rather intend this possibility under some *possible circumstances* whether they be real or not.[17]

This relaxation of the meaning criterion is important as marking the thin edge of the wedge. Nominalism begins to be left behind. It is no longer necessary for a proposition to be actually verifiable to be meaningful; it is sufficient if it would be possible to verify it. But the departure from nominalism is not so drastic as might appear, since the possible experience is reducible to an actual experience. "A *sentence* S is called *confirmable* . . . if the confirmation of S is reducible . . . to that of a class of observable predicates."[18] The possible experience is like a traditional paper bank note; the bank note had no value in itself, but had value only so far as it was based upon a piece of precious metal that could be produced under certain specified conditions. So a potentiality of experience has no reality *qua* potentiality; its only reality is that of the actual experience that could be produced under certain specified conditions.

However, in Carnap's discussion of dispositional predicates we see a more radical deviation from nominalism. He says, "Those predicates of the thing-language which are not observable, e.g., disposition terms, are reducible to observable predicates and hence confirmable."[19] The inter-

---

[16]R. Carnap, "Testability and Meaning," *Philosophy of Science*, vol. 3 (1936), pp. 419–71, and vol. 4 (1937), pp. 1–40.
[17]Ibid, vol. 3, p. 457.
[18]Ibid., p. 456.
[19]Ibid., p. 466.

esting question here is the reference to a nonobservable predicate. If this
means that there are properties that cannot be actualized in experience,
it is a complete break with the actualities of nominalism. I shall return
to this question in a moment. Before dealing with it I should like to show
that Ayer seems to talk in a very similar fashion. In reformulating the
verifiability criterion, Ayer talks of "indirect verification"; he says that
"a statement is indirectly verifiable if it satisfies the following conditions:
first, that in conjunction with certain other premises it entails one or
more directly verifiable statements which are not deducible from these
other premises alone; and secondly, that these other premises do not
include any statement that is not either analytic, or directly verifiable,
or capable of being indirectly verifiable."[20] Ayer criticizes even the less
rigorous formulation of the meaning criterion as "too harsh . . . for it
would seem to imply that it was illegitimate to introduce any term that
did not itself designate something observable."[21]

From both Carnap's treatment of dispositional properties and Ayer's
reformulation of the verifiability criterion it would appear, then, that
positivists will now allow as meaningful what is not, even in theory,
actually observable. The successive stages of the position seem to be:
(1) a term is meaningful only if its referent is actually observable; (2) a
term is meaningful if its referent is theoretically observable; (3) a term
is meaningful if its referent is actually and theoretically unobservable,
provided its referent has consequences that are actually or theoretically
observable.

These changes in the positivistic meaning criterion reveal an increasing shift away from nominalism. If we allow "actuality" to denote what
enters into human experience, that is, what is observed, we need to
introduce terminology for referring to objects that are not actualities. A

---

[20]A. J. Ayer, *Language, Truth and Logic* (London: Gollancz, 1947), p. 13. There is an
interesting anticipation of this formulation in the writings of Chauncey Wright, the
nineteenth-century American positivist. Wright says, "Thus, while ideal or transcendental
elements are admitted into scientific researches, though in themselves insusceptible of
simple verification, they must still show credentials from the senses, either by affording
from themselves consequences capable of sensuous verification, or by yielding such consequences in conjunction with ideas which by themselves are verifiable" Chauncey Wright,
Philosophical Discussions (New York: Holt, 1877), p. 47.
[21]Ayer, op. cit., p. 14.

set of definitions such as the following seems to be necessary:
(1) x is an actuality means x is observed; (2) x is an actualizable means x is not now an actuality but may in theory become an actuality; (3) x is a potentiality means x is not an actuality but is (a) actualizable or (b) has consequences which are either actual or actualizable; (4) x is real means x is either an actuality or a potentiality; (5) x is a fiction means x is neither an actuality nor a potentiality.

The above (1), the first part of (4), and (5) are clearly within the framework of the positivistic meaning criterion. What positivists would be less inclined to accept, and what Peirce would wish to maintain, is that (2) and (3) are not identifiable with any class of (1) and that (4) must include potentialities as well as actualities. In short, one might maintain these two theses: (a) the potential cannot be identified either logically or empirically with the actual, and (b) the potential is as real as the actual.

It has been generally recognized that a potentiality, e.g., a dispositional property, can not be logically defined in terms of actualities if by definable is meant translatable, i.e., that the definiens may, at discretion, be substituted for the definiendum. Such a definition would define solubility, for example, as, x is soluble means if x is put in water, then x will dissolve. If such a definition were accepted, then any object whatever could be shown to be soluble by the ordinary definition of the if-then relation according to which the relation holds if the antecedent is false, for we would merely need to substitute the phrase "if x is put in water, then x will dissolve" for the predicate "soluble" as applied to any object, x, and then show that x was never put in water, thus falsifying the antecedent and validating the relation and hence demonstrating the existence of the property.

To avoid this difficulty Carnap has proposed that we do not attempt to introduce dispositional predicates by translatability but by reduction, which is a process of introducing a term such as "soluble" by a series of sentences of the sort, "If x is put in water, then if x is soluble, then x dissolves."[22] The necessity for introducing dispositional predicates by

[22]Carnap, loc. cit., pp. 439 ff.

reduction is due to the fact that logically the dispositional predicate cannot be defined in terms of actualities, i.e., is not translatable into or identifiable with a class of actualities.

It is sometimes suggested that the impossibility of eliminating dispositional predicates by substituting sense-data predicates (eliminating potentialities by substituting actualities) is a purely logical difficulty that could be solved by a more careful analysis of the if-then relation as found in subjunctive conditionals. That this is not the case may be seen by noting that the difficulty that we have just seen on the logical level is also present on the epistemological level in empirical situations.

Suppose that I am about to release an ordinary pencil and I ask a scientist whether it will fall. He knows the law of gravitation and therefore asserts that it will fall. When he knows the proposition "The pencil, if released, will fall," what is it that he knows? Certainly he does not literally know the future actual event of the pencil falling. He cannot peer into the future and see something that has not yet occurred. We might say that he only anticipates this future event. But to anticipate is to know something that will be actualized only in the future. The event is not actualized now and hence cannot itself be an object of knowledge. What is known now is the potentiality of this event occurring in the future; this potentiality is real now, and it is the potentiality —not the future actuality—which is the object of knowledge.

A future actuality is never known *qua* actuality; it is always known only as a potentiality. What a scientist knows whenever he knows something about the future—and whenever he knows a law he does know something about the future—is a potentiality and not an actuality.[23] Peirce's position is that a definition of law can not be reduced to a statement about actualities; every law must contain an element of potentiality insofar as it denotes possibilities that are not now and which, if for example I do not release the pencil, may never become actualities.

---

[23]Of course, a scientist's knowledge of the future is not coercive. A botanist who knows Mendel's laws does not know whether there will be any sweet peas in 1990, but he does know that if there are any sweet peas in 1990 that are the descendants of any flower alive today, the descendants will exhibit certain characteristics that are potentially present in the contemporary flower. He does not know these future characteristics as actualities; he only knows them as potentialities.

There is, however, a difference between the potentiality involved in the pencil falling at some future time and the potentiality of a dispositional property. The potentiality of the pencil falling is what I have called an actualizable, that is, it may, under appropriate conditions, become actual. There is a one-to-one correlation between the potentiality of the pencil falling and the actuality of the pencil falling with reference to all the properties of each except those involved in the difference between being a potentiality and an actuality. This is not the case, however, with a dispositional property. A dispositional property is never actualizable. What are actualizable are certain consequences of the property but not the property itself. A dispositional property is a potentiality for acting in a certain manner. The disposition, as a disposition, cannot be identified with the acting. To say that a lump of sugar has solubility is not to say that it is dissolving now, but is to say that it has now the potentiality of dissolving at some future time. The actual dissolving is not the same as the potentiality—a piece of sugar that is actually dissolving is an instance of dissolution, not of solubility.

An adequate philosophy of science must admit both real laws and real dispositional properties. Both of these involve potentiality. Any philosophical approach that renders potentiality meaningless must be inadequate as a theoretical base for science. Nominalism, or the attempt to identify all meaning with actualities, does make potentiality meaningless. If all that we know are actualities, then the concept of potentiality is meaningless. The nominalist can ascribe meaning to the concept of an actual property or an actual instance of a law by telling me what experience may be expected at times when the property is actualized or the law is exhibited. But if he is to describe to me the meaning of a now potential property or a now potential law—i.e., a dispositional property or a present knowledge of a future regularity—he must not use experiences referring to the property or the law as actualized in future experience but must explain its nature *now* when it is unactualized. And the terms used to describe the unactualized entity are only meaningful on the nominalistic view if stated in terms of actualities. But what actualities can describe an "un-actuality"?

If we ask what a potentiality really is, there are, in general, only two possible answers. We can either make a Humean analysis of potentiality, in which case we argue that the potentiality is not really in the object but only an idea that we put into it, or we can argue with Peirce, that potentiality is a real feature of the object. If we accept the first alternative we have no basis for prediction as to how the object will behave. For if the potentiality is *merely* an idea in my mind, there is no reason why objects should act in accordance with my idea of how they will act. If in fact they did do so, I could never have a false view about a scientific law; if I ever got an idea into my head about how objects behaved, then they would act in that way. It is obvious that the world does not change its mode of behavior to adapt itself to my ideas but rather that the converse is the case.

IX

Peirce has often been referred to as a "seminal" philosopher. One of the more provocative of his remarks concerns the verifiability of metaphysics. In 1897 he wrote:

Thus, in brief, my philosophy may be described as the attempt of a physicist to make such conjecture as to the constitution of the universe as the methods of science may permit, with the aid of all that has been done by previous philosophers. I shall support my propositions by such arguments as I can. Demonstrative proof is not to be thought of. The demonstrations of the metaphysicians are all moonshine. The best that can be done is to supply a hypothesis not devoid of all likelihood, in the general line of growth of scientific ideas, and capable of being verified or refuted by future observers (1.7).

It has been a subject of some speculation as to what Peirce could have meant by the verification of a metaphysical proposition. Peirce has been dead for over fifty years. It might be fruitful to examine his metaphysics in the light of this statement in an effort to determine whether the line of growth of scientific ideas has verified or refuted it.[24]

Another way in which the matter might be put is this: What would

---

[24]The reader will find of interest an article that examines Peirce's evolutionism from this point of view; see Thomas A. Goudge, "Peirce's Evolutionism—After Half a Century," *Studies in the Philosophy of Charles Sanders Peirce, Second Series*, eds. Moore and Robin (Amherst: University of Massachusetts Press, 1964), p. 323 ff.

happen if metaphysics took physics seriously? What kind of a system would we get? Would it resemble that of Peirce? There is a great deal of similarity between Peirce's ideas and those recent philosophers such as Whitehead, Russell, Reichenbach, and Popper, who have taken science seriously.

The central doctrine of Peirce's metaphysics is his belief that there are real generals. Where does it stand in the light of contemporary science? The term "general," as we have seen, was applied by Peirce to entities that were indeterminate in respect to some property. Thus the concept of a "triangle" is indeterminate with respect to whether it is obtuse or acute. Insofar as the concept is indeterminate, it is general. We all understand how mathematical properties are general, but metaphysics must deal with physical objects. Are there any physical objects that are general?

Peirce tells us that a general property "surrenders to the interpreter the right of completing the determination for himself" (5.505). He says that he does not mean by a general sign, a vague sign. He does not mean that the object has a fully determinate structure but the observer is ignorant as to the character of some property. He means by "general," a property that is genuinely indeterminate—it has no fixed character in some respect.

Is there any interpretation of modern science in which there are genuinely indeterminate properties, that have no fixed character, and that leave their determination open?

This metaphysical question is translatable into an empirical hypothesis that would have the following operational form: There are real objects that have properties that extend over a range of interpretations any one of which may be selected by an observer. Such objects are real general objects.

If we take modern science seriously, does it appear to support the view that there are real general objects or to refute it? I do not feel that most physicists take relativity physics seriously enough and very few philosophers seem to me to do so. What is meant in relativity physics by saying that the property of length is relative? Does it mean that an object has some one length that is its real length and that measurements obtained by other observers are somehow "unreal"? Not on any possible interpretation of relativity.

The Lorentz transformation equation for length says that:

$$length = \sqrt{\frac{1 - v^2}{c^2}}$$

In this equation all the values on the right-hand side are constants except the one representing the velocity of the observer. It follows, therefore, that the length varies with the velocity of the observer. That is, the property of length extends over a range of interpretations any one of which may be selected by the observer if he only chooses the right velocity in relation to the object he is measuring. To say that there is some one length that remains unchanged through these transformations and which is "the" length is to make a statement that is not verifiable empirically and that would, if true, undermine the whole of relativity physics.

Now, how does one translate this range of interpretations into a scientific object? Do we say that there is some one interpretation that is unique, that is more real or more authoritative than any of the others? To do so is to revert immediately to an absolutistic or nonrelativity physics. On the other hand, if we take this operational result seriously, what can we say about lengths that extend continuously over a range? It seems to me that we can only say of length that it is a general property —that it extends over a range of interpretations, any one of which may be selected by an observer depending upon his velocity.

Since the Lorentz transformation equations cover time and mass measurements as well as measurements of distance, these properties also become general properties. In fact, the prescribed variations of mass have been experimentally verified with particles moving at high speeds in accelerators. Now, if the temporal and spatial dimensions of objects are general, and if the mass measurements show mass to be a general property, what remains that is particular in the physicalistic sense? It would seem to me that what we have are general objects not particular objects. The physicist may not wish to draw this conclusion, but what better can a metaphysician do?

Of course, we have physical evidence not only of a mass continuum and a space continuum but also of a time continuum. We all know that as we look out at the stars we are looking into the time continuum. We see some stars as they were a few years ago, others as they were centuries ago, and still others as they were thousands and millions of years ago. If we reverse our orientation, then we realize that observers on these stars will see our planet as it was years ago, centuries ago, or millions of years ago. If we occupied these stars would we see our own history unfold? Does it somehow still exist as part of the time continuum?[25]

However we answer this question, it appears to me that science at the macrocosmic level lends credence to the notion that there are real generals.

Let us look briefly at the microcosm. I think it is perfectly clear on at least one interpretation (the so-called Copenhagen or "hard" interpretation of subatomic physics) that what the principle of indeterminancy is saying is that small particles have either a generalized location or a generalized mass. In "The Architecture of Theories" Peirce wrote, "When we come to atoms, the presumption in favor of a simple law seems very slender. There is room for serious doubt whether the fundamental laws of mechanics hold good for single atoms, and it seems quite likely that they are capable of motion in more than three dimensions." This seems to me a remarkable statement to have been made in 1891. I believe that subsequent physics has lent credence to it in the principle of indeterminacy.

If we turn from physics to biology, what do we find? Are biological properties determinate or indeterminate? We know now that gene-determined biological characteristics are not as unilaterally determined by the chemistry of the chromosomes as we once thought. The genes apparently can act within a range of choices. Which choice will be made depends upon the environment as much as upon the genes. Temperature variation and diverse chemical conditions introduced into the envi-

[25]That intrepid explorer of the time continuum—the cartoon character Alley Oop—relies on just this principle. (Furthermore, he explores the continuum utilizing a time-machine invented by Dr. Wonmug—and as any astute student of German knows, "wonmug" is a translation of "Einstein," which in English means "one mug" of beer.)

ronment of the developing embryo operate to demonstrate the range of choices. For example, the number and position of the eyes of certain minnows are a function of the salinity of the sea water in which the eggs develop. If the amount of magnesium chloride in the water is excessive, the embryo will develop a centrally placed, single ("cyclopean") eye. In reporting this result, Stockard wrote,

> In other words, the genetic composition of these fishes causes them to develop two eyes in normal sea water, but the same genetic composition gives rise to a single cyclopean eye when an excess of magnesium chloride is added to the sea water. If sea water normally had the composition which causes fish to develop with the cyclopean eye, and an experimenter should develop the eggs of fish in a solution of the same composition as our ordinary sea water, he would find them giving rise to fish with two lateral eyes instead of the median one, and these two-eyed specimens would appear to this imaginary investigator as monsters.[26]

I suspect, myself, that the so-called higher animals are "higher" only because they are more general in their structure and behavior, and that man's success is due in large part to his having specialized in remaining general. He has retained his amateur status. People talk about a sex "instinct" and a food "instinct," but I suspect this is only loose talk.

I once asked a learned anthropologist what he thought the chances might be if an untutored male and female human were cast at an early age upon a desert isle, that they might learn the sex act well enough to reproduce their kind. He said he would not give them better than a fifty-fifty chance.

If someone were to invent a process tomorrow whereby human energy needs could be satisfied by some kind of photosynthesis—so that all one needed to do to get a balanced energy input cheaply and effectively would be to pass once a day in front of a machine that emitted certain kinds of electromagnetic waves—it is not unlikely that in a few generations "eating" as we know it would become some kind of a sin. The process of putting the cadavers of animals into the stomach would soon become more obnoxious than nudism (once "natural") is now. The point is that even eating is not an instinct.

[26]C. R. Stockard, *The Physical Basis of Personality* (New York: Norton, 1931), pp. 109–110.

The generality of human behavior is often cited by biologists. Bentley Glass says, "It remains true that man is the most plastic and malleable of animals in respect to his behavior, that his superiority over other animals resides in this, that by his intelligence he can make prompt and effective adjustment to altered surroundings, to a degree quite impossible for other species."[27]

What is it biologically that controls and orders and determines life? One sensitive observer sees on the biological scene something general —something more than a collection of particular individuals. In *The Firmament of Time*, Loren Eiseley has this to say:

Yet for all this flood of change, movement and destruction, there is an enormous stability about the morphological plans which are built into the great phyla—the major divisions of life. They have all, or most of them, survived since the first fossil records. They do not vanish. The species alter, one might say, but the *Form*, that greater animal which stretches across the millennia survives. . . .

Many years ago I was once, by accident, locked in a museum with which I had some association. In the evening twilight I found myself in a lengthy hall containing nothing but Crustacea of all varieties. I used to think they were a rather limited order of life, but as I walked about impatiently in my search for a guard, the sight began to impress, not to say overawe me.

The last light of sunset, coming through a window, gilded with red a huge Japanese crab on a pedestal at one end of the room. It was one of the stilt-walkers of the nightmare deeps, with a body the size of a human head carried tiptoe on three-foot legs like fire tongs. In the cases beside him there were crabs built and riveted like Sherman tanks, and there were crabs whose claws had been flattened into plates that clapped over their faces and left them shut up inside with little secrets. There were crabs covered with chitinous thorns that would have made them indigestible; there were crabs drawn out and thin, with delicate elongated pincers like the tools men use to manipulate at a distance in dangerous atomic furnaces.

There were crabs that planted sea growths on their backs and marched about like restless gardens. There were crabs as ragged as waterweed or as smooth as beach pebbles; there were crabs that climbed trees and crabs from beneath the polar ice. But the sea change was on them all. They were one, one great plan that flamed there on its pedestal in the sinister evening light, but they were

[27]Bentley Glass, *Science and Liberal Education* (Baton Rouge: Louisiana State University Press, 1959), p. 111.

also many and the touch of Maya, of illusion, lay upon them.

I was shivering a little by the time the guard came to me. Around us in the museum cases was an old pattern, out of the remote sea depths. It was alien to man. I would never underestimate it again. It is not the individual that matters; it is the Plan and the incredible potentialities within it. The forms within the Form are endless and their emergence into time is endless. I leaned there, gazing at that monster from whom the forms seemed flowing, like the last vertebrate on a world whose sun was dying. It was plain that they wanted the planet and meant to have it. One could feel the massed threat of them in this hall.[28]

Students of Peirce will be reminded of the formulation mentioned earlier in which Peirce expressed the problem of the reality of generals when he said, "The question . . . is whether *man, horse,* and other names of natural classes, correspond with anything . . . independent of our thoughts" (8.12). I take it that Eiseley would have agreed with Peirce that natural classes are not just human constructs, that they are biologically in things.

What conclusion do we draw from this kind of scientific situation as to the validity of Peirce's doctrine of the reality of generals? Certainly this kind of analysis does not give "demonstrative proof" of Peirce's metaphysics, but then he did not expect that. It does seem to me that the doctrine of real generals continues to be consistent with "the general line of growth of scientific ideas," as Peirce hoped it was.

I do not feel, however, that Peirce scholars, or philosophers generally, have taken this matter seriously enough. What seems to me at issue, and I feel strongly that this is what Peirce saw to be the real issue, is whether general potentiality is as real as individual particularity.

If we say that there are real general objects or real general forces we are certainly saying that there are, for example, a variety of potential lengths that now exist, any one of which can be actualized by selecting an appropriate frame of reference. The interesting philosophical question is, what is the ontological status of these potential lengths while they are potential? I do not find it useful to contrast potentiality with reality because I think potentiality is part of reality. Potentiality really exists. It exists in objects in many ways and is as ontologically real as

[28]Loren Eiseley, *The Firmament of Time* (New York: Atheneum, 1966), pp. 82–84.

anything else about them. It may, in fact, be all that is ontologically real.

There is a strong tendency in contemporary philosophy to talk about potentialities as "dispositions," and to define dispositional properties and then feel that the matter is taken care of. This seems to me a philosophically regressive interpretation. As indicated in the previous section these views define these properties in terms of their effects. Thus, "sugar has solubility" becomes "sugar will dissolve if put into water." But this seems to me to evade the issue. I do not want to know what effects may be produced in the future by solubility, I want to know what its nature is now. What is there in sugar right now that I am trying to characterize when I say sugar has solubility? I do not believe that a present potentiality can be defined in terms of future actualities. A present potentiality exists right now. It may or may not become actualized in the future. But if it never becomes actualized it still exists now as a potentiality. What is its character now as a potentiality?

This seems to me, as it did to Peirce, and I think it did to Aristotle, an important problem. If we can solve it, many of the problems about counter-factual propositions, about scientific processes, and about cause and effect will be solved with it. From the epistemological point of view a basic purpose of science is to know the future—to make predictions. What a scientist seeks to know is not past actualities—they are history —nor even present actualities, for the immediate present is beyond control. He seeks to know the future in order to control it so far as possible. His business is to assert meaningful propositions about events that are not yet actualized. In some cases, as a result of his knowledge of as yet unactualized events, he seeks to find means of preventing those events from ever becoming actualities.

If we accept Peirce's view that the potentiality is a real feature of the object, we must, if we are to make this assertion meaningful, deny that all that is real are particular determinate individuals. We must reject the nominalistic epistemology and admit a position that allows for real indeterminate potentialities. If we admit that the function of knowledge is to enable us to control the future, then we must take potentialities seriously, for the future as known in the present consists entirely of potentialities, some of which will be actualized and some of which will not. Any epistemological approach that holds that potentialities are meaningless cannot be adequate as a practical basis for human behavior nor as a theoretical basis for science. An epistemology that takes into account the facts of human behavior and the working practices of science must recognize that potentialities, while they cannot be identified with any class of individuals, are nevertheless real. And the reason they are real is because, as Peirce first showed us, the world is general.

Charles S. Peirce:
The Essential Writings

I. Preface to an Unwritten Book
1897–98

THESE FEW PARAGRAPHS may be seen as a short intellectual autobiography.* Peirce wrote them in 1897 and 1898, looking back on his intellectual growth and the factors that influenced him as he saw it. One of the pleasures of reading Peirce lies in the quality of his literary style. He combined a personal warmth of style and an intensely held set of convictions with an integrity and respect for truth that placed him in the tradition of those philosophers from Plato to Hume who have made philosophy a joy to pursue aesthetically as well as intellectually. This short selection reveals these traits to the discerning reader.

Preface†

1. To erect a philosophical edifice that shall outlast the vicissitudes of time, my care must be, not so much to set each brick with nicest accuracy, as to lay the foundations deep and massive. Aristotle built upon a few deliberately chosen concepts—such as matter and form, act and power—very broad, and in their outlines vague and rough, but solid, unshakable, and not easily undermined; and thence it has come to pass that Aristotelianism is babbled in every nursery, that "English Common Sense," for example, is thoroughly peripatetic, and that ordinary men

---

* *The Collected Papers of Charles Sanders Peirce*, ed. Charles Hartshorne and Paul Weiss, vol. I, (1.1–14) (Cambridge, Mass.: The Belknap Press of Harvard University Press, 1931). Copyright 1931, 1959 by the President and Fellows of Harvard College.

† 1 and 2 are from "A Guess at the Riddle" (c. 1898), see bk. III, ch. 3, §1 note. 3–7 and 8–14 are two fragments, (c. 1897).

live so completely within the house of the Stagyrite that whatever they
see out of the windows appears to them incomprehensible and metaphysical. Long it has been only too manifest that, fondly habituated
though we be to it, the old structure will not do for modern needs; and
accordingly, under Descartes, Hobbes, Kant, and others, repairs, alterations, and partial demolitions have been carried on for the last three
centuries. One system, also, stands upon its own ground; I mean the new
Schelling-Hegel mansion, lately run up in the German taste, but with
such oversights in its construction that, although brand new, it is already
pronounced uninhabitable. The undertaking this volume inaugurates is
to make a philosophy like that of Aristotle, that is to say, to outline a
theory so comprehensive that, for a long time to come, the entire work
of human reason, in philosophy of every school and kind, in mathematics, in psychology, in physical science, in history, in sociology, and in
whatever other department there may be, shall appear as the filling up
of its details. The first step toward this is to find simple concepts
applicable to every subject.

2. But before all else, let me make the acquaintance of my reader, and
express my sincere esteem for him and the deep pleasure it is to me to
address one so wise and so patient. I know his character pretty well, for
both the subject and the style of this book ensure his being one out of
millions. He will comprehend that it has not been written for the
purpose of confirming him in his preconceived opinions, and he would
not take the trouble to read it if it had. He is prepared to meet with
propositions that he is inclined at first to dissent from; and he looks to
being convinced that some of them are true, after all. He will reflect,
too, that the thinking and writing of this book has taken, I won't say
how long, quite certainly more than a quarter of an hour, and consequently fundamental objections of so obvious a nature that they must
strike everyone instantaneously will have occurred to the author, although the replies to them may not be of that kind whose full force can
be instantly apprehended.

3. The reader has a right to know how the author's opinions were
formed. Not, of course, that he is expected to accept any conclusions
that are not borne out by argument. But in discussions of extreme

difficulty, like these, when good judgment is a factor, and pure ratiocination is not everything, it is prudent to take every element into consideration. From the moment when I could think at all, until now, about forty years, I have been diligently and incessantly occupied with the study of methods [of] inquiry, both those that have been and are pursued and those that ought to be pursued. For ten years before this study began, I had been in training in the chemical laboratory. I was thoroughly grounded not only in all that was then known of physics and chemistry, but also in the way in which those who were successfully advancing knowledge proceeded. I have paid the most attention to the methods of the most exact sciences, have intimately communed with some of the greatest minds of our times in physical science, and have myself made positive contributions—none of them of any very great importance, perhaps—in mathematics, gravitation, optics, chemistry, astronomy, etc. I am saturated, through and through, with the spirit of the physical sciences. I have been a great student of logic, having read everything of any importance on the subject, devoting a great deal of time to medieval thought, without neglecting the works of the Greeks, the English, the Germans, the French, etc., and have produced systems of my own both in deductive and in inductive logic. In metaphysics, my training has been less systematic; yet I have read and deeply pondered upon all the main systems, never being satisfied until I was able to think about them as their own advocates thought.

4. The first strictly philosophical books that I read were of the classical German schools; and I became so deeply imbued with many of their ways of thinking that I have never been able to disabuse myself of them. Yet my attitude was always that of a dweller in a laboratory, eager only to learn what I did not yet know, and not that of philosophers bred in theological seminaries, whose ruling impulse is to teach what they hold to be infallibly true. I devoted two hours a day to the study of Kant's *Critic of the Pure Reason* for more than three years, until I almost knew the whole book by heart, and had critically examined every section of it. For about two years, I had long and almost daily discussions with Chauncey Wright, one of the most acute of the followers of J. S. Mill.

5. The effect of these studies was that I came to hold the classical German philosophy to be, upon its argumentative side, of little weight; although I esteem it, perhaps am too partial to it, as a rich mine of philosophical suggestions. The English philosophy, meager and crude, as it is, in its conceptions, proceeds by surer methods and more accurate logic. The doctrine of the association of ideas is, to my thinking, the finest piece of philosophical work of the prescientific ages. Yet I can but pronounce English sensationalism to be entirely destitute of any solid bottom. From the evolutionary philosophers I have learned little; although I admit that, however hurriedly their theories have been knocked together, and however antiquated and ignorant Spencer's *First Principles* and general doctrines, yet they are under the guidance of a great and true idea, and are developing it by methods that are in their main features sound and scientific.

6. The works of Duns Scotus have strongly influenced me. If his logic and metaphysics, not slavishly worshipped, but torn away from its medievalism, be adapted to modern culture, under continual wholesome reminders of nominalistic criticisms, I am convinced that it will go far toward supplying the philosophy that is best to harmonize with physical science. But other conceptions have to be drawn from the history of science and from mathematics.

7. Thus, in brief, my philosophy may be described as the attempt of a physicist to make such conjecture as to the constitution of the universe as the methods of science may permit, with the aid of all that has been done by previous philosophers. I shall support my propositions by such arguments as I can. Demonstrative proof is not to be thought of. The demonstrations of the metaphysicians are all moonshine. The best that can be done is to supply a hypothesis, not devoid of all likelihood, in the general line of growth of scientific ideas, and capable of being verified or refuted by future observers.

8. Religious infallibilism, caught in the current of the times, shows symptoms of declaring itself to be only practically speaking infallible; and when it has thus once confessed itself subject to gradations, there will remain over no relic of the good old tenth-century infallibilism, except that of the infallible scientists, under which head I include, not

merely the kind of characters that manufacture scientific catechisms and homilies, churches and creeds, and who are indeed "born missionaries," but all those respectable and cultivated persons who, having acquired their notions of science from reading, and not from research, have the idea that "science" means knowledge, while the truth is, it is a misnomer applied to the pursuit of those who are devoured by a desire to find things out. . . .

9. Though infallibility in scientific matters seems to me irresistibly comical, I should be in a sad way if I could not retain a high respect for those who lay claim to it, for they comprise the greater part of the people who have any conversation at all. When I say they lay claim to it, I mean they assume the functions of it quite naturally and unconsciously. The full meaning of the adage *Humanum est errare*, they have never waked up to. In those sciences of measurement that are the least subject to error—metrology, geodesy, and metrical astronomy—no man of self-respect ever now states his result, without affixing to it its *probable error;* and if this practice is not followed in other sciences it is because in those the probable errors are too vast to be estimated.

10. I am a man of whom critics have never found anything good to say. When they could see no opportunity to injure me, they have held their peace. The little laudation I have had has come from such sources, that the only satisfaction I have derived from it, has been from such slices of bread and butter as it might waft my way. Only once, as far as I remember, in all my lifetime have I experienced the pleasure of praise —not for what it might bring but in itself. That pleasure was beatific; and the praise that conferred it was meant for blame. It was that a critic said of me that I did not seem to be *absolutely sure of my own conclusions.* Never, if I can help it, shall that critic's eye ever rest on what I am now writing; for I owe a great pleasure to him; and, such was his evident animus, that should he find that out, I fear the fires of hell would be fed with new fuel in his breast.

11. My book will have no instruction to impart to anybody. Like a mathematical treatise, it will suggest certain ideas and certain reasons for holding them true; but then, if you accept them, it must be because you like my reasons, and the responsibility lies with you. Man is essen-

tially a social animal: but to be social is one thing, to be gregarious is another: I decline to serve as bellwether. My book is meant for people who *want to find out;* and people who want philosophy ladled out to them can go elsewhere. There are philosophical soup shops at every corner, thank God!

12. The development of my ideas has been the industry of thirty years. I did not know as I ever should get to publish them, their ripening seemed so slow. But the harvest time has come, at last, and to me that harvest seems a wild one, but of course it is not I who have to pass judgment. It is not quite you, either, individual reader; it is experience and history.

13. For years in the course of this ripening process, I used for myself to collect my ideas under the designation *fallibilism;* and indeed the first step toward *finding out* is to acknowledge you do not satisfactorily know already; so that no blight can so surely arrest all intellectual growth as the blight of cocksureness; and ninety-nine out of every hundred good heads are reduced to impotence by that malady—of whose inroads they are most strangely unaware!

14. Indeed, out of a contrite fallibilism, combined with a high faith in the reality of knowledge, and an intense desire to find things out, all my philosophy has always seemed to me to grow. . . .

II. Review of the Works of George Berkeley—1871

OF ALL THE DOCTRINES of Peirce there was none about which he felt
so strongly as he did about the views he held on scholastic realism. As
he put it later, he "first declared" for realism in this early review of the
works of Berkeley.* The question of exactly what Peirce meant by his
realism is still one of the most widely debated subjects among students
of his philosophy. The selections from the Berkeley review contain a
discussion of the realist-nominalist controversy in terms of its historical
development.

   This new edition of Berkeley's works is much superior to any of the
former ones. It contains some writings not in any of the other editions,
and the rest are given with a more carefully edited text. The editor has
done his work well. The introductions to the several pieces contain
analyses of their contents that will be found to provide the greatest
service to the reader. On the other hand, the explanatory notes that
disfigure every page seem to us altogether unnecessary and useless.
   Berkeley's metaphysical theories have at first sight an air of paradox
and levity very unbecoming to a bishop. He denies the existence of
matter, our ability to see distance, and the possibility of forming the
simplest general conception; while he admits the existence of Platonic
ideas; and argues the whole with a cleverness that every reader admits,
but which few are convinced by. His disciples seem to think the present

*Extracts from a review of Alexander Campbell Fraser's *The Works of George Berkeley,
D. D., formerly Bishop of Cloyne: including many of his Writings hitherto unpublished,*
four volumes (Oxford: Clarendon Press, 1871), *The North American Review,* 111 (October 1871), p. 449–472. Also *Collected Papers* (8.7–8.38).

moment a favorable one for obtaining for their philosophy a more patient hearing than it has yet got. It is true that we of this day are sceptical and not given to metaphysics, but so, say they, was the generation that Berkeley addressed, and for which his style was chosen; while it is hoped that the spirit of calm and thorough inquiry that is now, for once, almost the fashion, will save the theory from the perverse misrepresentations that formerly assailed it, and lead to a fair examination of the arguments that, in the minds of his sectators, put the truth of it beyond all doubt. But above all it is anticipated that the Berkeleyan treatment of that question of the validity of human knowledge and of the inductive process of science, that is now so much studied, is such as to command the attention of scientific men to the idealistic system. To us these hopes seem vain. The truth is that the minds from whom the spirit of the age emanates have now no interest in the only problems that metaphysics ever pretended to solve. The abstract acknowledgment of God, Freedom, and Immortality, apart from those other religious beliefs (that cannot possibly rest on metaphysical grounds) that alone may animate this, is now seen to have no practical consequence whatever. The world is getting to think of these creatures of metaphysics, as Aristotle of the Platonic ideas: τερετίσματα γάρ ἐστι, καὶ εἰ ἔστιν, οὐδὲν πρὸς τὸν λόγον ἐστίν. The question of the grounds of the validity of induction has, it is true, excited an interest, and may continue to do so (though the argument is now become too difficult for popular apprehension); but whatever interest it has had has been due to a hope that the solution of it would afford the basis for sure and useful maxims concerning the logic of induction,—a hope that would be destroyed so soon as it were shown that the question was a purely metaphysical one. This is the prevalent feeling, among advanced minds. It may not be just; but it exists. And its existence is an effectual bar (if there were no other) to the general acceptance of Berkeley's system. The few who do now care for metaphysics are not of that bold order of minds who delight to hold a position so unsheltered by the prejudices of common sense as that of the good bishop.

As a matter of history, however, philosophy must always be interesting. It is the best representative of the mental development of each age.

It is so even of ours, if we think what really is our philosophy. Metaphysical history is one of the chief branches of history, and ought to be expounded side by side with the history of society, of government, and of war; for in its relations with these we trace the significance of events for the human mind. The history of philosophy in the British Isles is a subject possessing more unity and entirety within itself than has usually been recognized in it. The influence of Descartes was never so great in England as that of traditional conceptions, and we can trace a continuity between modern and medieval thought there, which is wanting in the history of France, and still more, if possible, in that of Germany.

From very early times it has been the chief intellectual characteristic of the English to wish to effect everything by the plainest and directest means, without unnecessary contrivance. In war, for example, they rely more than any other people in Europe upon sheer hardihood, and rather despise military science. The main peculiarities of their system of law arise from the fact that every evil has been rectified as it became intolerable, without any thoroughgoing measure. The bill for legalizing marriage with a deceased wife's sister is yearly pressed because it supplies a remedy for an inconvenience actually felt; but nobody has proposed a bill to legalize marriage with a deceased husband's brother. In philosophy, this national tendency appears as a strong preference for the simplest theories, and a resistance to any complication of the theory as long as there is the least possibility that the facts can be explained in the simpler way. And, accordingly, British philosophers have always desired to weed out of philosophy all conceptions that could not be made perfectly definite and easily intelligible, and have shown strong nominalistic tendencies since the time of Edward I or even earlier. Berkeley is an admirable illustration of this national character, as well as of that strange union of nominalism with Platonism, which has repeatedly appeared in history, and has been such a stumbling block to the historians of philosophy.

The medieval metaphysic is so entirely forgotten, and has so close a historic connection with modern English philosophy, and so much bearing upon the truth of Berkeley's doctrine, that we may perhaps be pardoned a few pages on the nature of the celebrated controversy con-

cerning universals. And first let us set down a few dates. It was at the
very end of the eleventh century that the dispute concerning nominalism and realism, that had existed in a vague way before, began to attain
extraordinary proportions. During the twelfth century it was the matter
of most interest to logicians, when William of Champeaux, Abelard,
John of Salisbury, Gilbert de la Porrée, and many others, defended as
many different opinions. But there was no historic connection between
this controversy and those of scholasticism proper, the scholasticism of
Aquinas, Scotus, and Ockam. For about the end of the twelfth century
a great revolution of thought took place in Europe. What the influences
were that produced it requires new historical researches to say. No doubt
it was partly due to the crusades. But a great awakening of intelligence
did take place at that time. It requires, it is true, some examination to
distinguish this particular movement from a general awakening that had
begun a century earlier , and had been growing stronger ever since. But
now there was an accelerated impulse. Commerce was attaining new
importance, and was inventing some of her chief conveniences and
safeguards. Law, which had hitherto been utterly barbaric, began to be
a profession. The civil law was adopted in Europe, the canon law was
digested; the common law took some form. The Church, under Inno-
cent III was assuming the sublime functions of a moderator over kings.
And those orders of mendicant friars were established, two of which did
so much for the development of the scholastic philosophy. Art felt the
spirit of a new age, and there could hardly be a greater change than from
the highly ornate round-arched architecture of the twelfth century to
the comparatively simple Gothic of the thirteenth. Indeed, if any one
wishes to know what a scholastic commentary is like, and what the tone
of thought in it is, he has only to contemplate a Gothic cathedral. The
first quality of either is a religious devotion, truly heroic. One feels that
the men who did these works did really believe in religion as we believe
in nothing. We cannot easily understand how Thomas Aquinas can
speculate so much on the nature of angels, and whether ten thousand
of them could dance on a needle's point. But it was simply because he
held them for real. If they are real, why are they not more interesting
than the bewildering varieties of insects that naturalists study; or why

should the orbits of double stars attract more attention than spiritual intelligences? It will be said that we have no means of knowing anything about them. But that is on a par with censuring the schoolmen for referring questions to the authority of the Bible and of the Church. If they really believed in their religion, as they did, what better could they do? And if they found in these authorities testimony concerning angels, how could they avoid admitting it. Indeed, objections of this sort only make it appear still more clearly how much those were the ages of faith. And if the spirit was not altogether admirable, it is only because faith itself has its faults as a foundation for the intellectual character. The men of that time did fully believe and did think that, for the sake of giving themselves up absolutely to their great task of building or of writing, it was well worth while to resign all the joys of life. Think of the spirit in which Duns Scotus must have worked, who wrote his thirteen volumes in folio, in a style as condensed as the most condensed parts of Aristotle, before the age of thirty-four. Nothing is more striking in either of the great intellectual products of that age, than the complete absence of self-conceit on the part of the artist or philosopher. That anything of value can be added to his sacred and catholic work by its having the smack of individuality about it, is what he has never conceived. His work is not designed to embody *his* ideas, but the universal truth; there will not be one thing in it however minute, for which you will not find that he has his authority; and whatever originality emerges is of that inborn kind that so saturates a man that he cannot himself perceive it. The individual feels his own worthlessness in comparison with his task, and does not dare to introduce his vanity into the doing of it. Then there is no machine-work, no unthinking repetition about the thing. Every part is worked out for itself as a separate problem, no matter how analogous it may be in general to another part. And no matter how small and hidden a detail may be, it has been conscientiously studied, as though it were intended for ths eye of God. Allied to this character is a detestation of antithesis or the studied balancing of one thing against another, and of a too geometrical grouping,—a hatred of posing that is as much a moral trait as the others. Finally, there is nothing in which the scholastic philosophy and the Gothic architecture resemble one another more than in the gradually increasing sense of immensity that impresses the mind of the student as he learns to appreciate the real dimensions and cost of each. It is very unfortunate that the thirteenth, fourteenth, and fifteenth centuries should, under the name of the Middle Ages, be confounded with others, which they are in every respect as unlike as the Renaissance is from modern times. In the history of logic, the break between the twelfth and thirteenth centuries is so great that only one author of the former age is ever quoted in the latter. If this is to be attributed to the fuller acquaintance with the works of Aristotle, to what, we would ask, is this profounder study itself to be attributed, since it is now known that the knowledge of those works was not imported from the Arabs? The thirteenth century was realistic, but the question concerning universals was not as much agitated as several others. Until about the end of the century, scholasticism was somewhat vague, immature, and unconscious of its own power. Its greatest glory was in the first half of the fourteenth century. Then Duns Scotus,* a Briton (for whether Scotch, Irish, or English is disputed), first stated the realistic position consistently, and developed it with great fullness and applied it to all the different questions that depend upon it. His theory of "formalities" was the subtlest, except perhaps Hegel's logic, ever broached, and he was separated from nominalism only by the division of a hair. It is not therefore surprising that the nominalistic position was soon adopted by several writers, especially by the celebrated William of Ockam, who took the lead of this party by the thoroughgoing and masterly way in which he treated the theory and combined it with a then rather recent but now forgotten addition to the doctrine of logical terms. With Ockam, who died in 1347, scholasticism may be said to have culminated. After him the scholastic philosophy showed a tendency to separate itself from the religious element that alone could dignify it, and sunk first into extreme formalism and fancifulness, and then into the merited contempt of all men; just as the Gothic architecture had a very similar fate, at about the same time, and for much the same reasons.

*Died 1308.

The current explanations of the realist-nominalist controversy are equally false and unintelligible. They are said to be derived ultimately from Bayle's Dictionary; at any rate, they are not based on a study of the authors. "Few, very few, for a hundred years past," says Hallam, with truth, "have broken the repose of the immense works of the school-men." Yet it is perfectly possible so to state the matter that no one shall fail to comprehend what the question was, and how there might be two opinions about it. Are universals real? We have only to stop and consider a moment what was meant by the word *real*, when the whole issue soon becomes apparent. Objects are divided into figments, dreams, etc., on the one hand, and realities on the other. The former are those that exist only inasmuch as you or I or some man imagines them; the latter are those that have an existence independent of your mind or mine or that of any number of persons. The real is that which is not whatever we happen to think it, but is unaffected by what we may think of it. The question, therefore, is whether *man, horse*, and other names of natural classes, correspond with anything that all men, or all horses, really have in common, independent of our thought, or whether these classes are constituted simply by a likeness in the way in which our minds are affected by individual objects that have in themselves no resemblance or relationship whatsoever. Now that this is a real question that different minds will naturally answer in opposite ways, becomes clear when we think that there are two widely separated points of view, from which *reality*, as just defined, may be regarded. Where is the real, the thing independent of how we think it, to be found? There must be such a thing, for we find our opinions constrained; there is something, there-fore, that influences our thoughts, and is not created by them. We have, it is true, nothing immediately present to us but thoughts. Those thoughts, however, have been caused by sensations, and those sensations are constrained by something out of the mind. This thing out of the mind, which directly influences sensation, and through sensation thought, because it *is* out of the mind, is independent of how we think it, and is, in short, the real. Here is one view of reality, a very familiar one. And from this point of view it is clear that the nominalistic answer must be given to the question concerning universals. For, while from this standpoint it may be admitted to be true as a rough statement that one man is like another, the exact sense being that the realities external to the mind produce sensations that may be embraced under one conception, yet it can by no means be admitted that the two real men have really anything in common, for to say that they are both men is only to say that the one mental term or thought-sign "man" stands indifferently for either of the sensible objects caused by the two external realities; so that not even the two sensations have in themselves anything in common, and far less is it to be inferred that the external realities have. This conception of reality is so familiar, that it is unnecessary to dwell upon it; but the other, or realist conception, if less familiar, is even more natural and obvious. All human thought and opinion contains an arbitrary, accidental element, dependent on the limitations in circumstances, power, and bent of the individual; an element of error, in short. But human opinion universally tends in the long run to a definite form, which is the truth. Let any human being have enough information and exert enough thought upon any question, and the result will be that he will arrive at a certain definite conclusion, which is the same that any other mind will reach under sufficiently favorable circumstances. Suppose two men, one deaf, the other blind. One hears a man declare he means to kill another, hears the report of the pistol, and hears the victim cry; the other sees the murder done. Their sensations are affected in the highest degree with their individual peculiarities. The first information that their sensations will give them, their first inferences, will be more nearly alike, but still different; the one having, for example, the idea of a man shouting, the other of a man with a threatening aspect; but their final conclusions, the thought the remotest from sense, will be identical and free from the one-sidedness of their idiosyncrasies. There is, then, to every question a true answer, a final conclusion, to which the opinion of every man is constantly gravitating. He may for a time recede from it, but give him more experience and time for consideration, and he will finally approach it. The individual may not live to reach the truth; there is a residuum of error in every individual's opinions. No matter; it remains that there is a definite opinion to which the mind of man is, on the whole and in the long run, tending. On many questions the final agreement is already reached, on all it will be reached if time enough is given. The arbitrary will or other individual peculiarities of a sufficiently large number of minds may postpone the general agreement in that opinion indefinitely; but it cannot affect what the character of that opinion shall be when it is reached. This final opinion, then, is independent, not indeed of thought in general, but of all that is arbitrary and individual in thought; is quite independent of how you, or I, or any number of men think. Everything, therefore, that will be thought to exist in the final opinion is real, and nothing else. What is the POWER of external things, to affect the senses? To say that people sleep after taking opium because it has a soporific *power*, is that to say anything in the world but that people sleep after taking opium because they sleep after taking opium? To assert the existence of a power or potency, is it to assert the existence of anything actual? Or to say that a thing has a potential existence, is it to say that it has an actual existence? In other words, is the present existence of a power anything in the world but a regularity in future events relating to a certain thing regarded as an element that is to be taken account of beforehand, in the conception of that thing? If not, to assert that there are external things that can be known only as exerting a power on our sense, is nothing different from asserting that there is a general *drift* in the history of human thought that will lead it to one general agreement, one catholic consent. And any truth more perfect than this destined conclusion, any reality more absolute than what is thought in it, is a fiction of metaphysics. It is obvious how this way of thinking harmonizes with a belief in an infallible Church, and how much more natural it would be in the Middle Ages than in Protestant or positivist times.

This theory of reality is instantly fatal to the idea of a thing in itself, —a thing existing independent of all relation to the mind's conception of it. Yet it would by no means forbid, but rather encourage us, to regard the appearances of sense as only signs of the realities. Only, the realities that they represent would not be the unknowable cause of sensation, but *noumena*, or intelligible conceptions that are the last products of the mental action that is set in motion by sensation. The matter of sensation is altogether accidental; precisely the same information, practically, being capable of communication through different senses. And the catholic consent that constitutes the truth is by no means to be limited to men in this earthly life or to the human race, but extends to the whole communion of minds to which we belong, including some probably whose senses are very different from ours, so that in that consent no predication of a sensible quality can enter, except as an admission that so certain sorts of senses are affected. This theory is also highly favorable to a belief in external realities. It will, to be sure, deny that there is any reality that is absolutely incognizable in itself, so that it cannot be taken into the mind. But observing that "the external" means simply that which is independent of what phenomenon is immediately present, that is of how we may think or feel; just as "the real" means that which is independent of how we may think or feel *about* it; it must be granted that there are many objects of true science that are external, because there are many objects of thought that, if they are independent of that thinking whereby they are thought (that is, if they are real), are indisputably independent of all *other* thoughts and feelings.

It is plain that this view of reality is inevitably realistic; because general conceptions enter into all judgments, and therefore into true opinions. Consequently a thing in the general is as real as in the concrete. It is perfectly true that all white things have whiteness in them, for that is only saying, in another form of words, that all white things are white; but since it is true that real things possess whiteness, whiteness is real. It is a real that only exists by virtue of an act of thought knowing it, but that thought is not an arbitrary or accidental one dependent on any idiosyncrasies, but one that will hold in the final opinion.

This theory involves a phenomenalism. But it is the phenomenalism of Kant, and not that of Hume. Indeed, what Kant called his Copernican step was precisely the passage from the nominalistic to the realistic view of reality. It was the essence of his philosophy to regard the real object as determined by the mind. That was nothing else than to consider every conception and intuition that enters necessarily into the experience of an object, and that is not transitory and accidental, as having objective validity. In short, it was to regard the reality as the normal product of mental action, and not as the incognizable cause of it.

This realistic theory is thus a highly practical and common-sense position. Wherever universal agreement prevails, the realist will not be the one to disturb the general belief by idle and fictitious doubts. For according to him it is a consensus or common confession that constitutes reality. What he wants, therefore, is to see questions put to rest. And if a general belief, that is perfectly stable and immovable, can in any way be produced, though it be by the fagot and the rack, to talk of any error in such belief is utterly absurd. The realist will hold that the very same objects that are immediately present in our minds in experience really exist just as they are experienced out of the mind; that is, he will maintain a doctrine of immediate perception. He will not, therefore, sunder existence out of the mind and being in the mind as two wholly improportionable modes. When a thing is in such relation to the individual mind that that mind cognizes it, it is in the mind; and its being so in the mind will not in the least diminish its external existence. For he does not think of the mind as a receptacle, that if a thing is in, it ceases to be out of. To make a distinction between the true conception of a thing and the thing itself is, he will say, only to regard one and the same thing from two different points of view; for the immediate object of thought in a true judgment *is* the reality. The realist will, therefore, believe in the objectivity of all necessary conceptions, space, time, relation, cause, and the like.

No realist or nominalist ever expressed so definitely, perhaps, as is here done, his conception of reality. It is difficult to give a clear notion of an opinion of a past age, without exaggerating its distinctness. But careful examination of the works of the schoolmen will show that the distinction between these two views of the real—one as the fountain of the current of human thought, the other as the unmoving form to which it is flowing —is what really occasions their disagreement on the question concerning universals. The gist of all the nominalist's arguments will be found to relate to a *res extra animam*, while the realist defends his position only by assuming that the immediate object of thought in a true judgment is real. The notion that the controversy between realism and nominalism had anything to do with Platonic ideas is a mere product of the imagination, that the slightest examination of the books would suffice to disprove. . . .

Thus we see how large a part of the metaphysical ideas of today have come to us by inheritance from very early times, Berkeley being one of the intellectual ancestors whose labors did as much as anyone's to enhance the value of the bequest. The realistic philosophy of the last century has now lost all its popularity, except with the most conservative minds. And science as well as philosophy is nominalistic. The doctrine of the correlation of forces, the discoveries of Helmholtz, and the hypotheses of Liebig and of Darwin, have all that character of explaining familiar phenomena apparently of a peculiar kind by extending the operation of simple mechanical principles, which belongs to nominalism. Or if the nominalistic character of these doctrines themselves cannot be detected, it will at least be admitted that they are observed to carry along with them those daughters of nominalism,—sensationalism, phenomenalism, individualism, and materialism. That physical science is necessarily connected with doctrines of a debasing moral tendency will be believed by few. But if we hold that such an effect will not be produced by these doctrines on a mind that really understands them, we are accepting this belief, not on experience, which is rather against it, but on the strength of our general faith that what is really true it is good to believe and evil to reject. On the other hand, it is allowable to suppose that science has no essential affinity with the philosophical views with which it seems to be every year more associated. History cannot be held to exclude this supposition; and science as it exists is certainly much less nominalistic than the nominalists think it should be. [William] Whewell represents it quite as well as Mill. Yet a man who enters into the scientific thought of the day and has not materialistic tendencies is getting to be an impossibility. So long as there is a dispute between nominalism and realism, so long as the position we hold on the question is not determined by any proof *indisputable*, but is more or less a matter of inclination, a man as he gradually comes to feel the profound hostility of the two tendencies will, if he is not less than man, become engaged with one or other and can no more obey both than he can serve God and Mammon. If the two impulses are neutralized within him, the result simply is that he is left without any great intellectual motive. There is, indeed, no reason to suppose the logical question is in its own nature unsusceptible of solution. But that path out of the difficulty lies through the thorniest mazes of a science as dry as mathematics. Now there is a demand for mathematics; it helps to build bridges and drive engines, and therefore it becomes somebody's business to study it severely. But to have a philosophy is a matter of luxury; the only use of that is to make us feel comfortable and easy. It is a study for leisure hours; and we want it supplied in an elegant, an agreeable, an interesting form. The law of natural selection, that is the precise analog in another realm of the law of supply and demand, has the most immediate effect in fostering the other faculties of the understanding, for the men of mental power succeed in the struggle for life; but the faculty of philosophizing, except in the literary way, is not called for, and therefore a difficult question cannot be expected to reach solution until it takes some practical form. If anybody should have the good luck to find out the solution, nobody else would take the trouble to understand it. But though the question of realism and nominalism has its roots in the technicalities of logic, its branches reach about our life. The question whether the *genus homo* has any existence except as individuals, is the question whether there is anything of any more dignity, worth, and importance than individual happiness, individual aspirations and individual life. Whether men really have anything in common, so that the *community* is to be considered as an end in itself, and if so, what the relative value of the two factors is, is the most fundamental practical question in regard to every public institution the constitution of which we have it in our power to influence.

C. S. P.

III. Questions Concerning Certain Faculties Claimed for Man

THIS SERIES OF three papers appeared in 1868 in the *Journal of Speculative Philosophy.*[1] It represents an early but fairly detailed treatment of Peirce's epistemology.

In the first article he raises a series of questions about the nature of the knowledge process. He presents argumentation on each side of a question and then reaches a conclusion. His first question asks whether when we know something, we also know what the source of that knowledge is; i.e., do we know whether it is caused by a previous cognition or is it a direct intuition of something outside of thought? He concludes that we do not know the source of our knowledge by examination of it. Berkeley and Kant, for example, taught us that our cognitions of space are the result of inferences, not of intuitions. And yet prior to Berkeley's theory of vision, men thought that they had direct knowledge of space.

Peirce then examines our consciousness of self and asks whether, as Descartes held, we directly intuit the self. He draws the conclusion, remarkable for his time, that knowledge of the self is an inference (and hence learned), not intuited.

His third question asks whether we can intuit the difference between the quality of an experience, as to whether we are dreaming, imagining, or perceiving, for example. Again he concludes we cannot.

A fourth question asks whether we have any insights from introspection or whether all cognition is derived from observation. Again, Peirce answers that there is no reason for supposing that we have introspective

[1]Reprinted in *Collected Papers* at 5.213 ff., 5.264 ff., and 5.318 ff.

intuitions, and concludes that all cognitions must be derived from external observation.

In question five he turns to a somewhat different issue and asks whether we can think without signs. After arguing that we cannot, that every thought is a sign, he asks whether a sign can have any meaning if it is of something that cannot be known. He concludes that it cannot because no such incognizable could ever enter experience and thus could not be the object of a sign. Peirce has thus committed himself to the path that will in future years lead him to his pragmatic doctrine, for he has now said that the meaning of every sign must lie in the sense-experiences that it comes from and in those to which it will in the future lead us. In his final question, whether a cognition can be determined by something not a cognition, he argues the other side of the coin of his future theory of meaning, that any such cognition would be meaningless.

In the second article "Some Consequences of Four Incapacities," Peirce amplifies this position and shows that his epistemology is consistent with such elements in his metaphysics as his scholastic realism, his idealism, and his theory of truth as residing in the community of investigators. He, finally, drives home his argument that since the self is a learned entity, not an intuited entity, and since everything that is learned is a thought, that the self is a thought, or, more generally stated, since every thought is a sign, man himself is a sign.

The final article of the series is not included here. In it Peirce explores further consequences of his epistemology as they apply to logic. The discussion deals with such topics as are dear to the hearts of logicians: skepticism, the nature of logical reasoning, the parodoxes, and the uniformity of nature. He concludes that his epistemology is consistent with a social logic, but that such logic, and all logic, rests ultimately upon an act of faith, or hope: a belief that success is possible, that answers to our questions can be reached. Without this faith we would not look for answers and would not, therefore, find them if they exist. If answers do not exist we cannot find them anyway, but if they do exist we can only find them if we look for them, and we will only look for them if we believe they may be found. This act of faith, then, is at the base of all our methods of inquiry.

1. Questions Concerning Certain Faculties Claimed for Man

QUESTION 1. *Whether by the simple contemplation of a cognition, independently of any previous knowledge and without reasoning from sign, we are enabled rightly to judge whether that cognition has been determined by a previous cognition or whether it refers immediately to its object.*

Throughout this paper, the term *intuition* will be taken as signifying a cognition not determined by a previous cognition of the same object, and therefore so determined by something out of the consciousness.* Let me request the reader to note this. *Intuition* here will be nearly the same as "premise not itself a conclusion"; the only difference being that premises and conclusions are judgments, whereas an intuition may, as far as its definition states, be any kind of cognition whatever. But just as a conclusion (good or bad) is determined in the mind of the reasoner by its premise, so cognitions not judgments may be determined by previous cognitions; and a cognition not so determined, and therefore determined directly by the transcendental object, is to be termed an *intuition*.

Now, it is plainly one thing to have an intuition and another to know intuitively that it is an intuition, and the question is whether these two

---

*The word *intuitus* first occurs as a technical term in St. Anselm's *Monologium*. He wished to distinguish between our knowledge of God and our knowledge of finite things (and, in the next world, of God, also); and thinking of the saying of St. Paul, *Videmus nunc per speculum in ænigmate: tunc autem facie ad faciem*, he called the former *speculation* and the latter *intuition*. This use of "speculation" did not take root, because that word already had another exact and widely different meaning. In the Middle Ages the term "intuitive cognition" had two principal senses, first, as opposed to abstractive cognition, it meant the knowledge of the present as present, and this is its meaning in Anselm; but second, as no intuitive cognition was allowed to be determined by a previous cognition, it came to be used as the opposite of discursive cognition (see Scotus, In sentent. lib. 2, dist. 3, qu. 9), and this is nearly the sense in which I employ it. This is also nearly the sense in which Kant uses it, the former distinction being expressed by his *sensuous* and *nonsensuous*. (See Werke, herausg. Rosenkrantz, Thl. 2, S. 713, 31, 41, 100, u. s.w.) An enumeration of six meanings of intuition may be found in Hamilton's Reid, p. 759.

things, distinguishable in thought, are, in fact, invariably connected, so that we can always intuitively distinguish between an intuition and a cognition determined by another. Every cognition, as something present, is, of course, an intuition of itself. But the determination of a cognition by another cognition or by a transcendental object is not, at least so far as appears obviously at first, a part of the immediate content of that cognition, although it would appear to be an element of the action or passion of the transcendental *ego*, which is not, perhaps, in consciousness immediately; and yet this transcendental action or passion may invariably determine a cognition of itself, so that, in fact, the determination or nondetermination of the cognition by another may be a part of the cognition. In this case, I should say that we had an intuitive power of distinguishing an intuition from another cognition.

There is no evidence that we have this faculty, except that we seem to *feel* that we have it. But the weight of that testimony depends entirely on our being supposed to have the power of distinguishing in this feeling whether the feeling be the result of education, old associations, etc., or whether it is an intuitive cognition; or, in other words, it depends on presupposing the very matter testified to. Is this feeling infallible? And is this judgment concerning it infallible, and so on, *ad infinitum*? Supposing that a man really could shut himself up in such a faith, he would be, of course, impervious to the truth, "evidence-proof."

But let us compare the theory with the historic facts. The power of intuitively distinguishing intuitions from other cognitions has not prevented men from disputing very warmly as to which cognitions are intuitive. In the Middle Ages reason and external authority were regarded as two coordinate sources of knowledge, just as reason and the authority of intuition are now; only the happy device of considering the enunciations of authority to be essentially indemonstrable had not yet been hit upon. All authorities were not considered as infallible; any more than all reasons; but when Berengarius said that the authoritativeness of any particular authority must rest upon reason, the proposition was scouted as opinionated, impious, and absurd. Thus, the credibility of authority was regarded by men of that time simply as an ultimate premise, as a cognition not determined by a previous cognition of the same object, or, in our terms, as an intuition. It is strange that they should have thought so, if, as the theory now under discussion supposes, by merely contemplating the credibility of the authority, as a Fakir does his God, they could have seen that it was not an ultimate premise! Now, what if our *internal* authority should meet the same fate, in the history of opinions, as that external authority has met? Can that be said to be absolutely certain that many sane, well-informed, and thoughtful men already doubt?*

Every lawyer knows how difficult it is for witnesses to distinguish between what they have seen and what they have inferred. This is particularly noticeable in the case of a person who is describing the performances of a spiritual medium or of a professed juggler. The difficulty is so great that the juggler himself is often astonished at the discrepancy between the actual facts and the statement of an intelligent witness who has not understood the trick. A part of the very complicated

---

*The proposition of Berengarius is contained in the following quotation from his *De Sacra Cæna:* "*Maximi plane cordis est, per omnia ad dialecticam confugere, quia confugere ad eam ad rationem est confugere, quo qui non confugit, cum secundum rationem sit factus ad imaginem dei, suum honorem reliquit, nec potest renovari de die in diem ad imaginem dei.*" The most striking characteristic of medieval reasoning, in general is the perpetual resort to authority. When Fredigisus and others wish to prove that darkness is a thing, although they have evidently derived the opinion from nominalistic-Platonistic meditations, they argue the matter thus: "God called the darkness, night"; then, certainly, it is a thing, for otherwise before it had a name, there would have been nothing, not even a fiction to name. Abelard thinks it worth while to cite Boëthius, when he says that space has three dimensions, and when he says that an individual cannot be in two places at once. The author of *De Generibus et Speciebus,* a work of a superior order, in arguing against a Platonic doctrine, says that if whatever is universal is eternal, the *form* and matter of Socrates, being severally universal are both eternal, and that, therefore, Socrates was not created by God, but only put together, "*quod quantum a vero deviet, palam est.*" The authority is the final court of appeal. The same author, where in one place he doubts a statement of Boëthius, finds it necessary to assign a special reason why in this case it is not absurd to do so. *Exceptio probat regulam in casibus non exceptis.* Recognized authorities were certainly sometimes disputed in the twelfth century; their mutual contradictions insured that, and the authority of philosophers was regarded as inferior to that of theologians. Still, it would be impossible to find a passage where the authority of Aristotle is directly denied upon any logical question. "*Sunt et multi errores eius,*" says John of Salisbury, "*qui in scripturis tam Ethnicis, quam fidelibus poterunt inveniri: verum in logica parem habuisse non legitur.*" "*Sed nihil adversus Aristotelem,*" says Abelard, and in another place, "*Sed si Aristotelem Peripateticorum principem culpare possumus, quam amplius in hac arte recpimus?*" The idea of going without an authority, or of subordinating authority to reason, does not occur to him.

trick of the Chinese rings consists in taking two solid rings linked together, talking about them as though they were separate—taking it for granted, as it were—then pretending to put them together, and handing them immediately to the spectator that he may see that they are solid. The art of this consists in raising, at first, the strong suspicion that one is broken. I have seen McAlister do this with such success, that a person sitting close to him, with all his faculties straining to detect the illusion, would have been ready to swear that he saw the rings put together, and, perhaps, if the juggler had not professedly practiced deception, would have considered a doubt of it as a doubt of his own veracity. This certainly seems to show that it is not always very easy to distinguish between a premise and a conclusion, that we have no infallible power of doing so, and that in fact our only security in difficult cases is in some signs from which we can infer that a given fact must have been seen or must have been inferred. In trying to give an account of a dream, every accurate person must often have felt that it was a hopeless undertaking to attempt to disentangle waking interpretations and fillings out from the fragmentary images of the dream itself.

The mention of dreams suggests another argument. A dream, as far as its own content goes, is exactly like an actual experience. It is mistaken for one. And yet all the world believes that dreams are determined, according to the laws of the association of ideas, etc., by previous cognitions. If it be said that the faculty of intuitively recognizing intuitions is asleep, I reply that this is a mere supposition, without other support. Besides, even when we wake up, we do not find that the dream differed from reality, except by certain *marks*, darkness, and fragmentariness. Not unfrequently a dream is so vivid that the memory of it is mistaken for the memory of an actual occurrence.

A child has, as far as we know, all the perceptive powers of a man. Yet question him a little as to *how* he knows what he does. In many cases, he will tell you that he never learned his mother tongue; he always knew it, or he knew it as soon as he came to have sense. It appears, then, that *he* does not possess the faculty of distinguishing, by simple contemplation, between an intuition and a cognition determined by others.

There can be no doubt that before the publication of Berkeley's book on vision, it had generally been believed that the third dimension of space was immediately intuited, although, at present, nearly all admit that it is known by inference. We had been *contemplating* the object since the very creation of man, but this discovery was not made until we began to *reason* about it.

Does the reader know of the blind spot on the retina? Take a number of this journal, turn over the cover so as to expose the white paper, lay it sideways upon the table before which you must sit, and put two cents upon it, one near the left hand edge, and the other to the right. Put your left hand over your left eye, and with the right eye look *steadily* at the left hand cent. Then, with your right hand, move the right hand cent (which is now plainly seen) *towards* the left hand. When it comes to a place near the middle of the page it will disappear—you cannot see it without turning your eye. Bring it nearer to the other cent, or carry it further away, and it will reappear; but at that particular spot it cannot be seen. Thus it appears that there is a blind spot nearly in the middle of the retina; and this is confirmed by anatomy. It follows that the space we immediately see (when one eye is closed) is not, as we had imagined, a continuous oval, but is a ring, the filling up of which must be the work of the intellect. What more striking example could be desired of the impossibility of distinguishing intellectual results from intuitional data, by mere contemplation?

A man can distinguish different textures of cloth by feeling; but not immediately, for he requires to move his fingers over the cloth, which shows that he is obliged to compare the sensations of one instant with those of another.

The pitch of a tone depends upon the rapidity of the succession of the vibrations that reach the ear. Each of those vibrations produces an impulse upon the ear. Let a single such impulse be made upon the ear, and we know, experimentally, that it is perceived. There is, therefore, good reason to believe that each of the impulses forming a tone is perceived. Nor is there any reason to the contrary. So that this is the only admissible supposition. Therefore, the pitch of a tone depends upon the rapidity with which certain impressions are successively conveyed to the mind. These impressions must exist previously to any tone; hence, the sensation of pitch is determined by previous cognitions.

Nevertheless, this would never have been discovered by the mere contemplation of that feeling.

A similiar argument may be urged in reference to the perception of two dimensions of space. This appears to be an immediate intuition. But if we were to *see* immediately an extended surface, our retinas must be spread out in an extended surface. Instead of that, the retina consists of innumerable needles pointing towards the light, and whose distances from one another are decidedly greater than the *minimum visible*. Suppose each of those nerve points conveys the sensation of a little colored surface. Still, what we immediately see must even then be not a continuous surface but a collection of spots. Who could discover this by mere intuition? But all the analogies of the nervous system are against the supposition that the excitation of a single nerve can produce an idea as complicated as that of a space, however small. If the excitation of no one of these nerve points can immediately convey the impression of space, the excitation of all cannot do so. For, the excitation of each produces some impression (according to the analogies of the nervous system), hence, the sum of these impressions is a necessary condition of any perception produced by the excitation of all; or, in other terms, a perception produced by the excitation of all is determined by the mental impressions produced by the excitation of every one. This argument is confirmed by the fact that the existence of the perception of space can be fully accounted for by the action of faculties known to exist, without supposing it to be an immediate impression. For this purpose, we must bear in mind the following facts of physio-psychology: 1. The excitation of a nerve does not of itself inform us where the extremity of it is situated. If, by a surgical operation, certain nerves are displaced, our sensations from those nerves do not inform us of the displacement. 2. A single sensation does not inform us how many nerves or nerve points are excited. 3. We can distinguish between the impressions produced by the excitations of different nerve points. 4. The differences of impressions produced by different excitations of similar nerve points are similar. Let a momentary image be made upon the retina. By No. 2, the impression thereby produced will be indistinguishable from what might be produced by the excitation of some conceivable single nerve. It is not conceivable that the momentary excitation of a single nerve should give the sensation of space. Therefore, the momentary excitation of all the nerve points of the retina cannot, immediately or mediately, produce the sensation of space. The same argument would apply to any unchanging image on the retina. Suppose, however, that the image moves over the retina. Then the peculiar excitation that at one instant affects one nerve point, at a later instant will affect another. These will convey impressions which are very similar by 4, and yet which are distinguishable by 3. Hence, the conditions for the recognition of a relation between these impressions are present. There being, however, a very great number of nerve points affected by a very great number of successive excitations, the relations of the resulting impressions will be almost inconceivably complicated. Now, it is a known law of mind, that when phenomena of an extreme complexity are presented, which yet would be reduced to *order* or mediate simplicity by the application of a certain conception, that conception sooner or later arises in application to those phenomena. In the case under consideration, the conception of extension would reduce the phenomena to unity, and, therefore, its genesis is fully accounted for. It remains only to explain why the previous cognitions that determine it are not more clearly apprehended. For this explanation, I shall refer to a paper upon a new list of categories, § 5,* merely adding that just as we are able to recognize our friends by certain appearances, although we cannot possibly say what those appearances are and are quite unconscious of any process of reasoning, so in any case when the reasoning is easy and natural to us, however complex may be the premises, they sink into insignificance and oblivion proportionately to the satisfactoriness of the theory based upon them. This theory of space is confirmed by the circumstance that an exactly similar theory is imperatively demanded by the facts in reference to time. That the course of time should be immediately felt is obviously impossible. For, in that case, there must be an element of this feeling at each instant. But in an instant there is no duration and hence no immediate feeling of duration. Hence, no one of these elementary feelings is an immediate feeling of duration; and, hence the sum of all is not. On the other hand,

---

*Proceedings of the American Academy, May 14, 1867.

the impressions of any moment are very complicated,—containing all the images (or the elements of the images) of sense and memory, which complexity is reducible to mediate simplicity by means of the conception of time.*

We have, therefore, a variety of facts, all of which are most readily

*The above theory of space and time does not conflict with that of Kant so much as it appears to do. They are in fact the solutions of different questions. Kant, it is true, makes space and time intuitions, or rather forms of intuition, but it is not essential to his theory that intuition should mean more than "individual representation." The apprehension of space and time results, according to him, from a mental *process*,—the "Synthesis der Apprehension in der Anschauung." (See Critik d. reinen Vernunft. Ed. 1781, pp. 98 *et seq.*) My theory is merely an account of this synthesis.

The gist of Kant's Transcendental æsthetic is contained in two principles. First, that universal and necessary propositions are not given in experience. Second, that universal and necessary facts are determined by the conditions of experience in general. By a universal proposition is meant merely, one that asserts something of *all* of a sphere,—not necessarily one that all men believe. By a necessary proposition, is meant one that asserts what it does, not merely of the actual condition of things, but of every possible state of things; it is not meant that the proposition is one we cannot help believing. Experience, in Kant's first principle, cannot be used for a product of the objective understanding, but must be taken for the first impressions of sense with consciousness conjoined and worked up by the imagination into images, together with all that is logically deducible therefrom. In this sense, it may be admitted that universal and necessary propositions are not given in experience. But, in that case, neither are any inductive conclusions that might be drawn from experience, given in it. In fact, it is the peculiar function of induction to produce universal and necessary propositions. Kant points out, indeed, that the universality and necessity of scientific inductions are but the analog of philosophic universality and necessity; and this is true, in so far as it is never allowable to accept indefinite drawback. But this is owing to the insufficiency in the number of the instances; and whenever instances may be had in as large numbers as we please, *ad infinitum*, a truly universal and necessary proposition is inferable. As for Kant's second principle, that the truth of universal and necessary propositions is dependent upon the conditions of the general experience, it is no more nor less than the principle of Induction. I go to a fair and draw from the "grab-bag" twelve packages. Upon opening them, I find that every one contains a red ball. Here is a universal fact. It depends, then, on the condition of the experience. What is the condition of the experience? It is solely that the balls are the contents of packages drawn from that bag, that is, the only thing that determined the experience, was the drawing from the bag. I infer, then, according to the principle of Kant, that what is drawn from the bag will contain a red ball. This is induction. Apply induction not to any limited experience but to all human experience and you have the Kantian philosophy, so far as it is correctly developed.

Kant's successors, however, have not been content with his doctrine. Nor ought they to have been. For, there is this third principle: "Absolutely universal propositions must be analytic." For whatever is absolutely universal is devoid of all content or determination, for all determination is by negation. The problem, therefore, is not how universal propositions can be synthetical, but how universal propositions appearing to be synthetical can be evolved by thought alone from the purely indeterminate.

explained on the supposition that we have no intuitive faculty of distinguishing intuitive from mediate cognitions. Some arbitrary hypothesis may otherwise explain any one of these facts; this is the only theory that brings them to support one another. Moreover, no facts require the supposition of the faculty in question. Whoever has studied the nature of proof will see, then, that there are here very strong reasons for disbelieving the existence of this faculty. These will become still stronger when the consequences of rejecting it have, in this paper and in a following one, been more fully traced out.

QUESTION 2. *Whether we have an intuitive self-consciousness.*

Self-consciousness, as the term is here used, is to be distinguished both from consciousness generally, from the internal sense, and from pure apperception. Any cognition is a consciousness of the object as represented; by self-consciousness is meant a knowledge of ourselves. Not a mere feeling of subjective conditions of consciousness, but of our personal selves. Pure apperception is the self-assertion of THE *ego*; the self-consciousness here meant is the recognition of my *private* self. I know that *I* (not merely *the* I) exist. The question is, how do I know it; by a special intuitive faculty, or is it determined by previous cognitions?

Now, it is not self-evident that we have such an intuitive faculty, for it has just been shown that we have no intuitive power of distinguishing an intuition from a cognition determined by others. Therefore, the existence or nonexistence of this power is to be determined upon evidence, and the question is whether self-consciousness can be explained by the action of known faculties under conditions known to exist, or whether it is necessary to suppose an unknown cause for this cognition, and, in the latter case, whether an intuitive faculty of self-consciousness is the most probable cause which can be supposed.

It is first to be observed that there is no known self-consciousness to be accounted for in extremely young children. It has already been pointed out by Kant* that the late use of the very common word "I"

*Werke, vii. (2), 11.

with children indicates an imperfect self-consciousness in them, and that, therefore, so far as it is admissible for us to draw any conclusion in regard to the mental state of those who are still younger, it must be against the existence of any self-consciousness in them.

On the other hand, children manifest powers of thought much earlier. Indeed, it is almost impossible to assign a period at which children do not already exhibit decided intellectual activity in directions in which thought is indispensable to their well-being. The complicated trigonometry of vision, and the delicate adjustments of coordinated movement, are plainly mastered very early. There is no reason to question a similar degree of thought in reference to themselves.

A very young child may always be observed to watch its own body with great attention. There is every reason why this should be so, for from the child's point of view this body is the most important thing in the universe. Only what it touches has any actual and present feeling; only what it faces has any actual color; only what is on its tongue has any actual taste.

No one questions that, when a sound is heard by a child, he thinks, not of himself as hearing, but of the bell or other object as sounding. How when he wills to move a table? Does he then think of himself as desiring, or only of the table as fit to be moved? That he has the latter thought, is beyond question; that he has the former, must, until the existence of an intuitive self-consciousness is proved, remain an arbitrary and baseless supposition. There is no good reason for thinking that he is less ignorant of his own peculiar condition than the angry adult who denies that he is in a passion.

The child, however, must soon discover by observation that things that are thus fit to be changed are apt actually to undergo this change, after a contact with that peculiarly important body called Willy or Johnny. This consideration makes his body still more important and central, since it establishes a connection between the fitness of a thing to be changed and a tendency in this body to touch it before it is changed.

The child learns to understand the language; that is to say, a connection between certain sounds and certain facts becomes established in his mind. He has previously noticed the connection between these sounds and the motions of the lips of bodies somewhat similar to the central one, and has tried the experiment of putting his hand on those lips and has found the sound in that case to be smothered. He thus connects that language with bodies somewhat similar to the central one. By efforts so unenergetic that they should be called rather instinctive, perhaps, than tentative, he learns to produce those sounds. So he begins to converse.

It must be about this time that he begins to find that what these people about him say is the very best evidence of fact. So much so, that testimony is even a stronger mark of fact than *the facts themselves*, or rather than what must now be thought of as the *appearances* themselves. (I may remark, by the way, that this remains so through life; testimony will convince a man that he himself is mad.) A child hears it said that the stove is hot. But it is not, he says; and, indeed, that central body is not touching it, and only what that touches is hot or cold. But he touches it, and finds the testimony confirmed in a striking way. Thus, he becomes aware of ignorance, and it is necessary to suppose a *self* in which this ignorance can inhere. So testimony gives the first dawning of self-consciousness.

But, further, although usually appearances are either only confirmed or merely supplemented by testimony, yet there is a certain remarkable class of appearances that are continually contradicted by testimony. These are those predicates that *we* know to be emotional, but which *he* distinguishes by their connection with the movements of that central person, himself (that the table wants moving, etc.). These judgments are generally denied by others. Moreover, he has reason to think that others, also, have such judgments that are quite denied by all the rest. Thus, he adds to the conception of appearance as the actualization of fact, the conception of it as something *private* and valid only for one body. In short, *error* appears, and it can be explained only by supposing a *self* that is fallible.

Ignorance and error are all that distinguish our private selves from the absolute *ego* of pure apperception.

Now, the theory that, for the sake of perspicuity, has thus been stated in a specific form, may be summed up as follows: At the age at which we know children to be self-conscious, we know that they have been made aware of ignorance and error; and we know them to possess at that age powers of understanding sufficient to enable them to infer from ignorance and error their own existence. Thus we find that known faculties, acting under conditions known to exist, would rise to self-consciousness. The only essential defect in this account of the matter is, that while we know that children exercise *as much* understanding as is here supposed, we do not know that they exercise it in precisely this way. Still the supposition that they do so is infinitely more supported by facts, than the supposition of a wholly peculiar faculty of the mind.

The only argument worth noticing for the existence of an intuitive self-consciousness is this. We are more certain of our own existence than of any other fact; a premise cannot determine a conclusion to be more certain than it is itself; hence, our own existence cannot have been inferred from any other fact. The first premise must be admitted, but the second premise is founded on an exploded theory of logic. A conclusion cannot be more certain than that some one of the facts that support it is true, but it may easily be more certain than any one of those facts. Let us suppose, for example, that a dozen witnesses testify to an occurrence. Then my belief in that occurrence rests on the belief that each of those men is generally to be believed upon oath. Yet the fact testified to is made more certain than that any one of those men is generally to be believed. In the same way, to the developed mind of man, his own existence is supported by *every other fact*, and is, therefore, incomparably more certain than any one of these facts. But it cannot be said to be more certain than that there is another fact, since there is no doubt perceptible in either case.

It is to be concluded, then, that there is no necessity of supposing an intuitive self-consciousness, since self-consciousness may easily be the result of inference.

QUESTION 3. *Whether we have an intuitive power of distinguishing between the subjective elements of different kinds of cognitions.*

Every cognition involves something represented, or that of which we are conscious, and some action or passion of the self whereby it becomes represented. The former shall be termed the objective, the latter the subjective, element of the cognition. The cognition itself is an intuition of its objective element, that may therefore be called, also, the immediate object. The subjective element is not necessarily immediately known, but it is possible that such an intuition of the subjective element of a cognition of its character, whether that of dreaming, imagining, conceiving, believing, etc., should accompany every cognition. The question is whether this is so.

It would appear, at first sight, that there is an overwhelming array of evidence in favor of the existence of such a power. The difference between seeing a color and imagining it is immense. There is a vast difference between the most vivid dream and reality. And if we had no intuitive power of distinguishing between what we believe and what we merely conceive, we never, it would seem, could in any way distinguish them; since if we did so by reasoning, the question would arise whether the argument itself was believed or conceived, and this must be answered before the conclusion could have any force. And thus there would be a *regressus ad infinitum*. Besides, if we do not know that we believe, then, from the nature of the case, we do not believe.

But be it noted that we do not intuitively know the existence of this faculty. For it is an intuitive one, and we cannot intuitively know that a cognition is intuitive. The question is, therefore, whether it is necessary to suppose the existence of this faculty, or whether then the facts can be explained without this supposition.

In the first place, then, the difference between what is imagined or dreamed and what is actually experienced, is no argument in favor of the existence of such a faculty. For it is not questioned that there are distinctions in what is present to the mind, but the question is, whether independently of any such distinctions in the immediate *objects* of consciousness, we have any immediate power of distinguishing different modes of consciousness. Now, the very fact of the immense difference in the immediate objects of sense and imagination, sufficiently accounts for our distinguishing those faculties; and instead of being an argument in favor of the existence of an intuitive power of distinguishing the subjective elements of consciousness, it is a powerful reply to any such argument, so far as the distinction of sense and imagination is concerned.

Passing to the distinction of belief and conception, we meet the statement that the knowledge of belief is essential to its existence. Now, we can unquestionably distinguish a belief from a conception, in most cases, by means of a peculiar feeling of conviction; and it is a mere question of words whether we define belief as that judgment that is accompanied by this feeling, or as that judgment from which a man will act. We may conveniently call the former *sensational*, the latter *active* belief. That neither of these necessarily involves the other will surely be admitted without any recital of facts. Taking belief in the sensational sense, the intuitive power of reorganizing it will amount simply to the capacity for the sensation that accompanies the judgment. This sensation, like any other, is an object of consciousness; and therefore the capacity for it implies no intuitive recognition of subjective elements of consciousness. If belief is taken in the active sense, it may be discovered by the observation of external facts and by inference from the sensation of conviction that usually accompanies it.

Thus, the arguments in favor of this peculiar power of consciousness disappear, and the presumption is again against such a hypothesis. Moreover, as the immediate objects of any two faculties must be admitted to be different, the facts do not render such a supposition in any degree necessary.

QUESTION 4. *Whether we have any power of introspection, or whether our whole knowledge of the internal world is derived from the observation of external facts.*

It is not intended here to assume the reality of the external world. Only, there is a certain set of facts that are ordinarily regarded as external, while others are regarded as internal. The question is whether the latter are known otherwise than by inference from the former. By introspection, I mean a direct perception of the internal world, but not necessarily a perception of it *as* internal. Nor do I mean to limit the signification of the word to intuition, but would extend it to any knowledge of the internal world not derived from external observation.

There is one sense in which any perception has an internal object, namely, that every sensation is partly determined by internal conditions. Thus, the sensation of redness is as it is, owing to the constitution of the mind; and in this sense it is a sensation of something internal. Hence, we may derive a knowledge of the mind from a consideration of this sensation, but that knowledge would, in fact, be an inference from redness as a predicate of something external. On the other hand, there are certain other feelings—the emotions, for example—which appear to arise in the first place, not as predicates at all, and to be referable to the mind alone. It would seem, then, that by means of these, a knowledge of the mind may be obtained, that is not inferred from any character of outward things. The question is whether this is really so.

Although introspection is not necessarily intuitive, it is not self-evident that we possess this capacity; for we have no intuitive faculty of distinguishing different subjective modes of consciousness. The power, if it exists, must be known by the circumstance that the facts cannot be explained without it.

In reference to the above argument from the emotions, it must be admitted that if a man is angry, his anger implies, in general, no determinate and constant character in its object. But, on the other hand, it can hardly be questioned that there is some relative character in the outward thing that makes him angry, and a little reflection will serve to show that his anger consists in his saying to himself, "this thing is vile, abominable, etc.," and that it is rather a mark of returning reason to say, "I am angry." In the same way any emotion is a predication concerning some object, and the chief difference between this and an objective intellectual judgment is that while the latter is relative to human nature or to mind in general, the former is relative to the particular circumstances and disposition of a particular man at a particular time. What is here said of emotions in general is true in particular of the sense of beauty and of the moral sense. Good and bad are feelings that first arise as predicates, and therefore are either predicates of the not I, or are determined by previous cognitions (there being no intuitive power of distinguishing subjective elements of consciousness).

It remains, then, only to inquire whether it is necessary to suppose a particular power of introspection for the sake of accounting for the sense of willing. Now, volition, as distinguished from desire, is nothing but the power of concentrating the attention, of abstracting. Hence, the knowledge of the power of abstracting may be inferred from abstract objects, just as the knowledge of the power of seeing is inferred from colored objects.

It appears, therefore, that there is no reason for supposing a power of introspection; and, consequently, the only way of investigating a psychological question is by inference from external facts.

QUESTION 5. *Whether we can think without signs.*

This is a familiar question, but there is, to this day, no better argument in the affirmative than that thought must precede every sign. This assumes the impossibility of an infinite series. But Achilles, as a fact, will overtake the tortoise. *How* this happens is a question not necessary to be answered at present, as long as it certainly does happen.

If we seek the light of external facts, the only cases of thought that we can find are of thought in signs. Plainly, no other thought can be evidenced by external facts. But we have seen that only by external facts can thought be known at all. The only thought, then, that can possibly be cognized is thought in signs. But thought that cannot be cognized does not exist. All thought, therefore, must necessarily be in signs.

A man says to himself, "Aristotle is a man; *therefore*, he is fallible." Has he not, then, thought what he has not said to himself, that all men are fallible? The answer is, that he has done so, so far as this is said in his *therefore*. According to this, our question does not relate to *fact*, but is a mere asking for distinctness of thought.

From the proposition that every thought is a sign, it follows that every thought must address itself to some other, must determine some other, since that is the essence of a sign. This, after all, is but another form of the familiar axiom, that in intuition, i.e. in the immediate present, there is no thought, or, that all that is reflected upon has past. *Hinc loquor inde est.* That, since any thought, there must have been a thought, has its analog in the fact that, since any past time, there must have been an infinite series of times. To say, therefore, that thought cannot happen in an instant, but requires a time, is but another way of saying that every thought must be interpreted in another, or that all thought is in signs.

QUESTION 6. *Whether a sign can have any meaning, if by its definition it is the sign of something absolutely incognizable.*

It would seem that it can, and that universal and hypothetical propositions are instances of it. Thus, the universal proposition, "all ruminants are cloven-hoofed," speaks of a possible infinity of animals, and no matter how many ruminants may have been examined, the possibility must remain that there are others that have not been examined. In the case of a hypothetical proposition, the same thing is still more manifest; for such a proposition speaks not merely of the actual state of things, but of every possible state of things, all of which are not knowable, inasmuch as only one can so much as exist.

On the other hand, all our conceptions are obtained by abstractions and combinations of cognitions first occurring in judgments of experience. Accordingly, there can be no conception of the absolutely incognizable, since nothing of that sort occurs in experience. But the meaning of a term is the conception that it conveys. Hence, a term can have no such meaning.

If it be said that the incognizable is a concept compounded of the concept *not* and *cognizable*, it may be replied that *not* is a mere syncategorematic term and not a concept by itself.

If I think "white," I will not go so far as Berkeley and say that I think of a person seeing, but I will say that what I think is of the nature of a cognition, and so of anything else that can be experienced. Consequently, the highest concept that can be reached by abstractions from judgments of experience—and, therefore, the highest concept that can be reached at all—is the concept of something of the nature of a cognition. *Not*, then, or *what is other than*, if a concept, is a concept of the cognizable. Hence, not-cognizable, if a concept, is a concept of the form "A, not-A," and is, at least, self-contradictory. Thus, ignorance and error can only be conceived as correlative to a real knowledge and truth, which latter are of the nature of cognitions. Over against any cognition, there is an unknown but knowable reality; but over against all possible cognition, there is only the self-contradictory. In short, *cognizability* (in its widest sense) and *being* are not merely metaphysically the same, but are synonymous terms.

To the argument from universal and hypothetical propositions, the reply is, that though their truth cannot be cognized with absolute certainty, it may be probably known by induction.

QUESTION 7. *Whether there is any cognition not determined by a previous cognition.*

It would seem that there is or has been; for since we are in possession of cognitions, which are all determined by previous ones, and these by cognitions earlier still, there must have been a *first* in this series or else our state of cognition at any time is completely determined, according to logical laws, by our state at any previous time. But there are many facts against the last supposition, and therefore in favor of intuitive cognitions.

On the other hand, since it is impossible to know intuitively that a given cognition is not determined by a previous one, the only way in which this can be known is by hypothetic inference from observed facts. But to adduce the cognition by which a given cognition has been determined is to explain the determinations of that cognition. And it is the only way of explaining them. For something entirely out of consciousness that may be supposed to determine it, can, as such, only be known and only adduced in the determinate cognition in question. So, that to suppose that a cognition is determined solely by something absolutely external, is to suppose its determinations incapable of explanation. Now, this is a hypothesis that is warranted under no circumstances, inasmuch as the only possible justification for a hypothesis is that it explains the facts, and to say that they are explained and at the same time to suppose them inexplicable is self-contradictory.

If it be objected that the peculiar character of *red* is not determined by any previous cognition, I reply that that character is not a character of red as a cognition; for if there be a man to whom red things look as blue ones do to me and *vice versa*, that man's eyes teach him the same facts that they would if he were like me.

Moreover, we know of no power by which an intuition could be known. For, as the cognition is beginning, and therefore in a state of change, at only the first instant would it be intuition. And, therefore, the apprehension of it must take place in no time and be an event occupying no time.* Besides, all the cognitive faculties we know of are relative, and consequently their products are relations. But the cognition of a relation is determined by previous cognitions. No cognition not determined by a previous cognition, then, can be known. It does not exist, then, first, because it is absolutely incognizable, and second, because a cognition only exists so far as it is known.

The reply to the argument that there must be a first is as follows: In retracing our way from conclusions to premises, or from determined cognitions to those that determine them, we finally reach, in all cases, a point beyond which the consciousness in the determined cognition is more lively than in the cognition that determines it. We have a less lively consciousness in the cognition that determines our cognition of the third dimension than in the latter cognition itself; a less lively consciousness in the cognition that determines our cognition of a continuous surface (without a blind spot) than in this latter cognition itself; and a less lively consciousness of the impressions that determine the sensation of tone than of that sensation itself. Indeed, when we get near enough to the external this is the universal rule. Now let any horizontal line represent a cognition, and let the length of the line serve to measure (so to speak) the liveliness of consciousness in that cognition. A point, having no length, will, on this principle, represent an object quite out of consciousness. Let one horizontal line below another represent a cognition that determines the cognition represented by that other and which has the same object as the latter. Let the finite distance between two such lines represent that they are two different cognitions. With this aid to thinking, let us see whether "there must be a first." Suppose an inverted triangle $\bigtriangledown$ to be gradually dipped into water. At any date or instant, the surface of the water makes a horizontal line across that triangle. This line represents another cognition of the same object determined by the former, and having a livelier consciousness. The apex of

---

*This argument, however, only covers a part of the question. It does not go to show that there is no cognition undetermined except by another like it.

the triangle represents the object external to the mind that determines both these cognitions. The state of the triangle before it reaches the water represents a state of cognition that contains nothing that determines these subsequent cognitions. To say, then, that if there be a state of cognition by which all subsequent cognitions of a certain object are not determined, there must subsequently be some cognition of that object not determined by previous cognitions of the same object, is to say that when that triangle is dipped into the water there must be a sectional line made by the surface of the water lower than which no surface line had been made in that way. But draw the horizontal line where you will, as many horizontal lines as you please can be assigned at finite distances below it and below one another. For any such section is at some distance above the apex, otherwise it is not a line. Let this distance be a. Then there have been similar sections at the distances $\frac{1}{2}a$, $\frac{1}{4}a$, $\frac{1}{8}a$, $\frac{1}{16}a$, above the apex, and so on as far as you please. So that it is not true that there must be a first. Explicate the logical difficulties of this paradox (they are identical with those of the Achilles) in whatever way you may. I am content with the result, as long as your principles are fully applied to the particular case of cognitions determining one another. Deny motion, if it seems proper to do so; only then deny the process of determination of one cognition by another. Say that instants and lines are fictions; only say, also, that states of cognition and judgments are fictions. The point here insisted on is not this or the logical solution of the difficulty, but merely that cognition arises by a *process* of beginning, as any other change comes to pass.

In a subsequent paper I shall trace the consequences of these principles, in reference to the questions of reality, of individuality, and of the validity of the laws of logic.

2.   Some Consequences of Four Incapacities

Descartes is the father of modern philosophy, and the spirit of Cartesianism—that which principally distinguishes it from the scholasticism that it displaced—may be compendiously stated as follows:

1. It teaches that philosophy must begin with universal doubt; whereas scholasticism had never questioned fundamentals.

2. It teaches that the ultimate test of certainty is to be found in the individual consciousness; whereas scholasticism had rested on the testimony of sages and of the Catholic Church.

3. The multiform argumentation of the Middle Ages is replaced by a single thread of inference depending often upon inconspicuous premises.

4. Scholasticism had its mysteries of faith, but undertook to explain all created things. But there are many facts that Cartesianism not only does not explain, but renders absolutely inexplicable, unless to say that "God makes them so" is to be regarded as an explanation.

In some, or all of these respects, most modern philosophers have been, in effect, Cartesians. Now without wishing to return to scholasticism, it seems to me that modern science and modern logic require us to stand upon a very different platform from this.

1. We cannot begin with complete doubt. We must begin with all the prejudices that we actually have when we enter upon the study of philosophy. These prejudices are not to be dispelled by a maxim, for they are things that it does not occur to us *can* be questioned. Hence this initial scepticism will be a mere self-deception, and not real doubt; and no one who follows the Cartesian method will ever be satisfied until he has formally recovered all those beliefs that in form he has given up. It is, therefore, as useless a preliminary as going to the North Pole would be in order to get to Constantinpole by coming down regularly upon a meridian. A person may, it is true, in the course of his studies, find reason to doubt what he began by believing; but in that case he doubts because he has a positive reason for it, and not on account of the Cartesian maxim. Let us not pretend to doubt in philosophy what we do not doubt in our hearts.

2. The same formalism appears in the Cartesian criterion, which amounts to this: "Whatever I am clearly convinced of, is true." If I were really convinced, I should have done with reasoning, and should require

no test of certainty. But thus to make single individuals absolute judges of truth is most pernicious. The result is that metaphysicians will all agree that metaphysics has reached a pitch of certainty far beyond that of the physical sciences—only they can agree upon nothing else. In sciences in which men come to agreement, when a theory has been broached, it is considered to be on probation until this agreement is reached. After it is reached, the question of certainty becomes an idle one, because there is no one left who doubts it. We individually cannot reasonably hope to attain the ultimate philosophy we pursue; we can only seek it, therefore, for the community of philosophers. Hence, if disciplined and candid minds carefully examine a theory and refuse to accept it, this ought to create doubts in the mind of the author of the theory himself.

3. Philosophy ought to imitate the successful sciences in its methods, so far as to proceed only from tangible premises that can be subjected to careful scrutiny, and to trust rather to the multitude and variety of its arguments than to the conclusiveness of any one. Its reasoning should not form a chain that is no stronger than its weakest link, but a cable whose fibres may be ever so slender, provided they are sufficiently numerous and intimately connected.

4. Every unidealistic philosophy supposes some absolutely inexplicable, unanalyzable ultimate; in short, something resulting from mediation itself not susceptible of mediation. Now that anything *is* thus inexplicable can only be known by reasoning from signs. But the only justification of an inference from signs is that the conclusion explains the fact. To suppose the fact absolutely inexplicable is not to explain it, and hence this supposition is never allowable.

In the last number of this journal* will be found a piece entitled "Questions Concerning Certain Faculties Claimed for Man," that has been written in this spirit of opposition to Cartesianism. That criticism of certain faculties resulted in four denials, which for convenience may be here be repeated:

*[In this volume, pp. 64 ff.]

1. We have no power of introspection, but all knowledge of the internal world is derived by hypothetical reasoning from our knowledge of external facts.

2. We have no power of intuition, but every cognition is determined logically by previous cognitions.

3. We have no power of thinking without signs.

4. We have no conception of the absolutely incognizable.

These propositions cannot be regarded as certain; and, in order to bring them to a further test, it is now proposed to trace them out to their consequences. We may first consider the first alone; then trace the consequences of the first and second; then see what else will result from assuming the third also; and, finally, add the fourth to our hypothetical premises.

In accepting the first proposition, we must put aside all prejudices derived from a philosophy that bases our knowledge of the external world on our self-consciousness. We can admit no statement concerning what passes within us except as a hypothesis necessary to explain what takes place in what we commonly call the external world. Moreover when we have upon such grounds assumed one faculty or mode of action of the mind, we cannot, of course, adopt any other hypothesis for the purpose of explaining any fact that can be explained by our first supposition, but must carry the latter as far as it will go. In other words, we must, as far as we can do so without additional hypotheses, reduce all kinds of mental action to one general type.

The class of modifications of consciousness with which we must commence our inquiry must be one whose existence is indubitable, and whose laws are best known, and, therefore (since this knowledge comes from the outside), which most closely follows external facts; that is, it must be some kind of cognition. Here we may hypothetically admit the second proposition of the former paper, according to which there is no absolutely first cognition of any object, but cognition arises by a continuous process. We must begin, then, with a *process* of cognition, and with that process whose laws are best understood and most closely follow external facts. This is no other than the process of valid inference, which proceeds from its premise, A, to its conclusion, B, only if, as a matter of fact, such a proposition as B is always or usually true when such a proposition as A is true. It is a consequence, then, of the first two principles whose results we are to trace out, that we must, as far as we can, without any other supposition than that the mind reasons, reduce all mental action to the formula of valid reasoning.

But does the mind in fact go through the syllogistic process? It is certainly very doubtful whether a conclusion—as something existing in the mind independently, like an image—suddenly displaces two premises existing in the mind in a similar way. But it is a matter of constant experience, that if a man is made to believe in the premises, in the sense that he will act from them and will say that they are true, under favorable conditions he will also be ready to act from the conclusion and to say that that is true. Something, therefore, takes place within the organism that is equivalent to the syllogistic process.

A valid inference is either *complete* or *incomplete*. An incomplete inference is one whose validity depends upon some matter of fact not contained in the premises. This implied fact might have been stated as a premise, and its relations to the conclusion is the same whether it is explicitly posited or not, since it is at least virtually taken for granted; so that every valid incomplete argument is virtually complete. Complete arguments are divided into *simple* and *complex*. A complex argument is one that from three or more premises concludes what might have been concluded by successive steps in reasonings each of which is simple. Thus, a complex inference comes to the same thing in the end as a succession of simple inferences.

A complete, simple, and valid argument, or syllogism, is either *apodictic* or *probable*. An apodictic or deductive syllogism is one whose validity depends unconditionally upon the relation of the fact inferred to the facts posited in the premises. A syllogism whose validity should depend not merely upon its premises, but upon the existence of some other knowledge, would be impossible; for either this other knowledge would be posited, in which case it would be a part of the premises, or it would be implicitly assumed, in which case the inference would be incomplete. But a syllogism whose validity depends partly upon the *non-existence* of some other knowledge, is a *probable* syllogism.

A few examples will render this plain. The two following arguments are apodictic or deductive:

1. No series of days of which the first and last are different days of the week exceeds by one a multiple of seven days; now the first and last days of any leap year are different days of the week, and therefore no leap year consists of a number of days one greater than a multiple of seven.

2. Among the vowels there are no double letters; but one of the double letters *(w)* is compounded of two vowels: hence, a letter compounded of two vowels is not necessarily itself a vowel.

In both these cases, it is plain that as long as the premises are true, however other facts may be, the conclusions will be true. On the other hand, suppose that we reason as follows: "A certain man had the Asiatic cholera. He was in a state of collapse, livid, quite cold, and without perceptible pulse. He was bled copiously. During the process he came out of collapse, and the next morning was well enough to be about. Therefore, bleeding tends to cure the cholera." This is a fair probable inference, provided that the premises represent our whole knowledge of the matter. But if we knew, for example, that recoveries from cholera were apt to be sudden, and that the physician who had reported this case had known of a hundred other trials of the remedy without communicating the result, then the inference would lose all its validity.

The absence of knowledge which is essential to the validity of any probable argument relates to some question that is determined by the argument itself. This question, like every other, is whether certain objects have certain characters. Hence, the absence of knowledge is either whether besides the objects that, according to the premises, possess certain characters, any other objects possess them; or, whether besides the characters that, according to the premises, belong to certain objects, any other characters not necessarily involved in those belong to the same objects. In the former case, the reasoning proceeds as though all the objects that have certain characters were known, and this is *induction;* in the latter case, the inference proceeds as though all the characters requisite to the determination of a certain object or class were known, and this is *hypothesis.* This distinction, also, may be made more plain by examples.

Suppose we count the number of occurrences of the different letters in a certain English book, which we may call A. Of course, every new letter that we add to our count will alter the relative number of occurrences of the different letters; but as we proceed with our counting, this change will be less and less. Suppose that we find that as we increase the number of letters counted, the relative number of *e*'s approaches nearly 11¼ percent of the whole, that of the *t*'s 8½ percent, that of the *a*'s 8 percent, that of the *s*'s 7½ percent, etc. Suppose we repeat the same observations with half a dozen other English writings (which we may designate as B, C, D, E, F, G) with the like result. Then we may infer that in every English writing of some length, the different letters occur with nearly those relative frequencies.

Now this argument depends for its validity upon our *not* knowing the proportion of letters in any English writing besides A, B, C, D, E, F, and G. For if we know it in respect to H, and it is not nearly the same as in the others, our conclusion is destroyed at once; if it is the same, then the legitimate inference is from A, B, C, D, E, F, G, and H, and not from the first seven alone. This, therefore, is an *induction*.

Suppose, next, that a piece of writing in cipher is presented to us, without the key. Suppose we find that it contains something less than twenty-six characters, one of which occurs about 11 percent of all the times, another 8½ percent, another 8 percent, and another 7½ percent. Suppose that when we substitute for these *e*, *t*, *a*, and *s*, respectively, we are able to see how single letters may be substituted for each of the other characters so as to make sense in English, provided, however, that we allow the spelling to be wrong in some cases. If the writing is of any considerable length, we may infer with great probability that this is the meaning of the cipher.

The validity of this argument depends upon there being no other known characters of the writing in cipher that would have any weight in the matter; for if there are—if we know, for example, whether or not there is any other solution of it—this must be allowed its effect in supporting or weakening the conclusion. This, then, is *hypothesis*.

All valid reasoning is either deductive, inductive, or hypothetic; or else it combines two or more of these characters. Deduction is pretty well treated in most logical textbooks; but it will be necessary to say a few words about induction and hypothesis in order to render what follows more intelligible.

Induction may be defined as an argument that proceeds upon the assumption that all the members of a class or aggregate have all the characters that are common to all those members of this class concerning which it is known, whether they have these characters or not; or, in other words, which assumes that that is true of a whole collection that is true of a number of instances taken from it at random. This might be called statistical argument. In the long run, it must generally afford pretty correct conclusions from true premises. If we have a bag of beans partly black and partly white, by counting the relative proportions of the two colors in several different handfuls, we can approximate more or less to the relative proportions in the whole bag, since a sufficient number of handfuls would constitute all the beans in the bag. The central characteristic and key to induction is, that by taking the conclusion so reached as major premise of a syllogism, and the proposition stating that such and such objects are taken from the class in question as the minor premise, the other premise of the induction will follow from them deductively. Thus, in the above example we concluded that all books in English have about 11¼ percent of their letters *e*'s. From that as major premise, together with the proposition that A, B, C, D, E, F, and G are books in English, it follows deductively that A, B, C, D, E, F, and G have about 11¼ percent of their letters *e*'s. Accordingly, induction has been defined by Aristotle as the inference of the major premise of a syllogism from its minor premise and conclusion. The function of an induction is to substitute for a series of many subjects a single one that embraces them and an indefinite number of others. Thus it is a species of "reduction of the manifold to unity."

Hypothesis may be defined as an argument that proceeds upon the assumption that a character that is known necessarily to involve a certain number of others, may be probably predicated of any object that has all the characters that this character is known to involve. Just as induction may be regarded as the inference of the major premise of a syllogism, so hypothesis may be regarded as the inference of the minor premise, from the other two propositions. Thus, the example taken above consists of two such inferences of the minor premises of the following syllogisms:

1. Every English writing of some length in which such and such characters denote *e*, *t*, *a*, and *s*, has about 11¼ percent of the first sort of

marks, 8½ of the second, 8 of the third, and 7½ of the fourth;
This secret writing is an English writing of some length, in which such
and such characters denote e, t, a, and s, respectively:

∴ This secret writing has about 11¼ percent of its characters of the
first kind, 8½ of the second, 8 of the third, and 7½ of the fourth.

2. A passage written with such an alphabet makes sense when such and
such letters are severally substituted for such and such characters;
This secret writing is written with such an alphabet:

∴ This secret writing makes sense when such and such substitutions
are made.

The function of hypothesis is to substitute for a great series of predicates forming no unity in themselves, a single one (or small number) that
involves them all, together (perhaps) with an indefinite number of
others. It is, therefore, also a reduction of a manifold to unity.* Every

---

*Several persons versed in logic have objected that I have here quite misapplied the term
hypothesis, and that what I so designate is an argument from *analogy.* It is a sufficient
reply to say that the example of the cipher has been given as an apt illustration of
hypothesis by Descartes (Rule 10 Œuvres choisies: Paris, 1865, page 334), by Leibniz
(Nouv. Ess., lib. 4, ch. 12, § 13, Ed. Erdmann, p. 383 *b*), and (as I learn from D. Stewart;
Works, vol. 3, pp. 305 et seqq.) by Gravesande, Boscovich, Hartley, and G. L. Le Sage.
The term hypothesis has been used in the following senses: 1. For the theme or proposition
forming the subject of discourse. 2. For an assumption. Aristotle divides *theses* or propositions adopted without any reason into definitions and hypotheses. The latter are propositions stating the existence of something. Thus the geometer says, "Let there be a triangle."
3. For a condition in a general sense. We are said to seek other things than happiness
ἐξ ὑποθέσεως, conditionally. The best republic is the ideally perfect, the second the best
on earth, the third, the best ἐξ ὑποθέσεως, under the circumstances. Freedom is the
ὑπόθεσις or condition of democracy. 4. For the antecedent of a hypothetical proposition.
5. For an oratorical question that assumes facts. 6. In the Synopsis of Psellus, for the
reference of a subject to the things it denotes. 7. Most commonly in modern times, for
the conclusion of an argument from consequence and consequent to antecedent. This is
my use of the term. 8. For such a conclusion when too weak to be a theory accepted into
the body of a science.
     I give a few authorities to support the seventh use.
     Chauvin.—Lexicon Rationale, 1st Ed.—"Hypothesis est propositio, quæ assumitur ad
probandum aliam veritatem incognitam. Requirunt multi, ut hæc hypothesis vera esse
cognoscatur, etiam antequam appareat, an alia ex eâ deduci possint. Verum aiunt alii, hoc
unum desiderari, ut hypothesis pro vera admittatur, quod nempe ex hac talia deducitur,
quæ respondent phænomenis, et satisfaciunt omnibus difficultatibus, quæ hac parte in re,
et in iis quæ de ea apparent, occurrebant."
     Newton.—"Hactenus phænomena cŒlorum et maris nostri per vim gravitatis exposui,
sed causam gravitatis nondum assignavi. . . . Rationem vero harum gravitatis proprietatum
ex phænomenis nondum potui deducere, et hypotheses non fingo. Quicquid enim ex
phænomenis non deducitur, *hypothesis* vocanda est. . . . In hâc Philosophiâ Propositiones
deducuntur ex phænomenis, et redduntur generales per inductionem." Principia. *Ad fin.*

deductive syllogism may be put into the form

If *A*, then *B*;

But *A*:

∴ *B*.

And as the minor premise in this form appears as antecedent or reason of a hypothetical proposition, hypothetic inference may be called reasoning from consequent to antecedent.

The argument from analogy, which a popular writer upon logic calls reasoning from particulars to particulars, derives its validity from its combining the characters of induction and hypothesis, being analyzable

---

Sir Wm. Hamilton.—"*Hypotheses*, that is, propositions which are assumed with probability, in order to explain or prove something else which cannot otherwise be explained or proved."—Lectures on Logic (Am. Ed.), p. 188.

"The name of *hypothesis* is more emphatically given to provisory suppositions, which serve to explain the phenomena in so far as observed, but which are only asserted to be true, if ultimately confirmed by a complete induction."—Ibid, p. 364.

"When a phenomenon is presented which can be explained by no principle afforded through experience, we feel discontented and uneasy; and there arises an effort to discover some cause which may, at least provisionally, account for the outstanding phenomenon; and this cause is finally recognized as valid and true, if, through it, the given phenomenon is found to obtain a full and perfect explanation. The judgment in which a phenomenon is referred to such a problematic cause, is called a *Hypothesis.*"—Ibid, pp. 449, 450. See also Lectures on Metaphysics, p. 117.

J. S. Mill.—"An hypothesis is any supposition which we make (either without actual evidence, or on evidence avowedly insufficient), in order to endeavor to deduce from it conclusions in accordance with facts which are known to be real; under the idea that if the conclusions to which the hypothesis leads are known truths, the hypothesis itself either must be, or at least is likely to be true."—Logic (6th Ed.), vol. 2, p. 8.

Kant.—"*If all the consequents of a cognition are true, the cognition itself is true.* . . . It is allowable, therefore, to conclude from consequent to a reason, but without being able to determine this reason. From the complexus of all consequents alone can we conclude the truth of a determinate reason. . . . The difficulty with this *positive* and *direct* mode of inference *(modus ponens)* is that the totality of the consequents cannot be apodeictically recognized, and that we are therefore led by this mode of inference only to a probable and *hypothetically* true cognition *(Hypotheses).*"—Logik by Jäsche Werke; Ed. Rosenk. and Sch., vol. 3, p. 221.

"A hypothesis is the judgment of the truth of a reason on account of the sufficiency of the consequents."—Ibid, p. 262.

Herbart.—"We can make hypotheses, thence deduce consequents, and afterwards see whether the latter accord with experience. Such suppositions are termed hypotheses."—Einleitung; Werke, vol. 1, p. 53.

Beneke.—"Affirmative inferences from consequent to antecedent, or hypotheses."—System der Logik, vol. 2, p. 103.

There would be no difficulty in greatly multiplying these citations.

either into a deduction or an induction, or a deduction and a hypothesis.

But though inference is thus of three essentially different species, it also belongs to one genus. We have seen that no conclusion can be legitimately derived which could not have been reached by successions of arguments having two premises each, and implying no fact not asserted.

Either of these premises is a proposition asserting that certain objects have certain characters. Every term of such a proposition stands either for certain objects or for certain characters. The conclusion may be regarded as a proposition substituted in place of either premise, the substitution being justified by the fact stated in the other premise. The conclusion is accordingly derived from either premise by substituting either a new subject for the subject of the premise, or a new predicate for the predicate of the premise, or by both substitutions. Now the substitution of one term for another can be justified only so far as the term substituted represents only what is represented in the term replaced. If, therefore, the conclusion be denoted by the formula,

$$S \text{ is } P;$$

and this conclusion be derived, by a change of subject, from a premise which may on this account be expressed by the formula,

$$M \text{ is } P;$$

then the other premise must assert that whatever thing is represented by S is represented by M, or that

$$\text{Every } S \text{ is an } M;$$

while, if the conclusion, S is P, is derived from either premise by a change of predicate, that premise may be written

$$S \text{ is } M;$$

and the other premise must assert that whatever characters are implied in P are implied in M, or that

$$\text{Whatever is } M \text{ is } P.$$

In either case, therefore, the syllogism must be capable of expression in the form,

$$S \text{ is } M; M \text{ is } P:$$
$$\therefore \ S \text{ is } P.$$

Finally, if the conclusion differs from either of its premises, both in subject and predicate, the form of statement of conclusion and premise may be so altered that they shall have a common term. This can always be done, for if *P* is the premise and *C* the conclusion, they may be stated thus:

The state of things represented in *P* is real,

and

The state of things represented in *C* is real.

In this case the other premise must in some form virtually assert that every state of things such as is represented by *C* is the state of things represented in *P*.

All valid reasoning, therefore, is of one general form; and in seeking to reduce all mental action to the formulæ of valid inference, we seek to reduce it to one single type.

An apparent obstacle to the reduction of all mental action to the type of valid inferences is the existence of fallacious reasoning. Every argument implies the truth of a general principle of inferential procedure (whether involving some matter of fact concerning the subject of argument, or merely a maxim relating to a system of signs), according to which it is a valid argument. If this principle is false, the argument is a fallacy; but neither a valid argument from false premises, nor an exceedingly weak, but not altogether illegitimate, induction or hypothesis, however its force may be overestimated, however false its conclusion, is a fallacy.

Now words, taken just as they stand, if in the form of an argument, thereby do imply whatever fact may be necessary to make the argument conclusive; so that to the formal logician, who has to do only with the meaning of the words according to the proper principles of interpretation, and not with the intention of the speaker as guessed at from other indications, the only fallacies should be such as are simply absurd and contradictory, either because their conclusions are absolutely inconsistent with their premises, or because they connect propositions by a species of illative conjunction, by which they cannot under any circumstances be validly connected.

But to the psychologist an argument is valid only if the premises from which the mental conclusion is derived would be sufficient, if true, to justify it, either by themselves, or by the aid of other propositions that had previously been held for true. But it is easy to show that all inferences made by man, which are not valid in this sense, belong to four classes, viz.: 1. Those whose premises are false; 2. Those that have some little force, though only a little; 3. Those that result from confusion of one proposition with another; 4. Those that result from the indistinct apprehension, wrong application, or falsity, of a rule of inference. For, if a man were to commit a fallacy not of either of these classes, he would, from true premises conceived with perfect distinctness, without being led astray by any prejudice or other judgment serving as a rule of inference, draw a conclusion that had really not the least relevancy. If this could happen, calm consideration and care could be of little use in thinking, for caution only serves to insure our taking all the facts into account, and to make those that we do take account of, distinct; nor can coolness do anything more than to enable us to be cautious, and also to prevent our being affected by a passion in inferring that to be true that we wish were true, or that we fear may be true, or in following some other wrong rule of inference. But experience shows that the calm and careful consideration of the same distinctly conceived premises (including prejudices) will insure the pronouncement of the same judgment by all men. Now if a fallacy belongs to the first of these four classes and its premises are false, it is to be presumed that the procedure of the mind from these premises to the conlusion is either correct, or errs in one of the other three ways; for it cannot be supposed that the mere falsity of the premises should affect the procedure of reason when that falsity is not known to reason. If the fallacy belongs to the second class and has some force, however little, it is a legitimate probable argument, and belongs to the type of valid inference. If it is of the third class and results from the confusion of one proposition with another, this confusion must be owing to a resemblance between the two propositions; that is to say, the person reasoning, seeing that one proposition has some of the characters that belong to the other, concludes that it has all the essential characters of the other, and is equivalent to it. Now this is a hypothetic inference, which though it may be weak, and though its conclusion happens to be false, belongs to the type of valid inferences; and, there-fore, as the *nodus* of the fallacy lies in this confusion, the procedure of the mind in these fallacies of the third class conforms to the formula of valid inference. If the fallacy belongs to the fourth class, it either results from wrongly applying or misapprehending a rule of inference, and so is a fallacy of confusion, or it results from adopting a wrong rule of inference. In this latter case, this rule is in fact taken as a premise, and therefore the false conclusion is owing merely to the falsity of a premise. In every fallacy, therefore, possible to the mind of man, the procedure of the mind conforms to the formula of valid inference.

The third principle whose consequences we have to deduce is, that, whenever we think, we have present to the consciousness some feeling, image, conception, or other representation, which serves as a sign. But it follows from our own existence (that is proved by the occurrence of ignorance and error) that everything that is present to us is a phenome-nal manifestation of ourselves. This does not prevent its being a phe-nomenon of something without us, just as a rainbow is at once a manifestation both of the sun and of the rain. When we think, then, we ourselves, as we are at that moment, appear as a sign. Now a sign has, as such, three references: first, it is a sign *to* some thought which interprets it; second, it is a sign *for* some object to which in that thought it is equivalent; third, it is a sign, *in* some respect or quality, which brings it into connection with its object. Let us ask what the three correlates are to which a thought-sign refers.

1. When we think, to what thought does that thought-sign that is ourself address itself? It may, through the medium of outward expres-sion, that it reaches perhaps only after considerable internal develop-ment, come to address itself to thought of another person. But whether this happens or not, it is always interpreted by a subsequent thought of our own. If, after any thought, the current of ideas flows on freely, it follows the law of mental association. In that case, each former thought suggests something to the thought that follows it, i.e., is the sign of something to this latter. Our train of thought may, it is true, be inter-rupted. But we must remember that, in addition to the principal ele-ment of thought at any moment, there are a hundred things in our mind

to which but a small fraction of attention or consciousness is conceded. It does not, therefore, follow, because a new constitutent of thought gets the uppermost, that the train of thought that it displaces is broken off altogether. On the contrary, from our second principle, that there is no intuition or cognition not determined by previous cognitions, it follows that the striking in of a new experience is never an instantaneous affair, but is an *event* occupying time, and coming to pass by a continuous process. Its prominence in consciousness, therefore, must probably be the consummation of a growing process; and if so, there is no sufficient cause for the thought that had been the leading one just before, to cease abruptly and instantaneously. But if a train of thought ceases by gradually dying out, it freely follows its own law of association as long as it lasts, and there is no moment at which there is a thought belonging to this series, subsequent to which there is not a thought that interprets or repeats it. There is no exception, therefore, to the law that every thought-sign is translated or interpreted in a subsequent one, unless it be that all thought comes to an abrupt and final end in death.

2. The next question is: For what does the thought-sign stand—what does it name—what is its *suppositum?* The outward thing, undoubtedly, when a real outward thing is thought of. But still, as the thought is determined by a previous thought of the same object, it only refers to the thing through denoting this previous thought. Let us suppose, for example, that Toussaint is thought of, and first thought of as a *Negro*, but not distinctly as a man. If this distinctness is afterwards added, it is through the thought that a *Negro* is a *man;* that is to say, the subsequent thought, *man*, refers to the outward thing by being predicated of that previous thought, *Negro*, which has been had of that thing. If we afterwards think of Toussaint as a general, then we think that this Negro, this man, was a general. And so in every case the subsequent thought denotes what was thought in the previous thought.

3. The thought-sign stands for its object in the respect that is thought; that is to say, this respect is the immediate object of consciousness in the thought, or, in other words, it is the thought itself, or at least what the thought is thought to be in the subsequent thought to which it is a sign.

We must now consider two other properties of signs that are of great importance in the theory of cognition. Since a sign is not identical with the thing signified, but differs from the latter in some respects, it must plainly have some characters that belong to it in itself, and have nothing to do with its representative function. These I call the *material* qualities of the sign. As examples of such qualities, take in the word "man" its consisting of three letters—in a picture, its being flat and without relief. In the second place, a sign must be capable of being connected (not in the reason but really) with another sign of the same object, or with the object itself. Thus, words would be of no value at all unless they could be connected into sentences by means of a real copula that joins signs of the same thing. The usefulness of some signs—as a weathercock, a tally, etc.—consists wholly in their being really connected with the very things they signify. In the case of a picture such a connection is not evident, but it exists in the power of association that connects the picture with the brain-sign that labels it. This real, physical connection of a sign with its object, either immediately or by its connection with another sign, I call the *pure demonstrative application* of the sign. Now the representative function of a sign lies neither in its material quality nor in its pure demonstrative application; because it is something that the sign is, not in itself or in a real relation to its object, but that it is *to a thought*, while both of the characters just defined belong to the sign independently of its addressing any thought. And yet if I take all the things that have certain qualities and physically connect them with another series of things, each to each, they become fit to be signs. If they are not regarded as such they are not actually signs, but they are so in the same sense, for example, in which an unseen flower can be said to be *red*, this being also a term relative to a mental affection.

Consider a state of mind that is a conception. It is a conception by virtue of having a *meaning*, a logical comprehension; and if it is applicable to any object, it is because that object has the characters contained in the comprehension of this conception. Now the logical comprehension of a thought is usually said to consist of the thought contained in it; but thoughts are events, acts of the mind. Two thoughts are two events separated in time, and one cannot literally be contained in the other. It may be said that all thoughts exactly similar are regarded as one; and that to say that one thought contains another, means that it contains one exactly similar to that other. But how can two thoughts be similar? Two objects can only be *regarded* as similar if they are compared and brought together in the mind. Thoughts have no existence except in the mind; only as they are regarded do they exist. Hence, two thoughts cannot *be* similar unless they are brought together in the mind. But, as to their existence, two thoughts are separated by an interval of time. We are too apt to imagine that we can frame a thought similar to a past thought, by matching it with the latter, as though this past thought were still present to us. But it is plain that the knowledge that one thought is similar to or in any way truly representative of another, cannot be derived from immediate perception, but must be an hypothesis (unquestionably fully justifiable by facts), and that therefore the formation of such a representing thought must be dependent upon a real effective force behind consciousness, and not merely upon a mental comparison. What we must mean, therefore, by saying that one concept is contained in another, is that we normally represent one to be in the other; that is, that we form a particular kind of judgment,* of which the subject signifies one concept and the predicate the other.

No thought in itself, then, no feeling in itself, contains any others, but is absolutely simple and unanalyzable; and to say that it is composed of other thoughts and feelings, is like saying that a movement upon a straight line is composed of the two movements of which it is the resultant; that is to say, it is a metaphor, or fiction, parallel to the truth. Every thought, however artificial and complex, is, so far as it is immediately present, a mere sensation without parts, and therefore, in itself, without similarity to any other, but incomparable with any other and absolutely *sui generis.*† Whatever is wholly incomparable with anything

---

*A judgment concerning a minimum of information, for the theory of which see my paper on Comprehension and Extension, in the Proceedings of the American Academy of Arts and Sciences, vol. 7, p. 426.

†Observe that I say *in itself.* I am not so wild as to deny that my sensation of red today is like my sensation of red yesterday. I only say that the similarity can *consist* only in the physiological force behind consciousness,—which leads me to say, I recognize this feeling the same as the former one, and so does not consist in a community of sensation.

else is wholly inexplicable, because explanation consists in bringing things under general laws or under natural classes. Hence every thought, in so far as it is a feeling of a peculiar sort, is simply an ultimate, inexplicable fact. Yet this does not conflict with my postulate that that fact should be allowed to stand as inexplicable; for, on the one hand, we never can think, "This is present to me," since, before we have time to make the reflection, the sensation is past, and, on the other hand, when once past, we can never bring back the quality of the feeling as it was *in and for itself*, or know what it was like *in itself*, or even discover the existence of this quality except by a corollary from our general theory of ourselves, and then not in its idiosyncrasy, but only as something present. But, as something present, feelings are all alike and require no explanation, since they contain only what is universal. So that nothing that we can truly predicate of feelings is left inexplicable, but only something that we cannot reflectively know. So that we do not fall into the contradiction of making the Mediate immediable. Finally, no present actual thought (which is a mere feeling) has any meaning, any intellectual value; for this lies not in what is actually thought, but in what this thought may be connected with in representation by subsequent thoughts; so that the meaning of a thought is altogether something virtual. It may be objected, that if no thought has any meaning, all thought is without meaning. But this is a fallacy similar to saying, that, if in no one of the successive spaces that a body fills there is room for motion, there is no room for motion throughout the whole. At no one instant in my state of mind is there cognition or representation, but in the relation of my states of mind at different instants there is.* In short, the Immediate (and therefore in itself unsusceptible of mediation—the Unanalyzable, the Inexplicable, the Unintellectual) runs in a continuous stream through our lives; it is the sum total of consciousness, whose mediation, which is the continuity of it, is brought about by a real effective force behind consciousness.

Thus, we have in thought three elements; first the representative function that makes it a *representation;* second, the pure denotative

---

*Accordingly, just as we say that a body is in motion, and not that motion is in a body, we ought to say that we are in thought, and not that thoughts are in us.

application, or real connection, that brings one thought into *relation* with another; and third, the material quality, or how it feels, that gives thought its *quality.* *

That a sensation is not necessarily an intuition, or first impression of sense, is very evident in the case of the sense of beauty; and has been shown, upon page [68] of this volume, in the case of sound. When the sensation beautiful is determined by previous cognitions, it always arises as a predicate; that is, we think that something is beautiful. Whenever a sensation thus arises in consequence of others, induction shows that those others are more or less complicated. Thus, the sensation of a particular kind of sound arises in consequence of impressions upon the various nerves of the ear being combined in a particular way, and following one another with a certain rapidity. A sensation of color depends upon impressions upon the eye following one another in a regular manner, and with a certain rapidity. The sensation of beauty arises upon a manifold of other impressions. And this will be found to hold good in all cases. Secondly, all these sensations are in themselves simple, or more so than the sensations that give rise to them. Accordingly, a sensation is a simple predicate taken in place of a complex predicate; in other words, it fulfills the function of an hypothesis. But the general principle that every thing to which such and such a sensation belongs, has such and such a complicated series of predicates, is not one determined by reason (as we have seen), but is of an arbitrary nature. Hence, the class of hypothetic inferences that the arising of a sensation resembles, is that of reasoning from definition to definitum, in which the major premise is of an arbitrary nature. Only in this mode of reasoning, this premise is determined by the conventions of language, and expresses the occasion upon which a word is to be used; and in the formation of a sensation, it is determined by the constitution of our nature, and expresses the occasions upon which sensation, or a natural mental sign, arises. Thus, the sensation, so far as it represents something, is determined, according to a logical law, by previous cognitions; that is to say, these cognitions determine that there shall be a sensation. But so far as

*On quality, relation, and representation, see Proceedings of the American Academy of Arts and Sciences, vol. 7, p. 293.

the sensation is a mere feeling of a particular sort, it is determined only by an inexplicable, occult power; and so far, it is not a representation, but only the material quality of a representation. For just as in reasoning from definition to definitum, it is indifferent to the logician how the defined word shall sound, or how many letters it shall contain, so in the case of this constitutional word, it is not determined by an inward law how it shall feel in itself. A feeling, therefore, as a feeling, is merely the *material quality* of a mental sign.

But there is no feeling that is not also a representation, a predicate of something determined logically by the feelings that precede it. For if there are any such feelings not predicates, they are the emotions. Now every emotion has a subject. If a man is angry, he is saying to himself that this or that is vile and outrageous. If he is in joy, he is saying "this is delicious." If he is wondering, he is saying "this is strange." In short, whenever a man feels, he is thinking of *something*. Even those passions that have no definite object—as melancholy—only come to consciousness through tinging the *objects of thought*. That which makes us look upon the emotions more as affections of self than other cognitions, is that we have found them more dependent upon our accidental situation at the moment than other cognitions; but that is only to say that they are cognitions too narrow to be useful. The emotions, as a little observation will show, arise when our attention is strongly drawn to complex and inconceivable circumstances. Fear arises when we cannot predict our fate; joy, in the case of certain indescribable and peculiarly complex sensations. If there are some indications that something greatly for my interest, and which I have anticipated would happen, may not happen; and if, after weighing probabilities, and inventing safeguards, and straining for further information, I find myself unable to come to any fixed conclusion in reference to the future, in the place of that intellectual hypothetic inference that I seek, the feeling of *anxiety* arises. When something happens for which I cannot account, I *wonder*. When I endeavor to realize to myself what I never can do, a pleasure in the future, I *hope*. "I do not understand you," is the phrase of an angry man. The indescribable, the ineffable, the incomprehensible, commonly excite emotion; but nothing is so chilling as a scientific explanation. Thus an emotion is always a simple predicate substituted by an operation of the mind for a highly complicated predicate. Now if we consider that a very complex predicate demands explanation by means of an hypothesis, that that hypothesis must be a simpler predicate substituted for that complex one; and that when we have an emotion, an hypothesis, strictly speaking, is hardly possible—the analogy of the parts played by emotion and hypothesis is very striking. There is, it is true, this difference between an emotion and an intellectual hypothesis, that we have reason to say in the case of the latter, that to whatever the simple hypothetic predicate can be applied, of that the complex predicate is true; whereas, in the case of an emotion this is a proposition for which no reason can be given, but that is determined merely by our emotional constitution. But this corresponds precisely to the difference between hypothesis and reasoning from definition to definitum, and thus it would appear that emotion is nothing but sensation. There appears to be a difference, however, between emotion and sensation, and I would state it as follows:

There is some reason to think that, corresponding to every feeling within us, some motion takes place in our bodies. This property of the thought-sign, since it has no rational dependence upon the meaning of the sign, may be compared with what I have called the material quality of the sign; but it differs from the latter inasmuch as it is not essentially necessary that it should be felt in order that there should be any thought-sign. In the case of a sensation, the manifold of impressions that precede and determine it are not of a kind, the bodily motion corresponding to which comes from any large ganglion or from the brain, and probably for this reason the sensation produces no great commotion in the bodily organism; and the sensation itself is not a thought that has a very strong influence upon the current of thought except by virtue of the information it may serve to afford. An emotion, on the other hand, comes much later in the development of thought—I mean, further from the first beginning of the cognition of its object—and the thoughts that determine it already have motions corresponding to them in the brain, or the chief ganglion; consequently, it produces large movements in the body, and independently of its representative value, strongly affects the current of thought. The animal motions to which I allude, are, in the first place and obviously, blushing, blenching, staring, smiling, scowling, pouting, laughing, weeping, sobbing, wriggling, flinching, trembling, being petrified, sighing, snifling, shrugging, groaning, heartsinking, trepidation, swelling of the heart, etc. To these may, perhaps, be added, in the second place, other more complicated actions, that nevertheless spring from a direct impulse and not from deliberation.

That which distinguishes both sensations proper and emotions from the feeling of a thought, is that in the case of the two former the material quality is made prominent, because the thought has no relation of reason to the thoughts that determine it, which exists in the last case and detracts from the attention given to the mere feeling. By there being no relation of reason to the determining thoughts, I mean that there is nothing in the content of the thought that explains why it should arise only on occasion of these determining thoughts. If there is such a relation of reason, if the thought is essentially limited in its application to these objects, then the thought comprehends a thought other than itself; in other words, it is then a complex thought. An incomplex thought can, therefore, be nothing but a sensation or emotion, having no rational character. This is very different from the ordinary doctrine according to which the very highest and most metaphysical conceptions are absolutely simple. I shall be asked how such a conception of a *being* is to be analyzed, or whether I can ever define *one, two,* and *three,* without a diallele. Now I shall admit at once that neither of these conceptions can be separated into two others higher than itself; and in that sense, therefore, I fully admit that certain very metaphysical and eminently intellectual notions are absolutely simple. But though these concepts cannot be defined by genus and difference, there is another way in which they can be defined. All determination is by negation; we can first recognize any character only by putting an object which possesses it into comparison with an object which possesses it not. A conception, therefore, that was quite universal in every respect would be unrecognizable and impossible. We do not obtain the conception of Being, in the sense implied in the copula, by observing that all the things that we can think of have something in common, for there is no such thing to be observed. We get it by reflecting upon signs—words or thoughts

—we observe that different predicates may be attached to the same subject, and that each makes some conception applicable to the subject; then we imagine that a subject has something true of it merely because a predicate (no matter what) is attached to it—and that we call Being. The conception of being is, therefore, a conception about a sign—a thought, or word—and since it is not applicable to every sign, it is not primarily universal, although it is so in its mediate application to things. Being, therefore, may be defined; it may be defined, for example, as that which is common to the objects included in any class, and to the objects not included in the same class. But it is nothing new to say that metaphysical conceptions are primarily and at bottom thoughts about words, or thoughts about thoughts; it is the doctrine both of Aristotle (whose categories are parts of speech) and of Kant (whose categories are the characters of different kinds of propositions).

Sensation and the power of abstraction or attention may be regarded as, in one sense, the sole constituents of all thought. Having considered the former, let us now attempt some analysis of the latter. By the force of attention, an emphasis is put upon one of the objective elements of consciousness. This emphasis is, therefore, not itself an object of immediate consciousness; and in this respect it differs entirely from a feeling. Therefore, since the emphasis, nevertheless, consists in some effect upon consciousness, and so can exist only so far as it affects our knowledge; and since an act cannot be supposed to determine that which precedes it in time, this act can consist only in the capacity that the cognition emphasized has for producing an effect upon memory, or otherwise influencing subsequent thought. This is confirmed by the fact that attention is a matter of continuous quantity; for continuous quantity, so far as we know it, reduces itself in the last analysis to time. Accordingly, we find that attention does, in fact, produce a very great effect upon subsequent thought. In the first place, it strongly affects memory, a thought being remembered for a longer time the greater the attention originally paid to it. In the second place, the greater the attention, the closer the connection and the more accurate the logical sequence of thought. In the third place, by attention a thought may be recovered that has been forgotten. From these facts, we gather that attention is the power by which thought at one time is connected with and made to relate to thought at another time; or, to apply the conception of thought as a sign, that it is the *pure demonstrative application* of a thought-sign.

Attention is roused when the same phenomenon presents itself repeatedly on different occasions, or the same predicate in different subjects. We see that *A* has a certain character, that *B* has the same, *C* has the same; and this excites our attention, so that we say, "*These* have this character." Thus attention is an act of induction; but it is an induction that does not increase our knowledge, because our "these" covers nothing but the instances experienced. It is, in short, an argument from enumeration.

Attention produces effects upon the nervous system. These effects are habits, or nervous associations. A habit arises, when, having had the sensation of performing a certain act, *m*, on several occasions *a*, *b*, *c*, we come to do it upon every occurrence of the general event, *l*, of which *a*, *b*, and *c* are special cases. That is to say, by the cognition that

Every case of *a*, *b*, or *c*, is a case of *m*,

is determined the cognition that

Every case of *l* is a case of *m*.

Thus the formation of a habit is an induction, and is therefore necessarily connected with attention or abstraction. Voluntary actions result from the sensations produced by habits, as instinctive actions result from our original nature.

We have thus seen that every sort of modification of consciousness —Attention, Sensation, and Understanding—is an inference. But the objection may be made that inference deals only with general terms, and that an image, or absolutely singular representation, cannot therefore be inferred.

"Singular" and "individual" are equivocal terms. A singular may mean that which can be but in one place at one time. In this sense it is not opposed to general. *The sun* is a singular in this sense, but, as is explained in every good treatise on logic, it is a general term. I may have a very general conception of Hermolaus Barbarus, but still I conceive him only as able to be in one place at one time. When an image is said to be singular, it is meant that it is absolutely determinate in all respects. Every possible character, or the negative thereof, must be true of such an image. In the words of the most eminent expounder of the doctrine, the image of a man "must be either of a white, or a black, or a tawny; a straight, or a crooked; a tall, or a low, or a middle-sized man." It must be of a man with his mouth open or his mouth shut, whose hair is precisely of such and such a shade, and whose figure has precisely such and such proportions. No statement of Locke has been so scouted by all friends of images as his denial that the "idea" of a triangle must be either of an obtuse-angled, right-angled, or acute-angled triangle. In fact, the image of a triangle must be of one, each of whose angles is of a certain number of degrees, minutes, and seconds.

This being so, it is apparent that no man has a *true* image of the road to his office, or of any other real thing. Indeed he has no image of it at all unless he can not only recognize it, but imagines it (truly or falsely) in all its infinite details. This being the case, it becomes very doubtful whether we ever have any such thing as an image in our imagination. Please, reader, look at a bright red book, or other brightly colored object, and then shut your eyes and say whether you *see* that color, whether brightly or faintly—whether, indeed, there is anything like sight there. Hume and the other followers of Berkeley maintain that there is no difference between the sight and the memory of the red book except in "their different degrees of force and vivacity." "The colors which the memory employs," says Hume, "are faint and dull compared with those in which our original perceptions are clothed." If this were a correct statement of the difference, we should remember the book as being less red than it is; whereas, in fact, we remember the color with very great precision for a few moments [please to test this point, reader], although we do not see any thing like it. We carry away absolutely nothing of the color except the *consciousness that we could recognize it.* As a further proof of this, I will request the reader to try a little experiment. Let him call up, if he can, the image of a horse—not of one which he has ever seen, but of an imaginary one—and before reading further let him by contemplation* fix the image in his memory. . . . Has the reader done as requested? for I protest that it is not fair play to read further without doing so.——Now, the reader can say in general of what color that horse was, whether grey, bay, or black. But he probabably cannot say *precisely* of what shade it was. He cannot state this as exactly as he could just after having *seen* such a horse. But why, if he had an image in his mind that no more had the general color than it had the particular shade, has the latter vanished so instantaneously from his memory while the former still remains? It may be replied, that we always forget the details, before we do the more general characters; but that this answer is insufficient is, I think, shown by the extreme disproportion between the length of time that the exact shade of something looked at is remembered as compared with that instantaneous oblivion to the exact shade of the thing imagined, and the but slightly superior vividness of the memory of the thing seen as compared with the memory of the thing imagined.

The nominalists, I suspect, confound together thinking a triangle without thinking that it is either equilateral, isoceles, or scalene, and thinking a triangle without thinking whether it is equilateral, isoceles, or scalene.

---

*No person whose native tongue is English will need to be informed that contemplation is essentially (1) protracted, (2) voluntary, and (3) an action, and that it is never used for that which is set forth to the mind in this act. A foreigner can convince himself of this by the proper study of English writers. Thus, Locke (Essay concerning Human Understanding, Book II., chap. 19, § 1) says, "If it [an idea] be held there [in view] long under attentive consideration, 'tis *Contemplation*"; and again, (*Ibid.*, Book II., chap. 10, § 1) "Keeping the *Idea*, which is brought into it [the mind] for some time actually in view, which is called *Contemplation.*" This term is therefore unfitted to translate *Anschauung;* for this latter does not imply an act that is necessarily protracted or voluntary, and denotes most usually a mental presentation, sometimes a faculty, less often the reception of an impression in the mind, and seldom, if ever, an action. To the translation of *Anschauung* by intuition, there is, at least, no such insufferable objection. Etymologically the two words precisely correspond. The original philosophical meaning of intuition was a cognition of the present manifold in that character; and it is now commonly used, as a modern writer says, "to include all the products of the perceptive (external or internal) and imaginative faculties; every act of consciousness, in short, of which the immediate object is an *individual*, thing, act, or state of mind, presented under the condition of distinct existence in space and time." Finally, we have the authority of Kant's own example for translating his *Anschauung* by *Intuitus;* and, indeed, this is the common usage of Germans writing Latin. Moreover, *intuitiv* frequently replaces *anschauend* or anschaulich. If this constitutes a misunderstanding of Kant, it is one that is shared by himself and nearly all his countrymen.

It is important to remember that we have no intuitive power of distinguishing between one subjective mode of cognition and another; and hence often think that something is presented to us as a picture, while it is really constructed from slight data by the understanding. This is the case with dreams, as is shown by the frequent impossibility of giving an intelligible account of one without adding something which we feel was not in the dream itself. Many dreams, of which the waking memory makes elaborate and consistent stories, must probably have been in fact mere jumbles of these feelings of the ability to recognize this and that which I have just alluded to.

I will now go so far as to say that we have no images even in actual perception. It will be sufficent to prove this in the case of vision; for if no picture is seen when we look at an object, it will not be claimed that hearing, touch, and the other senses, are superior to sight in this respect. That the picture is not painted on the nerves of the retina is absolutely certain, if, as physiologists inform us, these nerves are needle-points pointing to the light and at distances, considerably greater than the *minimum visible*. The same thing is shown by our not being able to perceive that there is a large blind spot near the middle of the retina. If, then, we have a picture before us when we see, it is one constructed by the mind at the suggestion of previous sensations. Supposing these sensations to be signs, the understanding by reasoning from them could attain all the knowledge of outward things that we derive from sight, while the sensations are quite inadequate to forming an image or representation absolutely determinate. If we have such an image or picture, we must have in our minds a representation of a surface that is only a part of every surface we see, and we must see that each part, however small, has such and such a color. If we look from some distance at a speckled surface, it seems as if we did not see whether it were speckled or not; but if we have an image before us, it must appear to us either as speckled, or as not speckled. Again, the eye by education comes to distinguish minute differences of color; but if we see only absolutely determinate images, we must, no less before our eyes are trained than afterwards, see each color as particularly such and such a shade. Thus to suppose that we have an image before us when we see, is not only a hypothesis that explains nothing whatever, but is one that actually creates difficulties that require new hypotheses in order to explain them away.

One of these difficulties arises from the fact that the details are less easily distinguished than, and forgotten before, the general circumstances. Upon this theory, the general features exist in the details: the details are, in fact, the whole picture. It seems, then, very strange that that which exists only secondarily in the picture should make more impression than the picture itself. It is true that in an old painting the details are not easily made out; but this is because we know that the blackness is the result of time, and is no part of the picture itself. There is no difficulty in making out the details of the picture as it looks at present; the only difficulty is in guessing what it used to be. But if we have a picture on the retina, the minutest details are there as much as, nay, more than, the general outline and significancy of it. Yet that which must actually be seen, it is extremely difficult to recognize; while that which is only abstracted from what is seen is very obvious.

But the conclusive argument against our having any images, or absolutely determinate representations in perception, is that in that case we have the materials in each such representation for an infinite amount of conscious cognition, which we yet never become aware of Now there is no meaning in saying that we have something in our minds that never has the least effect on what we are conscious of knowing. The most that can be said is, that when we see we are put in a condition in which we are able to get a very large and perhaps indefinitely great amount of knowledge of the visible qualities of objects.

Moreover, that perceptions are not absolutely determinate and singular is obvious from the fact that each sense is an abstracting mechanism. Sight by itself informs us only of colors and forms. No one can pretend that the images of sight are determinate in reference to taste. They are, therefore, so far general that they are neither sweet nor nonsweet, bitter nor nonbitter, having savor or insipid.

The next question is whether we have any general conceptions except in judgments. In perception, where we know a thing as existing, it is plain that there is a judgment that the thing exists, since a mere general concept of a thing is in no case a cognition of it as existing. It has usually been said, however, that we can call up any concept without making any judgment; but it seems that in this case we only arbitrarily suppose ourselves to have an experience. In order to conceive the number 7, I suppose, that is, I arbitrarily make the hypothesis or judgment, that there are certain points before my eyes, and I judge that these are seven. This seems to be the most simple and rational view of the matter, and I may add that it is the one that has been adopted by the best logicians. If this be the case, what goes by the name of the association of images is in reality an association of judgments. The association of ideas, is said to proceed according to three principles—those of resemblance, of contiguity, and of causality. But it would be equally true to say that signs denote what they do on the three principles of resemblance, contiguity, and causality. There can be no question that anything *is* a sign of whatever is associated with it by resemblance, by contiguity, or by causality: nor can there be any doubt that any sign recalls the thing signified. So, then, the association of ideas consists in this, that a judgment occasions another judgment, of which it is the sign. Now this is nothing less nor more than inference.

Everything in which we take the least interest creates in us its own particular emotion, however slight this may be. This emotion is a sign and a predicate of the thing. Now, when a thing resembling this thing is presented to us, a similar emotion arises; hence, we immediately infer that the latter is like the former. A formal logician of the old school may say that in logic no term can enter into the conclusion that had not been contained in the premises, and that therefore the suggestion of something new must be essentially different from inference. But I reply that that rule of logic applies only to those arguments that are technically called completed. We can and do reason—

Elias was a man;
∴ He was mortal.

And this argument is just as valid as the full syllogism, although it is so only because the major premise of the latter happens to be true. If to pass from the judgment "Elias was a man" to the judgment "Elias was mortal," without actually saying to one's self that "All men are mortal," is not inference, then the term "inference" is used in so restricted a sense that inferences hardly occur outside of a logic-book.

What is here said of association by resemblance is true of all association. All association is by signs. Everything has its subjective or emotional qualities, which are attributed either absolutely or relatively, or by conventional imputation to anything that is a sign of it. And so we reason,

The sign is such and such;

∴ The sign is that thing.

This conclusion receiving, however, a modification, owing to other considerations, so as to become—

The sign is almost (is representative of) that thing.

We come now to the consideration of the last of the four principles whose consequences we were to trace; namely, that the absolutely incognizable is absolutely inconceivable. That upon Cartesian principles the very realities of things can never be known in the least, most competent persons must long ago have been convinced. Hence the breaking forth of idealism, which is essentially anti-Cartesian, in every direction, whether among empiricists (Berkeley, Hume), or among no-ologists (Hegel, Fichte). The principle now brought under discussion is directly idealistic; for, since the meaning of a word is the conception it conveys, the absolutely incognizable has no meaning because no conception attaches to it. It is, therefore, a meaningless word; and, consequently, whatever is meant by any term as "the real" is cognizable in some degree, and so is of the nature of a cognition, in the objective sense of that term.

At any moment we are in possession of certain information, that is, of cognitions that have been logically derived by induction and hypothesis from previous cognitions that are less general, less distinct, and of which we have a less lively consciousness. These in their turn have been derived from others still less general, less distinct, and less vivid; and so on back to the ideal* which is quite singular, and quite out of consciousness. This ideal first is the particular thing-in-itself. It does not exist as

---

*By an ideal I mean the limit that the possible cannot attain.

such. That is, there is no thing that is in-itself in the sense of not being relative to the mind, though things that are relative to the mind doubtless are, apart from that relation. The cognitions which thus reach us by this infinite series of inductions and hypotheses (which though infinite *a parte ante logice*, is yet as one continuous process not without a beginning *in time*) or of two kinds, the true and the untrue, or cognitions whose objects are *real* and those whose objects are *unreal*. And what do we mean by the real? It is a conception that we must first have had when we discovered that there was an unreal, an illusion; that is, when we first corrected ourselves. Now the distinction for which alone this fact logically called, was between an *ens* relative to private inward determinations, to the negations belonging to idiosyncrasy, and an *ens* such as would stand in the long run. The real, then, is that which, sooner or later, information and reasoning would finally result in, and which is therefore independent of the vagaries of me and you. Thus, the very origin of the conception of reality shows that this conception essentially involves the notion of a COMMUNITY, without definite limits, and capable of a definite increase of knowledge. And so those two series of cognitions—the real and the unreal—consist of those which, at a time sufficiently future, the community will always continue to reaffirm; and of those which, under the same conditions, will ever after be denied. Now, a proposition whose falsity can never be discovered, and the error of which therefore is absolutely incognizable, contains, upon our principle, absolutely no error. Consequently, that which is thought in these cognitions is the real, as it really is. There is nothing, then, to prevent our knowing outward things as they really are, and it is most likely that we do thus know them in numberless cases, although we can never be absolutely certain of doing so in any special case.

But it follows that since no cognition of ours is absolutely determinate, generals must have a real existence. Now this scholastic realism is usually set down as a belief in metaphysical fictions. But, in fact, a realist is simply one who knows no more recondite reality than that which is represented in a true representation. Since, therefore, the word "man" is true of something, that which "man" means is real. The nominalist must admit that man is truly applicable to something; but he believes that there is beneath this a thing in itself, an incognizable reality. His is the metaphysical figment. Modern nominalists are mostly superficial men, who do not know as the more thorough Roscellinus and Ockam did, that a reality that has no representation is one that has no relation and no quality. The great argument for nominalism is that there is no man unless there is some particular man. That, however, does not affect the realism of Scotus; for although there is no man of whom all further determination can be denied, yet there is a man, abstraction being made of all further determination. There is a real difference between man irrespective of what the other determinations may be, and man with this or that particular series of determinations, although undoubtedly this difference is only relative to the mind and not *in re*. Such is the position of Scotus.* Ockam's great objection is, there can be no real distinction that is not *in re*, in the thing-in-itself; but this begs the question, for it is itself based only on the notion that reality is something independent of representative relation.†

Such being the nature of reality in general, in what does the reality of the mind consist? We have seen that the content of consciousness, the entire phenomenal manifestation of mind, is a sign resulting from inference. Upon our principle, therefore, that the absolutely incognizable does not exist, so that the phenomenal manifestation of a substance is the substance, we must conclude that the mind is a sign developing according to the laws of inference. What distinguishes a man from a word? There is a distinction doubtless. The material qualities, the forces that constitute the pure denotative application, and the meaning of the human sign, are all exceedingly complicated in comparison with those of the word. But these differences are only relative. What other is there? It may be said that man is conscious, while a word is not. But consciousness is a very vague term. It may mean that emotion which accompanies the reflection that we have animal life. This is a consciousness that is dimmed when animal life is at its ebb in old age, or sleep, but that is

---

*"Eadem natura est, quæ in existentia per gradum singularitatis est determinata, et in intellectu, hoc est ut habet relationem ad intellectum ut cognitum ad cognoscens, est indeterminata."—Quæst. Subtillissimæ, lib. 7, qu. 18.
†See his argument *Summa logices*, part. 1, cap. 16.

not dimmed when the spiritual life is at its ebb; which is the more lively the better *animal* a man is, but that is not so, the better *man* he is. We do not attribute this sensation to words, because we have reason to believe that it is dependent upon the possession of an animal body. But this consciousness, being a mere sensation, is only a part of the *material quality* of the man-sign. Again, consciousness is sometimes used to signify the *I think*, or unity in thought; but the unity is nothing but consistency, or the recognition of it. Consistency belongs to every sign, so far as it is a sign; and therefore every sign, since it signifies primarily that it is a sign, signifies its own consistency. The man-sign acquires information, and comes to mean more than he did before. But so do words. Does not electricity mean more now than it did in the days of Franklin? Man makes the word, and the word means nothing that the man has not made it mean, and that only to some man. But since man can think only by means of words or other external symbols, these might turn round and say: "You mean nothing we have not taught you, and then only so far as you address some word as the interpretant of your thought." In fact, therefore, men and words reciprocally educate each other; each increase of a man's information involves and is involved by, a corresponding increase of a word's information.

Without fatiguing the reader by stretching this parallelism too far, it is sufficient to say that there is no element whatever of man's consciousness that had not something corresponding to it in the word; and the reason is obvious. It is that the word or sign that man uses *is* the man himself. For, as, the fact that every thought is a sign, taken in conjunction with the fact that life is a train of thought, proves that man is a sign; so, that every thought is an *external* sign, proves that man is an external sign. That is to say, the man and the external sign are identical, in the same sense in which the words *homo* and *man* are identical. Thus my language is the sum total of myself; for the man is the thought.

It is hard for man to understand this, because he persists in identifying himself with his will, his power over the animal organism, with brute force. Now the organism is only an instrument of thought. But the identity of a man consists in the *consistency* of what he does and thinks, and consistency is the intellectual character of a thing; that is, is its expressing something.

Finally, as what anything really is, is what it may finally come to be known to be in the ideal state of complete information, so that reality depends on the ultimate decision of the community; so thought is what it is, only by virtue of its addressing a future thought that is in its value as thought identical with it; though more developed. In this way, the existence of thought now, depends on what is to be hereafter; so that it has only a potential existence, dependent on the future thought of the community.

The individual man, since his separate existence is manifested only by ignorance and error, so far as he is anything apart from his fellows, and from what he and they are to be, is only a negation. This is man.

        *   *   *   "proud man,
Most ignorant of what he's most assured,
His glassy essence."

IV. Illustrations of the Logic of Science

A DECADE AFTER the series on "Certain Faculties Claimed for Man," Peirce published in 1877–78, the *Popular Science Monthly* Series "Illustrations of the Logic of Science."[1] The series is represented here in what were to be his two most famous articles "The Fixation of Belief" and "How to Make Our Ideas Clear." Many themes from the earlier papers recur. Most particularly there is the emphasis on the dependence of logic on actual thought processes—on logic as something man has learned by experimenting with good and poor forms of reasoning—a theme that was to have great influence on John Dewey's notion of experimental logics. In the second paper on "How to Make Our Ideas Clear," he carries these notions through more consistently than he had done before and formulates the pragmatic maxim for the first time.

In applying the pragmatic theory of definition to the notion of "reality" he produces his theory of the role of the community of investigators as the group whose ultimate opinion determines what truth and reality are. Finally he focuses attention on an entirely new theme when he associates reality with the practical. Dewey was later to describe pragmatism as the doctrine that reality has practical character. This new focus is to be contrasted with the Christian view that reality has religious character, or the Greek view that reality has metaphysical character. Here we meet for the first time the scientific insistence that reality has practical character—that to know reality is to know what may influence and determine practice and behavior, what may control the quality of life so as to mold the world nearer to our desires. This idea is now so familiar as to seem banal, but the trauma produced by the transition to this view of reality from the older religious and metaphysical views

[1] Reprinted in *Collected Papers* at 5.358 ff., 5.388 ff., 2.645 ff., 2.669 ff., 6.395 ff., and 2.619 ff.

undoubtedly was a major source of the objections to pragmatism that were to become so vehement in the writings of the opponents of the view when it was developed by James and Dewey.

1. The Fixation of Belief

I

Few persons care to study logic, because everybody conceives himself to be proficient enough in the art of reasoning already. But I observe that this satisfaction is limited to one's own ratiocination, and does not extend to that of other men.

We come to the full possession of our power of drawing inferences the last of all our faculties, for it is not so much a natural gift as a long and difficult art. The history of its practice would make a grand subject for a book. The medieval schoolmen, following the Romans, made logic the earliest of a boy's studies after grammar, as being very easy. So it was, as they understood it. Its fundamental principle, according to them, was, that all knowledge rests on either authority or reason; but that whatever is deduced by reason depends ultimately on a premise derived from authority. Accordingly, as soon as a boy was perfect in the syllogistic procedure, his intellectual kit of tools was held to be complete.

To Roger Bacon, that remarkable mind who in the middle of the thirteenth century was almost a scientific man, the schoolmen's conception of reasoning appeared only an obstacle to truth. He saw that experience alone teaches anything—a proposition that to us seems easy to understand, because a distinct conception of experience has been handed down to us from former generations; that to him also seemed perfectly clear, because its difficulties had not yet unfolded themselves. Of all kinds of experience, the best, he thought, was interior illumination, that teaches many things about Nature that the external senses could never discover, such as the transubstantiation of bread.

Four centuries later the more celebrated Bacon, in the first book of his "Novum Organum," gave his clear account of experience as something that must be open to verification and re-examination. But, superior as Bacon's conception is to earlier notions, a modern reader who is not in awe of his grandiloquence is chiefly struck by the inadequacy of his view of scientific procedure. That we have only to make some crude experiments, to draw up briefs of the results in certain blank forms, to go through these by rule, checking off everything disproved and setting down the alternatives, and that thus in a few years physical science would be finished up—what an idea! "He wrote on science like a Lord Chancellor," indeed.

The early scientists, Copernicus, Tycho Brahe, Kepler, Galileo, and Gilbert, had methods more like those of their modern brethren. Kepler undertook to draw a curve through the places of Mars;* and his greatest service to science was in impressing on men's minds that this was the thing to be done if they wished to improve astronomy; that they were not to content themselves with inquiring whether one system of epicycles was better than another, but that they were to sit down to the figures and find out what the curve, in truth, was. He accomplished this by his incomparable energy and courage, blundering along in the most inconceivable way (to us), from one irrational hypothesis to another, until, after trying twenty-two of these, he fell, by the mere exhaustion of his invention, upon the orbit that a mind well furnished with the weapons of modern logic would have tried almost at the outset.†

In the same way, every work of science great enough to be remembered for a few generations affords some exemplification of the defective state of the art of reasoning of the time when it was written; and each chief step in science has been a lesson in logic. It was so when Lavoisier and his contemporaries took up the study of chemistry. The old chemist's maxim had been *"Lege, lege, lege, labora, ora, et relege."* Lavoisier's method was not to read and pray, not to dream that some long and complicated chemical process would have a certain effect, to put it into practice with dull patience, after its inevitable failure to dream that with

---

*Not quite so, but as nearly so as can be told in a few words.

†Editor's note: In 1893 Peirce added the following note to this manuscript: "I am ashamed at being obliged to confess that this volume contains a very false and foolish remark about Kepler. When I wrote it I had never studied the original book as I have since. It is now my deliberate opinion that it is the most marvelous piece of inductive reasoning I have been able to find."

some modification it would have another result, and to end by publishing the last dream as a fact: his way was to carry his mind into his laboratory, and to make of his alembics and cucurbits instruments of thought, giving a new conception of reasoning, as something that was to be done with one's eyes open, by manipulating real things instead of words and fancies.

The Darwinian controversy is, in large part, a question of logic. Darwin proposed to apply the statistical method to biology. The same thing had been done in a widely different branch of science, the theory of gases. Though unable to say what the movements of any particular molecule of a gas would be on a certain hypothesis regarding the constitution of this class of bodies, Clausius and Maxwell were yet able, by the application of the doctrine of probabilities, to predict that in the long run such and such a proportion of the molecules would, under given circumstances, acquire such und such velocities; that there would take place, every second, such and such a number of collisions, etc.; and from these propositions were able to deduce certain properties of gases, especially in regard to their heat relations. In like manner, Darwin, while unable to say what the operation of variation and natural selection in any individual case will be, demonstrates that in the long run they will adapt animals to their circumstances. Whether or not existing animal forms are due to such action, or what position the theory ought to take, forms the subject of a discussion in which questions of fact and questions of logic are curiously interlaced.

II

The object of reasoning is to find out, from the consideration of what we already know, something else that we do not know. Consequently, reasoning is good if it be such as to give a true conclusion from true premises, and not otherwise. Thus, the question of its validity is purely one of fact and not of thinking. A being the premises and B the conclusion, the question is, whether these facts are really so related that if A is, B is. If so, the inference is valid; if not, not. It is not in the least the question whether, when the premises are accepted by the mind, we feel an impulse to accept the conclusion also. It is true that we do generally reason correctly by nature. But that is an accident; the true conclusion would remain true if we had no impulse to accept it; and the false one would remain false, though we could not resist the tendency to believe in it.

We are, doubtless, in the main logical animals, but we are not perfectly so. Most of us, for example, are naturally more sanguine and hopeful than logic would justify. We seem to be so constituted that in the absence of any facts to go upon we are happy and self-satisfied; so that the effect of experience is continually to contract our hopes and aspirations. Yet a lifetime of the application of this corrective does not usually eradicate our sanguine disposition. Where hope is unchecked by any experience, it is likely that our optimism is extravagant. Logicality in regard to practical matters is the most useful quality an animal can possess, and might, therefore, result from the action of natural selection; but outside of these it is probably of more advantage to the animal to have his mind filled with pleasing and encouraging visions, independently of their truth; and thus, upon unpractical subjects, natural selection might occasion a fallacious tendency of thought.

That which determines us, from given premises, to draw one inference rather than another, is some habit of mind, whether it be constitutional or acquired. The habit is good or otherwise, according as it produces true conclusions from true premises or not; and an inference is regarded as valid or not, without reference to the truth or falsity of its conclusion specially, but according as the habit that determines it is such as to produce true conclusions in general or not. The particular habit of mind that governs this or that inference may be formulated in a proposition whose truth depends on the validity of the inferences which the habit determines; and such a formula is called a *guiding principle* of inference. Suppose, for example, that we observe that a rotating disk of copper quickly comes to rest when placed between the poles of a magnet, and we infer that this will happen with every disk of copper. The guiding principle is, that what is true of one piece of copper is true of another. Such a guiding principle with regard to copper would be much safer than with regard to many other substances—brass, for example.

A book might be written to signalize all the most important of these guiding principles of reasoning. It would probably be, we must confess, of no service to a person whose thought is directed wholly to practical subjects, and whose activity moves along thoroughly beaten paths. The problems that present themselves to such a mind are matters of routine that he has learned once for all to handle in learning his business. But let a man venture into an unfamiliar field, or where his results are not continually checked by experience, and all history shows that the most masculine intellect will ofttimes lose his orientation and waste his efforts in directions that bring him no nearer to his goal, or even carry him entirely astray. He is like a ship in the open sea, with no one on board who understands the rules of navigation. And in such a case some general study of the guiding principles of reasoning would be sure to be found useful.

The subject could hardly be treated, however, without being first limited; since almost any fact may serve as a guiding principle. But it so happens that there exists a division among facts, such that in one class are all those that are absolutely essential as guiding principles, while in the others are all that have any other interest as objects of research. This division is between those that are necessarily taken for granted in asking whether a certain conclusion follows from certain premises, and those that are not implied in that question. A moment's thought will show that a variety of facts are already assumed when the logical question is first asked. It is implied, for instance, that there are such states of mind as doubt and belief—that a passage from one to the other is possible, the object of thought remaining the same, and that this transition is subject to some rules that all minds are alike bound by. As these are facts that we must already know before we can have any clear conception of reasoning at all, it cannot be supposed to be any longer of much interest to inquire into their truth or falsity. On the other hand, it is easy to believe that those rules of reasoning that are deduced from the very idea of the process are the ones that are the most essential; and, indeed, that so long as it conforms to these it will, at least, not lead to false conclusions from true premises. In point of fact, the importance of what may be deduced from the assumptions involved in the logical question turns out to be greater than might be supposed, and this for reasons that it is difficult to exhibit at the outset. The only one that I shall here mention is, that conceptions that are really products of logical reflection, without being readily seen to be so, mingle with our ordinary thoughts, and are frequently the causes of great confusion. This is the case, for example, with the conception of quality. A quality as such is never an object of observation. We can see that a thing is blue or green, but the quality of being blue and the quality of being green are not things that we see; they are products of logical reflection. The truth is, that common sense, or thought as it first emerges above the level of the narrowly practical, is deeply imbued with that bad logical quality to which the epithet *metaphysical* is commonly applied; and nothing can clear it up but a severe course of logic.

III

We generally know when we wish to ask a question and when we wish to pronounce a judgment, for there is a dissimilarity between the sensation of doubting and that of believing.

But this is not all that distinguishes doubt from belief. There is a practical difference. Our beliefs guide our desires and shape our actions. The Assassins, or followers of the Old Man of the Mountain, used to rush into death at his least command, because they believed that obedience to him would insure everlasting felicity. Had they doubted this, they would not have acted as they did. So it is with every belief, according to its degree. The feeling of believing is a more or less sure indication of there being established in our nature some habit that will determine our actions. Doubt never has such an effect.

Nor must we overlook a third point of difference. Doubt is an uneasy and dissatisfied state from which we struggle to free ourselves and pass into the state of belief; while the latter is a calm and satisfactory state that we do not wish to avoid, or to change to a belief in anything else.* On the contrary, we cling tenaciously, not merely to believing, but to believing just what we do believe.

*I am not speaking of secondary effects occasionally produced by the interference of other impulses.

Thus, both doubt and belief have positive effects upon us, though very different ones. Belief does not make us act at once, but puts us into such a condition that we shall behave in a certain way, when the occasion arises. Doubt has not the least effect of this sort, but stimulates us to action until it is destroyed. This reminds us of the irritation of a nerve and the reflex action produced thereby; while for the analog of belief, in the nervous system, we must look to what are called nervous associations—for example, to that habit of the nerves in consequence of which the smell of a peach will make the mouth water.

IV

The irritation of doubt causes a struggle to attain a state of belief. I shall term this struggle *inquiry*, though it must be admitted that this is sometimes not a very apt designation.

The irritation of doubt is the only immediate motive for the struggle to attain belief. It is certainly best for us that our beliefs should be such as may truly guide our actions so as to satisfy our desires; and this reflection will make us reject any belief that does not seem to have been so formed as to insure this result. But it will only do so by creating a doubt in the place of that belief. With the doubt, therefore, the struggle begins, and with the cessation of doubt it ends. Hence, the sole object of inquiry is the settlement of opinion. We may fancy that this is not enough for us, and that we seek, not merely an opinion, but a true opinion. But put this fancy to the test, and it proves groundless; for as soon as a firm belief is reached we are entirely satisfied, whether the belief be true or false. And it is clear that nothing out of the sphere of our knowledge can be our object, for nothing that does not affect the mind can be the motive for a mental effort. The most that can be maintained is that we seek for a belief that we shall *think* to be true. But we think each one of our beliefs to be true, and, indeed, it is mere tautology to say so.

That the settlement of opinion is the sole end of inquiry is a very important proposition. It sweeps away, at once, various vague and erroneous conceptions of proof. A few of these may be noticed here.

1. Some philosophers have imagined that to start an inquiry it was only necessary to utter a question or set it down upon paper, and have even recommended us to begin our studies with questioning everything! But the mere putting of a proposition into the interrogative form does not stimulate the mind to any struggle after belief. There must be a real and living doubt, and without this all discussion is idle.

2. It is a very common idea that a demonstration must rest on some ultimate and absolutely indubitable propositions. These, according to one school, are first principles of a general nature; according to another, are first sensations. But, in point of fact, an inquiry, to have that completely satisfactory result called demonstration, has only to start with propositions perfectly free from all actual doubt. If the premises are not in fact doubted at all, they cannot be more satisfactory than they are.

3. Some people seem to love to argue a point after all the world is fully convinced of it. But no further advance can be made. When doubt ceases, mental action on the subject comes to an end; and, if it did go on, it would be without a purpose.

V

If the settlement of opinion is the sole object of inquiry, and if belief is of the nature of a habit, why should we not attain the desired end, by taking any answer to a question that we may fancy, and constantly reiterating it to ourselves, dwelling on all that may conduce to that belief, and learning to turn with contempt and hatred from anything that might disturb it? This simple and direct method is really pursued by many men. I remember once being entreated not to read a certain newspaper lest it might change my opinion upon free trade. "Lest I might be entrapped by its fallacies and misstatements," was the form of expression. "You are not," my friend said, "a special student of political economy. You might, therefore, easily be deceived by fallacious arguments upon the subject. You might, then, if you read this paper, be led to believe in protection. But you admit that free trade is the true doctrine; and you do not wish to believe what is not true." I have often known this system to be deliberately adopted. Still oftener, the instinctive dislike of an undecided state of mind, exaggerated into a vague dread of doubt, makes men cling spasmodically to the views they already take. The man feels that if he only holds to his belief without wavering it will be entirely satisfactory. Nor can it be denied that a steady and immovable faith yields great peace of mind. It may, indeed, give rise to inconveniences, as if a man should resolutely continue to believe that fire would not burn him, or that he would be eternally damned if he received his *ingesta* otherwise than through a stomach pump. But then the man who adopts this method will not allow that its inconveniences are greater than its advantages. He will say, "I hold steadfastly to the truth, and the truth is always wholesome." And in many cases it may very well be that the pleasure he derives from his calm faith overbalances any inconveniences resulting from its deceptive character. Thus, if it be true that death is annihilation, then the man who believes that he will certainly go straight to heaven when he dies, provided he has fulfilled certain simple observances in this life, has a cheap pleasure that will not be followed by the least disappointment. A similar consideration seems to have weight with many persons in religious topics, for we frequently hear it said, "Oh, I could not believe so-and-so, because I should be wretched if I did." When an ostrich buries its head in the sand as danger approaches, it very likely takes the happiest course. It hides the danger, and then calmly says there is no danger; and, if it feels perfectly sure there is none, why should it raise its head to see? A man may go through life, systematically keeping out of view all that might cause a change in his opinions, and if he only succeeds—basing his method, as he does, on two fundamental psychological laws—I do not see what can be said against his doing so. It would be an egotistical impertinence to object that his procedure is irrational, for that only amounts to saying that his method of settling belief is not ours. He does not propose to himself to be rational, and, indeed, will often talk with scorn of man's weak and illusive reason. So let him think as he pleases.

But this method of fixing belief, which may be called the method of tenacity, will be unable to hold its ground in practice. The social impulse is against it. The man who adopts it will find that other men think differently from him, and it will be apt to occur to him, in some saner moment, that their opinions are quite as good as his own, and this will shake his confidence in his belief. This conception, that another man's thought or sentiment may be equivalent to one's own, is a distinctly new step, and a highly important one. It arises from an impulse too strong in man to be suppressed, without danger of destroying the human species. Unless we make ourselves hermits, we shall necessarily influence each other's opinions; so that the problem becomes how to fix belief, not in the individual merely, but in the community.

Let the will of the state act, then, instead of that of the individual. Let an institution be created that shall have for its object to keep correct doctrines before the attention of the people, to reiterate them perpetually, and to teach them to the young; having at the same time power to prevent contrary doctrines from being taught, advocated, or expressed. Let all possible causes of a change of mind be removed from men's apprehensions. Let them be kept ignorant, lest they should learn of some reason to think otherwise than they do. Let their passions be enlisted, so that they may regard private and unusual opinions with hatred and horror. Then, let all men who reject the established belief be terrified into silence. Let the people turn out and tar and feather such men, or let inquisitions be made into the manner of thinking of suspected persons, and, when they are found guilty of forbidden beliefs, let them be subjected to some signal punishment. When complete agreement could not otherwise be reached, a general massacre of all who have not thought in a certain way has proved a very effective means of settling opinion in a country. If the power to do this be wanting, let a list of opinions be drawn up, to which no man of the least independence of thought can assent, and let the faithful be required to accept all these propositions, in order to segregate them as radically as possible from the influence of the rest of the world.

This method has, from the earliest time, been one of the chief means of upholding correct theological and political doctrines, and of preserving their universal or catholic character. In Rome, especially, it has been practised from the days of Numa Pompilius to those of Pius Nonus. This is the most perfect example in history; but wherever there is a priesthood —and no religion has been without one—this method has been more or less made use of. Wherever there is an aristocracy, or a guild, or any association of a class of men whose interests depend or are supposed to depend on certain propositions, there will be inevitably found some traces of this natural product of social feeling. Cruelties always accompany this system; and when it is consistently carried out, they become atrocities of the most horrible kind in the eyes of any rational man. Nor should this occasion surprise, for the officer of a society does not feel justified in surrendering the interests of that society for the sake of mercy, as he might his own private interests. It is natural, therefore, that sympathy and fellowship should thus produce a most ruthless power.

In judging this method of fixing belief, which may be called the method of authority, we must, in the first place, allow its immeasurable mental and moral superiority to the method of tenacity. Its success is proportionately greater; and, in fact, it has over and over again worked the most majestic results. The mere structures of stone that it has caused to be put together—in Siam, for example, in Egypt, and in Europe— have many of them a sublimity hardly more than rivaled by the greatest works of Nature. And, except the geological epochs, there are no periods of time so vast as those that are measured by some of these organized faiths. If we scrutinize the matter closely, we shall find that there has not been one of their creeds that has remained always the same; yet the change is so slow as to be imperceptible during one person's life, so that individual belief remains sensibly fixed. For the mass of mankind, then, there is perhaps no better method than this. If it is their highest impulse to be intellectual slaves, then slaves they ought to remain.

But no institution can undertake to regulate opinions upon every subject. Only the most important ones can be attended to, and on the rest men's minds must be left to the action of natural causes. This imperfection will be no source of weakness so long as men are in such a state of culture that one opinion does not influence another—that is, so long as they cannot put two and two together. But in the most priest-ridden states some individuals will be found who are raised above that condition. These men possess a wider sort of social feeling; they see that men in other countries and in other ages have held to very different doctrines from those that they themselves have been brought up to believe; and they cannot help seeing that it is the mere accident of their having been taught as they have, and of their having been surrounded with the manners and associations they have, that has caused them to believe as they do and not far differently. And their candor cannot resist the reflection that there is no reason to rate their own views at a higher value than those of other nations and other centuries; and this gives rise to doubts in their minds.

They will further perceive that such doubts as these must exist in their minds with reference to every belief that seems to be determined by the caprice either of themselves or of those who originated the popular opinions. The willful adherence to a belief, and the arbitrary forcing of it upon others, must, therefore, both be given up, and a new method of settling opinions must be adopted, which shall not only produce an impulse to believe, but shall also decide what proposition it is that is to be believed. Let the action of natural preferences be unimpeded, then, and under their influence let men, conversing together and regarding matters in different lights, gradually develop beliefs in harmony with natural causes. This method resembles that by which conceptions of art have been brought to maturity. The most perfect example of it is to be found in the history of metaphysical philosophy. Systems of this sort have not usually rested upon any observed facts, at least not in any great degree. They have been chiefly adopted because their fundamental propositions seemed "agreeable to reason." This is an apt expression; it does not mean that which agrees with experience, but that which we find ourselves inclined to believe. Plato, for example, finds it agreeable to reason that the distances of the celestial spheres from one another should be proportional to the different lengths of strings that produce harmonious chords. Many philosophers have been led to their main conclusions by considerations like this; but this is the lowest and least developed form that the method takes, for it is clear that another man might find Kepler's theory, that the celestial spheres are proportional to the inscribed and circumscribed spheres of the different regular solids, more agreeable to *his* reason. But the shock of opinions will soon lead men to rest on preferences of a far more universal nature. Take, for example, the doctrine that man only acts selfishly—that is, from the consideration that acting in one way will afford him more pleasure than acting in another. This rests on no fact in the world, but it has had a wide acceptance as being the only reasonable theory.

This method is far more intellectual and respectable from the point of view of reason than either of the others that we have noticed. But its failure has been the most manifest. It makes of inquiry something similar to the development of taste; but taste, unfortunately, is always more or less a matter of fashion, and accordingly metaphysicians have never come to any fixed agreement, but the pendulum has swung backward and forward between a more material and a more spiritual philosophy, from the earliest times to the latest. And so from this, which has been called the *a priori* method, we are driven, in Lord Bacon's phrase, to a true induction. We have examined into this *a priori* method as something that promised to deliver our opinions from their accidental and capricious element. But development, while it is a process that eliminates the effect of some casual circumstances, only magnifies that of others. This method, therefore, does not differ in a very essential way from that of authority. The government may not have lifted its finger to influence my convictions; I may have been left outwardly quite free to choose, we will say, between monogamy and polygamy, and, appealing to my conscience only, I may have concluded that the latter practice is in itself licentious. But when I come to see that the chief obstacle to the spread of Christianity among a people of as high culture as the Hindus has been a conviction of the immorality of our way of treating women, I cannot help seeing that, though governments do not interfere, sentiments in their development will be very greatly determined by accidental causes. Now, there are some people, among whom I must suppose that my reader is to be found, who, when they see that any belief of theirs is determined by any circumstance extraneous to the facts, will from that moment not merely admit in words that that belief is doubtful, but will experience a real doubt of it, so that it ceases to be a belief.

To satisfy our doubts, therefore, it is necessary that a method should be found by which our beliefs may be caused by nothing human, but by some external permanency—by something upon which our thinking has no effect. Some mystics imagine that they have such a method in a private inspiration from on high. But that is only a form of the method of tenacity, in which the conception of truth as something public is not yet developed. Our external permanency would not be external, in our sense, if it was restricted in its influence to one individual. It must be something which affects, or might affect, every man. And, though these affections are necessarily as various as are individual conditions, yet the method must be such that the ultimate conclusion of every man shall be the same. Such is the method of science. Its fundamental hypothesis, restated in more familiar language, is this: There are real things, whose characters are entirely independent of our opinions about them; those realities affect our senses according to regular laws, and, though our sensations are as different as our relations to the objects, yet, by taking advantage of the laws of perception, we can ascertain by reasoning how things really are, and any man, if he has sufficient experience and reason enough about it, will be led to the one true conclusion. The new conception here involved is that of reality. It may be asked how I know that there are any realities. If this hypothesis is the sole support of my method of inquiry, my method of inquiry must not be used to support my hypothesis. The reply is this: 1. If investigation cannot be regarded as proving that there are real things, it at least does not lead to a contrary conclusion; but the method and the conception on which it is based remain ever in harmony. No doubts of the method, therefore, necessarily arise from its practice, as is the case with all the others. 2. The feeling that gives rise to any method of fixing belief is a dissatisfaction at two repugnant propositions. But here already is a vague concession that there is some *one* thing to which a proposition should conform. Nobody, therefore, can really doubt that there are realities, or, if he did, doubt would not be a source of dissatisfaction. The hypothesis, therefore, is one that every mind admits. So that the social impulse does not cause me to doubt it. 3. Everybody uses the scientific method about a great many things, and only ceases to use it when he does not know how to apply it. 4. Experience of the method has not led me to doubt it, but, on the contrary, scientific investigation has had the most wonderful triumphs in the way of settling opinion. These afford the explanation of my not doubting the method or the hypothesis which it supposes; and not having any doubt, nor believing that anybody else whom I could influence has, it would be the merest babble for me to say more about it. If there be anybody with a living doubt upon the subject, let him consider it.

To describe the method of scientific investigation is the object of this series of papers. At present I have only room to notice some points of contrast between it and other methods of fixing belief.

This is the only one of the four methods that presents any distinction of a right and a wrong way. If I adopt the method of tenacity and shut myself out from all influences, whatever I think necessary to doing this is necessary according to that method. So with the method of authority: The state may try to put down heresy by means which, from a scientific point of view, seem very ill-calculated to accomplish its purposes; but the only test *on that method* is what the state thinks, so that it cannot pursue the method wrongly. So with the *a priori* method. The very essence of it is to think as one is inclined to think. All metaphysicians will be sure to do that, however they may be inclined to judge each other to be perversely wrong. The Hegelian system recognizes every natural tendency of thought as logical, although it be certain to be abolished by counter-tendencies. Hegel thinks there is a regular system in the succession of these tendencies, in consequence of which, after drifting one way and the other for a long time, opinion will at last go right. And it is true that metaphysicians get the right ideas at last; Hegel's system of Nature represents tolerably the science of that day; and one may be sure that whatever scientific investigation has put out of doubt will presently receive *a priori* demonstration on the part of the metaphysicians. But with the scientific method the case is different. I may start with known and observed facts to proceed to the unknown; and yet the rules that I follow in doing so may not be such as investigation would approve. The test of whether I am truly following the method is not an immediate appeal to my feelings and purposes, but, on the contrary, itself involves the application of the method. Hence it is that bad reasoning as well as good reasoning is possible; and this fact is the foundation of the practical side of logic.

It is not to be supposed that the first three methods of settling opinion present no advantage whatever over the scientific method. On the contrary, each has some peculiar convenience of its own. The *a priori* method is distinguished for its comfortable conclusions. It is the nature of the process to adopt whatever belief we are inclined to, and there are certain flatteries to the vanity of man that we all believe by nature, until we are awakened from our pleasing dream by some rough facts. The method of authority will always govern the mass of mankind; and those who wield the various forms of organized force in the state will never be convinced that dangerous reasoning ought not to be suppressed in some way. If liberty of speech is to be untrammeled from the grosser forms of constraint, then uniformity of opinion will be secured by a moral terrorism to which the respectability of society will give its thorough approval. Following the method of authority is the path of peace. Certain nonconformities are permitted; certain others (considered unsafe) are forbidden. These are different in different countries and in different ages; but, wherever you are, let it be known that you seriously hold a tabooed belief, and you may be perfectly sure of being treated with a cruelty less brutal but more refined than hunting you like a wolf. Thus, the greatest intellectual benefactors of mankind have never dared, and dare not now, to utter the whole of their thought; and thus a shade of *prima facie* doubt is cast upon every proposition that is considered essential to the security of society. Singularly enough, the persecution does not all come from without; but a man torments himself and is oftentimes most distressed at finding himself believing propositions that he has been brought up to regard with aversion. The peaceful and sympathetic man will, therefore, find it hard to resist the temptation to submit his opinions to authority. But most of all I admire the method of tenacity for its strength, simplicity, and directness. Men who pursue it are distinguished for their decision of character, which becomes very easy with such a mental rule. They do not waste time in trying to make up their minds what they want, but, fastening like lightning upon whatever alternative comes first, they hold to it to the end, whatever happens, without an instant's irresolution. This is one of the splendid qualities that generally accompany brilliant, unlasting success. It is impossible not to envy the man who can dismiss reason, although we know how it must turn out at last.

Such are the advantages that the other methods of settling opinion have over scientific investigation. A man should consider well of them; and then he should consider that, after all, he wishes his opinions to coincide with the fact, and that there is no reason why the results of these three methods should do so. To bring about this effect is the prerogative of the method of science. Upon such considerations he has to make his choice—a choice that is far more than the adoption of any intellectual opinion, which is one of the ruling decisions of his life, to which, when once made, he is bound to adhere. The force of habit will sometimes cause a man to hold on to old beliefs, after he is in a condition to see that they have no sound basis. But reflection upon the state of the case will overcome these habits, and he ought to allow reflection its full weight. People sometimes shrink from doing this, having an idea that beliefs are wholesome which they cannot help feeling rest on nothing. But let such persons suppose an analogous though different case from their own. Let them ask themselves what they would say to a reformed Mussulman who should hesitate to give up his old notions in regard to the relations of the sexes; or to a reformed Catholic who should still shrink from reading the Bible. Would they not say that these persons ought to consider the matter fully, and clearly understand the new doctrine, and then ought to embrace it, in its entirety? But, above all, let it be considered that what is more wholesome than any particular belief is integrity of belief, and that to avoid looking into the support of any belief from a fear that it may turn out rotten is quite as immoral as it is disadvantageous. The person who confesses that there is such a thing as truth, which is distinguished from falsehood simply by this, that if acted on it will carry us to the point we aim at and not astray, and then, though convinced of this, dares not know the truth and seeks to avoid it, is in a sorry state of mind indeed.

Yes, the other methods do have their merits: a clear logical conscience does cost something—just as any virtue, just as all that we cherish, costs us dear. But we should not desire it to be otherwise. The genius of a man's logical method should be loved and reverenced as his bride, whom he has chosen from all the world. He need not condemn the others; on the contrary, he may honor them deeply, and in doing so he only honors her the more. But she is the one that he has chosen, and he knows that he was right in making that choice. And having made it, he will work and fight for her, and will not complain that there are blows to take, hoping that there may be as many and as hard to give, and will strive to be the worthy knight and champion of her from the blaze of whose splendors he draws his inspiration and his courage.

2. How to Make Our Ideas Clear

I

Whoever has looked into a modern treatise on logic of the common sort will doubtless remember the two distinctions between *clear* and *obscure* conceptions, and between *distinct* and *confused* conceptions. They have lain in the books now for nigh two centuries, unimproved and unmodified, and are generally reckoned by logicians as among the gems of their doctrine.

A clear idea is defined as one that is so apprehended that it will be recognized wherever it is met with, and so that no other will be mistaken for it. If it fails of this clearness, it is said to be obscure.

This is rather a neat bit of philosophical terminology; yet, since it is clearness that they were defining, I wish the logicians had made their definition a little more plain. Never to fail to recognize an idea, and under no circumstances to mistake another for it, let it come in how recondite a form it may, would indeed imply such prodigious force and clearness of intellect as is seldom met with in this world. On the other hand, merely to have such an acquaintance with the idea as to have become familiar with it, and to have lost all hesitancy in recognizing it in ordinary cases, hardly seems to deserve the name of clearness of apprehension, since after all it only amounts to a subjective feeling of mastery that may be entirely mistaken. I take it, however, that when the logicians speak of "clearness," they mean nothing more than such a familiarity with an idea, since they regard the quality as but a small merit, that needs to be supplemented by another, which they call *distinctness*.

A distinct idea is defined as one that contains nothing that is not clear. This is technical language; by the *contents* of an idea logicians understand whatever is contained in its definition. So that an idea is *distinctly* apprehended, according to them, when we can give a precise definition of it, in abstract terms. Here the professional logicians leave the subject; and I would not have troubled the reader with what they have to say, if it were not such a striking example of how they have been slumbering through ages of intellectual activity, listlessly disregarding the enginery of modern thought, and never dreaming of applying its lessons to the improvement of logic. It is easy to show that the doctrine that familiar use and abstract distinctness make the perfection of apprehension has its only true place in philosophies that have long been extinct; and it is now time to formulate the method of attaining to a more perfect clearness of thought, such as we see and admire in the thinkers of our own time.

When Descartes set about the reconstruction of philosophy, his first step was to (theoretically) permit skepticism and to discard the practice of the schoolmen of looking to authority as the ultimate source of truth. That done, he sought a more natural fountain of true principles, and professed to find it in the human mind; thus passing, in the most direct way, from the method of authority to that of apriority, as described in my first paper. Self-consciousness was to furnish us with our fundamental truths, and to decide what was agreeable to reason. But since, evidently, not all ideas are true, he was led to note, as the first condition of infallibility, that they must be clear. The distinction between an idea *seeming* clear and really being so, never occurred to him. Trusting to introspection, as he did, even for a knowledge of external things, why should he question its testimony in respect to the contents of our own minds? But then, I suppose, seeing men, who seemed to be quite clear and positive, holding opposite opinions upon fundamental principles, he was further led to say that clearness of ideas is not sufficient, but that they need also to be distinct, i.e., to have nothing unclear about them. What he probably meant by this (for he did not explain himself with precision) was, that they must sustain the test of dialectical examination; that they must not only seem clear at the outset, but that discussion must never be able to bring to light points of obscurity connected with them.

Such was the distinction of Descartes, and one sees that it was precisely on the level of his philosophy. It was somewhat developed by Leibniz. This great and singular genius was as remarkable for what he failed to see as for what he saw. That a piece of mechanism could not do work perpetually without being fed with power in some form, was a thing perfectly apparent to him; yet he did not understand that the machinery of the mind can only transform knowledge, but never originate it, unless it be fed with facts of observation. He thus missed the most essential point of the Cartesian philosophy, which is, that to accept propositions that seem perfectly evident to us is a thing that, whether it be logical or illogical, we cannot help doing. Instead of regarding the matter in this way, he sought to reduce the first principles of science to formulas that cannot be denied without self-contradiction, and was apparently unaware of the great difference between his position and that of Descartes. So he reverted to the old formalities of logic, and, above all, abstract definitions played a great part in his philosophy. It was quite natural, therefore, that on observing that the method of Descartes labored under the difficulty that we may seem to ourselves to have clear apprehensions of ideas that in truth are very hazy, no better remedy occurred to him than to require an abstract definition of every important term. Accordingly, in adopting the distinction of *clear* and *distinct* notions, he described the latter quality as the clear apprehension of everything contained in the definition; and the books have ever since copied his words. There is no danger that his chimerical scheme will ever again be overvalued. Nothing new can ever be learned by analyzing definitions. Nevertheless, our existing beliefs can be set in order by this process, and order is an essential element of intellectual economy, as of every other. It may be acknowledged, therefore, that the books are right in making familiarity with a notion the first step toward clearness of apprehension, and the defining of it the second. But in omitting all mention of any higher perspicuity of thought, they simply mirror a

philosophy that was exploded a hundred years ago. That much-admired
"ornament of logic"—the doctrine of clearness and distinctness—may
be pretty enough, but it is high time to relegate to our cabinet of
curiosities the antique *bijou*, and to wear about us something better
adapted to modern uses.

The very first lesson that we have a right to demand that logic shall
teach us is, how to make our ideas clear; and a most important one it
is, depreciated only by minds who stand in need of it. To know what
we think, to be masters of our own meaning, will make a solid foundation
for great and weighty thought. It is most easily learned by those whose
ideas are meager and restricted; and far happier they than such as wallow
helplessly in a rich mud of conceptions. A nation, it is true, may, in the
course of generations, overcome the disadvantage of an excessive wealth
of language and its natural concomitant, a vast, unfathomable deep of
ideas. We may see it in history, slowly perfecting its literary forms,
sloughing at length its metaphysics, and, by virtue of the untirable
patience that is often a compensation, attaining great excellence in every
branch of mental acquirement. The page of history is not yet unrolled
that is to tell us whether such a people will or will not in the long run
prevail over one whose ideas (like the words of their language) are few,
but which possesses a wonderful mastery over those which it has. For
an individual, however, there can be no question that a few clear ideas
are worth more than many confused ones. A young man would hardly
be persuaded to sacrifice the greater part of his thoughts to save the rest;
and the muddled head is the least apt to see the necessity of such a
sacrifice. Him we can usually only commiserate, as a person with a
congenital defect. Time will help him, but intellectual maturity with
regard to clearness comes rather late, an unfortunate arrangement of
Nature, inasmuch as clearness is of less use to a man settled in life, whose
errors have in great measure had their effect, than it would be to one
whose path lies before him. It is terrible to see how a single unclear idea,
a single formula without meaning, lurking in a young man's head, will
sometimes act like an obstruction of inert matter in an artery, hindering
the nutrition of the brain, and condemning its victim to pine away in
the fullness of his intellectual vigor and in the midst of intellectual

plenty. Many a man has cherished for years as his hobby some vague shadow of an idea, too meaningless to be positively false; he has, nevertheless, passionately loved it, has made it his companion by day and by night, and has given to it his strength and his life, leaving all other occupations for its sake, and in short has lived with it and for it, until it has become, as it were, flesh of his flesh and bone of his bone; and then he has waked up some bright morning to find it gone, clean vanished away like the beautiful Melusina of the fable, and the essence of his life gone with it. I have myself known such a man; and who can tell how many histories of circle-squarers, metaphysicians, astrologers, and what not, may not be told in the old German story?

II

The principles set forth in the first of these papers lead, at once, to a method of reaching a clearness of thought of a far higher grade than the "distinctness" of the logicians. We have there found that the action of thought is excited by the irritation of doubt, and ceases when belief is attained; so that the production of belief is the sole function of thought. All these words, however, are too strong for my purpose. It is as if I had described the phenomena as they appear under a mental microscope. Doubt and belief, as the words are commonly employed, relate to religious or other grave discussions. But here I use them to designate the starting of any question, no matter how small or how great, and the resolution of it. If, for instance, in a horse-car, I pull out my purse and find a five-cent nickel and five coppers, I decide, while my hand is going to the purse, in which way I will pay my fare. To call such a question doubt, and my decision belief, is certainly to use words very disproportionate to the occasion. To speak of such a doubt as causing an irritation that needs to be appeased, suggests a temper that is uncomfortable to the verge of insanity. Yet, looking at the matter minutely, it must be admitted that, if there is the least hesitation as to whether I shall pay the five coppers or the nickel (as there will be sure to be, unless I act from some previously contracted habit in the matter), though irritation is too strong a word, yet I am excited to such small mental activity as may be necessary to deciding how I shall act. Most frequently doubts arise from some indecision, however momentary, in our action. Sometimes it is not so. I have, for example, to wait in a railway station, and to pass the time I read the advertisements on the walls. I compare the advantages of different trains and different routes that I never expect to take, merely fancying myself to be in a state of hesitancy, because I am bored with having nothing to trouble me. Feigned hesitancy, whether feigned for mere amusement or with a lofty purpose, plays a great part in the production of scientific inquiry. However the doubt may originate, it stimulates the mind to an activity that may be slight or energetic, calm or turbulent. Images pass rapidly through consciousness, one incessantly melting into another, until at last, when all is over —it may be in a fraction of a second, in an hour, or after long years— we find ourselves decided as to how we should act under such circumstances as those which occasioned our hesitation. In other words, we have attained belief.

In this process we observe two sorts of elements of consciousness, the distinction between which may best be made clear by means of an illustration. In a piece of music there are the separate notes, and there is the air. A single tone may be prolonged for an hour or a day, and it exists as perfectly in each second of that time as in the whole taken together; so that, as long as it is sounding, it might be present to a sense from which everything in the past was as completely absent as the future itself. But it is different with the air, the performance of which occupies a certain time, during the portions of which only portions of it are played. It consists in an orderliness in the succession of sounds that strike the ear at different times; and to perceive it there must be some continuity of consciousness that makes the events of a lapse of time present to us. We certainly only perceive the air by hearing the separate notes; yet we cannot be said to directly hear it, for we hear only what is present at the instant, and an orderliness of succession cannot exist in an instant. These two sorts of objects, what we are *immediately* conscious of and what we are *mediately* conscious of, are found in all consciousness. Some elements (the sensations) are completely present at every instant so long as they last, while others (like thought) are actions having beginning, middle, and end, and consist in a congruence in the succession of sensations that flow through the mind. They cannot be immediately present to us, but must cover some portion of the past or future. Thought is a thread of melody running through the succession of our sensations.

We may add that just as a piece of music may be written in parts, each part having its own air, so various systems of relationship of succession subsist together between the same sensations. These different systems are distinguished by having different motives, ideas, or functions. Thought is only one such system, for its sole motive, idea, and function is to produce belief, and whatever does not concern that purpose belongs to some other system of relations. The action of thinking may incidentally have other results; it may serve to amuse us, for example, and among *dilettanti* it is not rare to find those who have so perverted thought to the purposes of pleasure that it seems to vex them to think that the questions upon which they delight to exercise it may ever get finally settled; and a positive discovery that takes a favorite subject out of the arena of literary debate is met with ill-concealed dislike. This disposition is the very debauchery of thought. But the soul and meaning of thought, abstracted from the other elements that accompany it, though it may be voluntarily thwarted, can never be made to direct itself toward anything but the production of belief. Thought in action has for its only possible motive the attainment of thought at rest; and whatever does not refer to belief is no part of the thought itself.

And what, then, is belief? It is the demicadence that closes a musical phrase in the symphony of our intellectual life. We have seen that it has just three properties: First, it is something that we are aware of; second, it appeases the irritation of doubt; and, third, it involves the establishment in our nature of a rule of action, or, say for short, a *habit*. As it appeases the irritation of doubt, which is the motive for thinking, thought relaxes, and comes to rest for a moment when belief is reached. But, since belief is a rule for action, the application of which involves further doubt and further thought, at the same time that it is a stopping place, it is also a new starting place for thought. That is why I have permitted myself to call it thought at rest, although thought is essentially an action. The *final* upshot of thinking is the exercise of volition, and of this thought no longer forms a part; but belief is only a stadium of mental action, an effect upon our nature due to thought, which will influence future thinking.

The essence of belief is the establishment of a habit, and different beliefs are distinguished by the different modes of action to which they give rise. If beliefs do not differ in this respect, if they appease the same doubt by producing the same rule of action, then no mere differences in the manner of consciousness of them can make them different beliefs, any more than playing a tune in different keys is playing different tunes. Imaginary distinctions are often drawn between beliefs that differ only in their mode of expression—the wrangling that ensues is real enough, however. To believe that any objects are arranged as in Fig. 1, and to believe that they are arranged as in Fig. 2, are one and the same belief; yet it is conceivable that a man should assert one proposition and deny the other. Such false distinctions do as much harm as the confusion of beliefs really different, and are among the pitfalls of which we ought constantly to beware, especially when we are upon metaphysical ground. One singular deception of this sort, that often occurs, is to mistake the sensation produced by our own unclearness of thought for a character of the object we are thinking. Instead of perceiving that the obscurity is purely subjective, we fancy that we contemplate a quality of the object that is essentially mysterious; and if our conception be afterward presented to us in a clear form we do not recognize it as the same, owing to the absence of the feeling of unintelligibility. So long as this deception lasts, it obviously puts an impassable barrier in the way of perspicuous thinking; so that it equally interests the opponents of rational thought to perpetuate it, and its adherents to guard against it.

Another such deception is to mistake a mere difference in the grammatical construction of two words for a distinction between the ideas they express. In this pedantic age, when the general mob of writers attend so much more to words than to things, this error is common enough. When I just said that thought is an *action*, and that it consists in a *relation*, although a person performs an action but not a relation, which can only be the result of an action, yet there was no inconsistency in what I said, but only a grammatical vagueness.

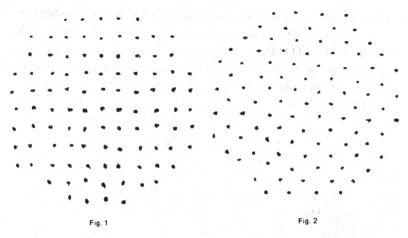

Fig. 1   Fig. 2

From all these sophisms we shall be perfectly safe so long as we reflect that the whole function of thought is to produce habits of action; and that whatever there is connected with a thought, but irrelevant to its purpose, is an accretion to it, but no part of it. If there be a unity among our sensations that has no reference to how we shall act on a given occasion, as when we listen to a piece of music, why we do not call that thinking. To develop its meaning, we have, therefore, simply to determine what habits it produces, for what a thing means is simply what habits it involves. Now, the identity of a habit depends on how it might lead us to act, not merely under such circumstances as are likely to arise, but under such as might possibly occur, no matter how improbable they may be. What the habit is depends on *when* and *how* it causes us to act. As for the *when*, every stimulus to action is derived from perception; as for the *how*, every purpose of action is to produce some sensible result. Thus, we come down to what is tangible and practical, as the root of every real distinction of thought, no matter how subtle it may be; and there is no distinction of meaning so fine as to consist in anything but a possible difference of practice.

To see what this principle leads to, consider in the light of it such a doctrine as that of transubstantiation. The Protestant churches generally hold that the elements of the sacrament are flesh and blood only in a topical sense; they nourish our souls as meat and the juice of it would our bodies. But the Catholics maintain that they are literally just that; although they possess all the sensible qualities of wafer cakes and diluted wine. But we can have no conception of wine except what may enter into a belief, either—

1. That this, that, or the other, is wine; or,
2. That wine possesses certain properties.

Such beliefs are nothing but self-notifications that we should, upon occasion, act in regard to such things as we believe to be wine according to the qualities that we believe wine to possess. The occasion of such action would be some sensible perception, the motive of it to produce some sensible result. Thus our action has exclusive reference to what affects the senses, our habit has the same bearing as our action, our belief the same as our habit, our conception the same as our belief; and we can consequently mean nothing by wine but what has certain effects, direct or indirect, upon our senses; and to talk of something as having all the sensible characters of wine, yet being in reality blood, is senseless jargon. Now, it is not my object to pursue the theological question; and having used it as a logical example I drop it, without caring to anticipate the theologian's reply. I only desire to point out how impossible it is that we should have an idea in our minds that relates to anything but conceived sensible effects of things. Our idea of anything *is* our idea of its sensible effects; and if we fancy that we have any other we deceive ourselves, and mistake a mere sensation accompanying the thought for a part of the thought itself. It is absurd to say that thought has any meaning unrelated to its only function. It is foolish for Catholics and Protestants to fancy themselves in disagreement about the elements of the sacrament, if they agree in regard to all their sensible effects, here or hereafter.

It appears, then, that the rule for attaining the third grade of clearness of apprehension is as follows: Consider what effects, that might conceivably have practical bearings, we conceive the object of our conception to have. Then, our conception of these effects is the whole of our conception of the object.

III

Let us illustrate this rule by some examples; and, to begin with the simplest one possible, let us ask what we mean by calling a thing *hard*. Evidently that it will not be scratched by many other substances. The whole conception of this quality, as of every other, lies in its conceived effects. There is absolutely no difference between a hard thing and a soft thing so long as they are not brought to the test. Suppose, then, that a diamond could be crystallized in the midst of a cushion of soft cotton, and should remain there until it was finally burned up. Would it be false to say that that diamond was soft? This seems a foolish question, and would be so, in fact, except in the realm of logic. There such questions are often of the greatest utility as serving to bring logical principles into sharper relief than real discussions ever could. In studying logic we must not put them aside with hasty answers, but must consider them with attentive care, in order to make out the principles involved. We may, in the present case, modify our question, and ask what prevents us from saying that all hard bodies remain perfectly soft until they are touched, when their hardness increases with the pressure until they are scratched. Reflection will show that the reply is this: There would be no *falsity* in such modes of speech. They would involve a modification of our present usage of speech with regard to the words hard and soft, but not of their meanings. For they represent no fact to be different from what it is; only they involve arrangements of facts that would be exceedingly maladroit. This leads us to remark that the question of what would occur under circumstances which do not actually arise is not a question of fact, but only of the most perspicuous arrangement of them. For example, the question of free will and fate in its simplest form, stripped of verbiage, is something like this: I have done something of which I am ashamed; could I, by an effort of the will, have resisted the temptation, and done otherwise? The philosophical reply is, that this is not a question of fact, but only of the arrangement of facts. Arranging them so as to exhibit what is particularly pertinent to my question—namely, that I ought to blame myself for having done wrong—it is perfectly true to say that, if I had willed to do otherwise than I did, I should have done otherwise.

On the other hand, arranging the facts so as to exhibit another impor-tant consideration, it is equally true that, when a temptation has once been allowed to work, it will, if it has a certain force, produce its effect, let me struggle how I may. There is no objection to a contradiction in what would result from a false supposition. The *reductio ad absurdum* consists in showing that contradictory results would follow from a hy-pothesis that is consequently judged to be false. Many questions are involved in the free will discussion, and I am far from desiring to say that both sides are equally right. On the contrary, I am of the opinion that one side denies important facts, and that the other does not. But what I do say is, that the above single question was the origin of the whole doubt; that, had it not been for this question, the controversy would never have arisen; and that this question is perfectly solved in the manner that I have indicated.

Let us next seek a clear idea of weight. This is another very easy case. To say that a body is heavy means simply that, in the absence of opposing force, it will fall. This (neglecting certain specifications of how it will fall, etc., that exist in the mind of the physicist who uses the word) is evidently the whole conception of weight. It is a fair question whether some particular facts may not *account* for gravity; but what we mean by the force itself is completely involved in its effects.

This leads us to undertake an account of the idea of force in general. This is the great conception that developed in the early part of the seventeenth century from the rude idea of a cause, and constantly improved upon since, has shown us how to explain all the changes of motion that bodies experience, and how to think about all physical phenomena; that has given birth to modern science, and changed the face of the globe; and that, aside from its more special uses, has played a principal part in directing the course of modern thought, and in furthering modern social development. It is therefore, worth some pains to comprehend it. According to our rule, we must begin by asking what is the immediate use of thinking about force; and the answer is, that we thus account for changes of motion. If bodies were left to themselves, without the intervention of forces, every motion would continue unchanged both in velocity and in direction. Furthermore, change of motion never takes place abruptly; if its direction is changed, it is always through a curve without angles; if its velocity alters, it is by degrees. The gradual changes that are constantly taking place are conceived by geometers to be compounded together according to the rules of the parallelogram of forces. If the reader does not already know what this is, he will find it, I hope, to his advantage to endeavor to follow the following explanation; but if mathematics are insupportable to him, pray let him skip three paragraphs rather than that we should part company here.

A *path* is a line whose beginning and end are distinguished. Two paths are considered to be equivalent, which, beginning at the same point, lead to the same point. Thus the two paths, A B C D E and A F G H E, are equivalent. Paths that do *not* begin at the same point are considered to be equivalent, provided that, on moving either of them without turning it, but keeping it always parallel to its original position, when its beginning coincides with that of the other path, the ends also coincide. Paths are considered as geometrically added together, when one begins where the other ends; thus the path A E is conceived to be a sum of A B, B C, C D, and DE. In the parallelogram of Fig. 4 the diagonal $A C$ is the sum of $A B$ and $B C$; or, since $A D$ is geometrically equivalent to $B C$, $A C$ is the geometrical sum of $A B$ and $A D$.

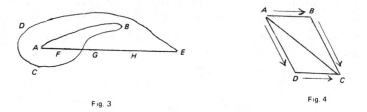

Fig. 3   Fig. 4

All this is purely conventional. It simply amounts to this: that we choose to call paths having the relations I have described equal or added. But, though it is a convention, it is a convention with a good reason. The rule for geometrical addition may be applied not only to paths, but to any other things that can be represented by paths. Now, as a path is determined by the varying direction and distance of the point that moves over it from the starting point, it follows that anything that from its beginning to its end is determined by a varying direction and a varying magnitude is capable of being represented by a line. Accordingly, *velocities* may be represented by lines, for they have only directions and rates. The same thing is true of *accelerations*, or changes of velocities. This is evident enough in the case of velocities; and it becomes evident for accelerations if we consider that precisely what velocities are to positions—namely, states of change of them—that accelerations are to velocities.

The so-called "parallelogram of forces" is simply a rule for compounding accelerations. The rule is, to represent the accelerations by paths, and then to geometrically add the paths. The geometers, however, not only use the "parallelogram of forces" to compound different accelerations, but also to resolve one acceleration into a sum of several. Let *A B* (Fig. 5) be the path that represents a certain acceleration—say, such a change in the motion of a body that at the end of one second the body will, under the influence of that change, be in a position different from what it would have had if its motion had continued unchanged such that a path equivalent to *A B* would lead from the latter position to the former. This acceleration may be considered as the sum of the accelerations represented by *A C* and *C B*. It may also be considered as the sum of the very different accelerations represented by *A D* and *D B*, where *A D* is almost the opposite of *A C*. And it is clear that there is an immense variety of ways in which *A B* might be resolved into the sum of two accelerations.

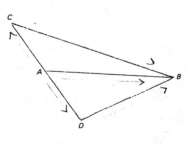

Fig. 5

After this tedious explanation, which I hope, in view of the extraordinary interest of the conception of force, may not have exhausted the reader's patience, we are prepared at last to state the grand fact that this conception embodies. This fact is that if the actual changes of motion that the different particles of bodies experience are each resolved in its appropriate way, each component acceleration is precisely such as is prescribed by a certain law of Nature, according to which bodies in the relative positions that the bodies in question actually have at the moment,* always receive certain accelerations, which, being compounded by geometrical addition, give the acceleration that the body actually experiences.

This is the only fact that the idea of force represents, and whoever will take the trouble clearly to apprehend what this fact is, perfectly comprehends what force is. Whether we ought to say that a force *is* an acceleration, or that it *causes* an acceleration, is a mere question of propriety of language, that has no more to do with our real meaning than the difference between the French idiom *"Il fait froid"* and its English equivalent *"It is cold."* Yet it is surprising to see how this simple affair has muddled men's minds. In how many profound treatises is not force spoken of as a "mysterious entity," which seems to be only a way of confessing that the author despairs of ever getting a clear notion of what the word means! In a recent admired work on "Analytic Mechanics" it is stated that we understand precisely the effect of force, but what force itself is we do not understand! This is simply a self-contradiction. The idea that the word force excites in our minds has no other function than to affect our actions, and these actions can have no reference to force otherwise than through its effects. Consequently, if we know what the effects of force are, we are acquainted with every fact that is implied in saying that a force exists, and there is nothing more to know. The truth is, there is some vague notion afloat that a question may mean something that the mind cannot conceive; and when some hairsplitting philosophers have been confronted with the absurdity of such a view, they have invented an empty distinction between positive and negative concep-

*Possibly the velocities also have to be taken into account.

tions, in the attempt to give their non-idea a form not obviously nonsensical. The nullity of it is sufficiently plain from the considerations given a few pages back; and, apart from those considerations, the quibbling character of the distinction must have struck every mind accustomed to real thinking.

IV

Let us now approach the subject of logic, and consider a conception that particularly concerns it, that of *reality*. Taking clearness in the sense of familiarity, no idea could be clearer than this. Every child uses it with perfect confidence, never dreaming that he does not understand it. As for clearness in its second grade, however, it would probably puzzle most men, even among those of a reflective turn of mind, to give an abstract definition of the real. Yet such a definition may perhaps be reached by considering the points of difference between reality and its opposite, fiction. A figment is a product of somebody's imagination; it has such characters as his thought impresses upon it. That whose characters are independent of how you or I think is an external reality. There are, however, phenomena within our own minds, dependent upon our thought, which are at the same time real in the sense that we really think them. But though their characters depend on how we think, they do not depend on what we think those characters to be. Thus, a dream has a real existence as a mental phenomenon, if somebody has really dreamt it; that he dreamt so and so does not depend on what anybody thinks was dreamt, but is completely independent of all opinion on the subject. On the other hand, considering, not the fact of dreaming, but the thing dreamt, it retains its peculiarities by virtue of no other fact than that it was dreamt to possess them. Thus we may define the real as that whose characters are independent of what anybody may think them to be.

But, however satisfactory such a definition may be found, it would be a great mistake to suppose that it makes the idea of reality perfectly clear. Here, then, let us apply our rules. According to them, reality, like every other quality, consists in the peculiar sensible effects that things partaking of it produce. The only effect that real things have is to cause belief, for all the sensations that they excite emerge into consciousness in the form of beliefs. The question therefore is, how is true belief (or belief in the real) distinguished from false belief (or belief in fiction). Now, as we have seen in the former paper, the ideas of truth and falsehood, in their full development, appertain exclusively to the scientific method of settling opinion. A person who arbitrarily chooses the propositions that he will adopt can use the word truth only to emphasize the expression of his determination to hold on to his choice. Of course, the method of tenacity never prevailed exclusively; reason is too natural to men for that. But in the literature of the Dark Ages we find some fine examples of it. When Scotus Erigena is commenting upon a poetical passage in which hellebore is spoken of as having caused the death of Socrates, he does not hesitate to inform the inquiring reader that Helleborus and Socrates were two eminent Greek philosophers, and that the latter having been overcome in argument by the former took the matter to heart and died of it! What sort of an idea of truth could a man have who could adopt and teach, without the qualification of a perhaps, an opinion taken so entirely at random? The real spirit of Socrates, who I hope would have been delighted to have been "overcome in argument," because he would have learned something by it, is in curious contrast with the naive idea of the glossist, for whom discussion would seem to have been simply a struggle. When philosophy began to awake from its long slumber, and before theology completely dominated it, the practice seems to have been for each professor to seize upon any philosophical position he found unoccupied and which seemed a strong one, to entrench himself in it, and to sally forth from time to time to give battle to the others. Thus, even the scanty records we possess of those disputes enable us to make out a dozen or more opinions held by different teachers at one time concerning the question of nominalism and realism. Read the opening part of the "Historia Calamitatum" of Abelard, who was certainly as philosophical as any of his contemporaries, and see the spirit of combat that it breathes. For him, the truth is simply his particular stronghold. When the method of authority prevailed, the truth meant little more than the Catholic faith. All the efforts of the scholastic doctors are directed toward harmonizing their faith in Aristotle and their faith in the Church, and one may search their ponderous folios through without finding an argument that goes any further. It is noticeable that where different faiths flourish side by side, renegades are looked upon with contempt even by the party whose belief they adopt; so completely has the idea of loyalty replaced that of truth seeking. Since the time of Descartes, the defect in the conception of truth has been less apparent. Still, it will sometimes strike a scientific man that the philosophers have been less intent on finding out what the facts are, than on inquiring what belief is most in harmony with their system. It is hard to convince a follower of the a priori method by adducing facts; but show him that an opinion he is defending is inconsistent with what he has laid down elsewhere, and he will be very apt to retract it. These minds do not seem to believe that disputation is ever to cease; they seem to think that the opinion that is natural for one man is not so for another, and that belief will, consequently, never be settled. In contenting themselves with fixing their own opinions by a method that would lead another man to a different result, they betray their feeble hold of the conception of what truth is.

On the other hand, all the followers of science are fully persuaded that the processes of investigation, if only pushed far enough, will give one certain solution to every question to which they can be applied. One man may investigate the velocity of light by studying the transits of Venus and the aberration of the stars; another by the oppositions of Mars and the eclipses of Jupiter's satellites; a third by the method of Fizeau; a fourth by that of Foucault; a fifth by the motions of the curves of Lissajoux; a sixth, a seventh, an eighth, and a ninth, may follow the different methods of comparing the measures of statical and dynamical electricity. They may at first obtain different results, but, as each perfects his method and his processes, the results will move steadily together toward a destined center. So with all scientific research. Different minds may set out with the most antagonistic views, but the progress of investigation carries them by a force outside of themselves to one and the same conclusion. This activity of thought by which we are carried, not where we wish, but to a foreordained goal, is like the operation of destiny. No modification of the point of view taken, no selection of other facts for study, no natural bent of mind even, can enable a man to escape the predestinate opinion. This great law is embodied in the conception of truth and reality. The opinion that is fated* to be ultimately agreed to by all who investigate, is what we mean by the truth, and the object represented in this opinion is the real. That is the way I would explain reality.

But it may be said that this view is directly opposed to the abstract definition that we have given of reality, inasmuch as it makes the characters of the real to depend on what is ultimately thought about them. But the answer to this is that, on the one hand, reality is independent, not necessarily of thought in general, but only of what you or I or any finite number of men may think about it; and that, on the other hand, though the object of the final opinion depends on what that opinion is, yet what that opinion is does not depend on what you or I or any man thinks. Our perversity and that of others may indefinitely postpone the settlement of opinion; it might even conceivably cause an arbitrary proposition to be universally accepted as long as the human race should last. Yet even that would not change the nature of the belief, which alone could be the result of investigation carried sufficiently far; and if, after the extinction of our race, another should arise with faculties and disposition for investigation, that true opinion must be the one that they would ultimately come to. "Truth crushed to earth shall rise again," and the opinion that would finally result from investigation does not depend on how anybody may actually think. But the reality of that which is real does depend on the real fact that investigation is destined to lead, at last, if continued long enough, to a belief in it.

But I may be asked what I have to say to all the minute facts of history, forgotten never to be recovered, to the lost books of the ancients, to the buried secrets.

> Full many a gem of purest ray serene
>   The dark, unfathomed caves of ocean bear;
> Full many a flower is born to blush unseen,
>   And waste its sweetness on the desert air.

---

*Fate means merely that which is sure to come true, and can [in no way] be avoided. It is a superstition to suppose that a certain sort of events are ever fated, and it is another to suppose that the word fate can never be freed from its superstitious taint We are all fated to die.

Do these things not really exist because they are hopelessly beyond the reach of our knowledge? And then, after the universe is dead (according to the prediction of some scientists), and all life has ceased forever, will not the shock of atoms continue though there will be no mind to know it? To this I reply that, though in no possible state of knowledge can any number be great enough to express the relation between the amount of what rests unknown to the amount of the known, yet it is un-philosophical to suppose that, with regard to any given question (which has any clear meaning), investigation would not bring forth a solution of it, if it were carried far enough. Who would have said, a few years ago, that we could ever know of what substances stars are made whose light may have been longer in reaching us than the human race has existed? Who can be sure of what we shall not know in a few hundred years? Who can guess what would be the result of continuing the pursuit of science for ten thousand years, with the activity of the last hundred? And if it were to go on for a million, or a billion, or any number of years you please, how is it possible to say that there is any question what might not ultimately be solved?

But it may be objected, "Why make so much of these remote consid-erations, especially when it is your principle that only practical distinc-tions have a meaning?" Well, I must confess that it makes very little difference whether we say that a stone on the bottom of the ocean, in complete darkness, is brilliant or not—that is to say, that it *probably* makes no difference, remembering always that that stone *may* be fished up tomorrow. But that there are gems at the bottom of the sea, flowers in the untraveled desert, etc., are propositions which, like that about a diamond being hard when it is not pressed, concern much more the arrangement of our language than they do the meaning of our ideas.

It seems to me, however, that we have, by the application of our rule, reached so clear an apprehension of what we mean by reality, and of the fact that the idea rests on, that we should not, perhaps, be making a pretension so presumptuous as it would be singular, if we were to offer a metaphysical theory of existence for universal acceptance among those who employ the scientific method of fixing belief. However, as metaphy-sics is a subject much more curious than useful, the knowledge of which, like that of a sunken reef, serves chiefly to enable us to keep clear of it, I will not trouble the reader with any more ontology at this moment. I have already been led much further into that path than I should have desired; and I have given the reader such a dose of mathematics, psychology, and all that is most abstruse, that I fear he may already have left me, and that what I am now writing is for the compositor and proofreader exclusively. I trusted to the importance of the subject. There is no royal road to logic, and really valuable ideas can only be had at the price of close attention. But I know that in the matter of ideas the public prefer the cheap and nasty; and in my next paper I am going to return to the easily intelligible, and not wander from it again. The reader who has been at the pains of wading through this month's paper shall be rewarded in the next one by seeing how beautifully what has been developed in this tedious way can be applied to the ascertainment of the rules of scientific reasoning.

We have, hitherto, not crossed the threshold of scientific logic. It is certainly important to know how to make our ideas clear, but they may be ever so clear without being true. How to make them so, we have next to study. How to give birth to those vital and procreative ideas that multiply into a thousand forms and diffuse themselves everywhere, advancing civilization and making the dignity of man, is an art not yet reduced to rules, but of the secret of which the history of science affords some hints.

V. A Guess at the Riddle

In *The Monist* series of 1891–93,[1] Peirce developed the basic concepts of his metaphysics. In the first essay, "The Architecture of Theories," he advises us that a system of metaphysics should be developed by utilizing the basic ideas of its time. He reviews the thought of his day and finds among its basic ideas the notion of law in dynamics and of evolution in cosmogony. In psychology he finds his basic categorial triad of first feelings, second sensations, and third concepts. He discusses the law of habit as a tendency to generalization; explores the mind-body problem and comes down on the side of an objective idealism. In mathematics he examines the notions of generalization and continuity. In logic he rediscovers his three categories.

Taking these ideas as the ones from which a metaphysics appropriate to the times would have to be constructed, he suggests, at the conclusion of the essay, what some of the characteristics of such a metaphysics would be. The base of his metaphysics is a doctrine of tychism, of absolute chance in the world. This chance is exemplified in the law of mind, which is not absolute as physical laws are. By virtue of the existence of chance, or uncertainty, an element of life is allowed in what would otherwise be a dead universe simply running down under the principles of mechanics.

To justify this metaphysics it is necessary to refute the dominant scientific metaphysics of his day—the metaphysics of a mechanistic universe. The second paper, "The Doctrine of Necessity Examined," reviews the arguments for a mechanistic view of the universe and undertakes to refute them.

The third paper examines the law of mind, which is defined as the

---

[1]Reprinted in *Collected Papers* 6.7 ff., 6.35 ff., 6.102 ff., 6.238 ff., 6.287 ff. See 5.436 for an intended sixth article that never appeared.

law that ideas tend to spread continously, to affect other ideas, and to become generalized. This doctrine of a tendency toward continuity and generalization is given the name synechism. The synechistic view is developed to show that since ideas can only be affected by ideas, matter must be a form of mind—"mind hide-bound with habits." This gives us an objective idealism that is combined with tychism and synechism (the tendency toward spreading and generalization) to make for a "thoroughgoing evolutionism."

The fourth paper on "Man's Glassy Essence" begins with a rather heavy dose of molecular physics that serves as an introduction to a discussion of the characteristics of protoplasm. We are then taken through a more detailed analysis of the relation between mind and matter, the development of feeling (consciousness) and of personality.

In the final paper in this series we examine the notion of love as the dynamic through which evolution occurs. Peirce sees love as an all-encompassing force. He here borrows an idea from Henry James (the elder) that true love loves not only what is like it (which is simply self-love), but loves also what is most unlike it (other love), so that love becomes a force that includes everything: "Love, recognizing germs of loveliness in the hateful, gradually warms it into life, and makes it lovely" —a doctrine not unlike what is known nowadays as "flower power." This force is called by Peirce agapasm, and is considered by him to be the creative force that moves the evolutionary process. He sets this doctrine as the antithesis of Darwinism's notion of the survival of the fittest, which he sees as extolling cruelty as the force that moves evolution.

1. The Architecture of Theories

Of the fifty or hundred systems of philosophy that have been advanced at different times of the world's history, perhaps the larger number have been not so much results of historical evolution as happy thoughts that have accidently occurred to their authors. An idea that has been found interesting and fruitful has been adopted, developed, and forced to yield explanations of all sorts of phenomena. The English have been particularly given to this way of philosophising; witness, Hobbes,

Hartley, Berkeley, James, Mill. Nor has it been by any means useless labor; it shows us what the true nature and value of the ideas developed are, and in that way affords serviceable materials for philosophy. Just as if a man, being seized with the conviction that paper was a good material to make things of, were to go to work to build a *papier mâché* house, with roof of roofing-paper, foundations of pasteboard, windows of paraffined paper, chimneys, bath tubs, locks, etc., all of different forms of paper, his experiment would probably afford valuable lessons to builders, while it would certainly make a detestable house, so those one-idea'd philosophies are exceedingly interesting and instructive, and yet are quite unsound.

The remaining systems of philosophy have been of the nature of reforms, sometimes amounting to radical revolutions, suggested by certain difficulties that have been found to beset systems previously in vogue; and such ought certainly to be in large part the motive of any new theory. This is like partially rebuilding a house. The faults that have been committed are, first, that the dilapidations have generally not been sufficiently thoroughgoing, and second, that not sufficient pain has been taken to bring the additions into deep harmony with the really sound parts of the old structure.

When a man is about to build a house, what a power of thinking he has to do before he can safely break ground! With what pains he has to excogitate the precise wants that are to be supplied! What a study to ascertain the most available and suitable materials, to determine the mode of construction to which those materials are best adapted, and to answer a hundred such questions! Now without riding the metaphor too far, I think we may safely say that the studies preliminary to the construction of a great theory should be at least as deliberate and thorough as those that are preliminary to the building of a dwelling-house.

That systems ought to be constructed architectonically has been preached since Kant, but I do not think the full import of the maxim has by any means been apprehended. What I would recommend is that every person who wishes to form an opinion concerning fundamental problems, should first of all make a complete survey of human knowledge, should take note of all the valuable ideas in each branch of science, should observe in just what respect each has been successful and where it has failed, in order that in the light of the thorough acquaintance so attained of the available materials for a philosophical theory and of the nature and strength of each, he may proceed to the study of what the problem of philosophy consists in, and of the proper way of solving it. I must not be understood as endeavoring to state fully all that these preparatory studies should embrace; on the contrary, I purposely slur over many points, in order to give emphasis to one special recommendation, namely, to make a systematic study of the conceptions out of which a philosophical theory may be built, in order to ascertain what place each conception may fitly occupy in such a theory, and to what uses it is adapted.

The adequate treatment of this single point would fill a volume, but I shall endeavor to illustrate my meaning by glancing at several sciences and indicating conceptions in them serviceable for philosophy. As to the results to which long studies thus commenced have led me, I shall just give a hint at their nature.

We may begin with dynamics—field in our day of perhaps the grandest conquest human science has ever made—I mean the law of the conservation of energy. But let us revert to the first step taken by modern scientific thought—and a great stride it was—the inauguration of dynamics by Galileo. A modern physicist on examining Galileo's works is surprised to find how little experiment had to do with the establishment of the foundations of mechanics. His principal appeal is to common sense and *il lume naturale*. He always assumes that the true theory will be found to be a simple and natural one. And we can see why it should indeed be so in dynamics. For instance, a body left to its own inertia moves in a straight line, and a straight line appears to us the simplest of curves. In *itself*, no curve is simpler than another. A system of straight lines has intersections precisely corresponding to those of a system of like parabolas similarly placed, or to those of any one of an infinity of systems of curves. But the straight line appears to us simple, because, as Euclid says, it lies evenly between its extremities; that is, because viewed endwise it appears as a point. That is, again, because light moves in straight lines. Now, light moves in straight lines because of the part that the straight line plays in the laws of dynamics. Thus it is that our minds having been formed under the influence of phenomena governed by the laws of mechanics, certain conceptions entering into those laws become implanted in our minds, so that we readily guess at what the laws are. Without such a natural prompting, having to search blindfold for a law that would suit the phenomena, our chance of finding it would be as one to infinity. The further physical studies depart from phenomena that have directly influenced the growth of the mind, the less we can expect to find the laws that govern them "simple" that is, composed of a few conceptions natural to our minds.

The researches of Galileo, followed up by Christiaan Huygens and others, led to those modern conceptions of Force and Law, which have revolutionized the intellectual world. The great attention given to mechanics in the seventeenth century soon so emphasised these conceptions as to give rise to the Mechanical Philosophy, or doctrine that all the phenomena of the physical universe are to be explained upon mechanical principles. Newton's great discovery imparted a new impetus to this tendency. The old notion that heat consists in an agitation of corpuscles was now applied to the explanation of the chief properties of gases. The first suggestion in this direction was that the pressure of gases is explained by the battering of the particles against the walls of the containing vessel, which explained Boyle's law of the compressibility of air. Later, the expansion of gases, Avogadro's chemical law, the diffusion and viscosity of gases, and the action of Sir William Crookes's radiometer were shown to be consequences of the same kinetical theory; but other phenomena, such as the ratio of the specific heat at constant volume to that at constant pressure require additional hypotheses, which we have little reason to suppose are simple, so that we find ourselves quite afloat. In like manner with regard to light, that it consists of vibrations was almost proved by the phenomena of diffraction, while those of polarization showed the excursions of the particles to be perpendicular to the line of propagation; but the phenomena of dispersion, etc., require additional hypotheses that may be very complicated. Thus, the further progress of molecular speculation appears quite uncertain. If hypotheses are to be tried haphazardly or simply because they will suit certain phenomena, it will occupy the mathematical physicists of the world say half a century on the average to bring each theory to the test, and since the number of possible theories may go up into the trillions, only one of which can be true, we have little prospect of making further solid additions to the subject in our time. When we come to atoms, the presumption in favor of a simple law seems very slender. There is room for serious doubt whether the fundamental laws of mechanics hold good for single atoms, and it seems quite likely that they are capable of motion in more than three dimensions.

To find out much more about molecules and atoms, we must search out a natural history of laws of nature, which may fulfill that function that the presumption in favor of simple laws fulfilled in the early days of dynamics, by showing us what kind of laws we have to expect and by answering such questions as this: Can we with reasonable prospect of not wasting time, try the supposition that atoms attract one another inversely as the seventh power of their distances, or can we not? To suppose universal laws of nature capable of being apprehended by the mind and yet having no reason for their special forms, but standing inexplicable and irrational, is hardly a justifiable position. Uniformities are precisely the sort of facts that need to be accounted for. That a pitched coin should sometimes turn up heads and sometimes tails calls for no particular explanation; but if it shows heads every time, we wish to know how this result has been brought about. Law is *par excellence* the thing that wants a reason.

Now the only possible way of accounting for the laws of nature and for uniformity in general is to suppose them results of evolution. This supposes them not to be absolute, not to be obeyed precisely. It makes an element of indeterminacy, spontaneity, or absolute chance in nature. Just as, when we attempt to verify any physical law, we find our observations cannot be precisely satisfied by it, and rightly attribute the discrepancy to errors of observation, so we must suppose far more minute discrepancies to exist owing to the imperfect cogency of the law itself, to a certain swerving of the facts from any definite formula.

Herbert Spencer wishes to explain evolution upon mechanical principles. This is illogical, for four reasons. First, because the principle of evolution requires no extraneous cause; since the tendency to growth can be supposed itself to have grown from an infinitesimal germ accidentally started. Second, because law ought more than anything else to be supposed a result of evolution. Third, because exact law obviously never can produce heterogeneity out of homogeneity; and arbitrary heterogeneity is the feature of the universe the most manifest and characteristic. Fourth, because the law of the conservation of energy is equivalent to the proposition that all operations governed by mechanical laws are reversible; so that an immediate corollary from it is that growth is not explicable by those laws, even if they be not violated in the process of growth. In short, Spencer is not a philosophical evolutionist, but only a half-evolutionist—or, if you will, only a semi-Spencerian. Now philosophy requires thoroughgoing evolutionism or none.

The theory of Darwin was that evolution had been brought about by the action of two factors: first, heredity, as a principle making offspring nearly resemble their parents, while yet giving room for "sporting," or accidental variations—for very slight variations often, for wider ones rarely; and, second, the destruction of breeds or races that are unable to keep the birth rate up to the death rate. This Darwinian principle is plainly capable of great generalization. Wherever there are large numbers of objects, having a tendency to retain certain characters unaltered, this tendency, however, not being absolute but giving room for chance variations, then, if the amount of variation is absolutely limited in certain directions by the destruction of everything that reaches those limits, there will be a gradual tendency to change in directions of departure from them. Thus, if a million players sit down to bet at an even game, since one after another will get ruined, the average wealth of those who remain will perpetually increase. Here is indubitably a genuine formula of possible evolution, whether its operation accounts for much or little in the development of animal and vegetable species.

The Lamarckian theory also supposes that the development of species has taken place by a long series of insensible changes, but it supposes that those changes have taken place during the lives of the individuals, in consequence of effort and exercise, and that reproduction plays no part in the process except in preserving these modifications. Thus, the Lamarckian theory only explains the development of characters for which individuals strive, while the Darwinian theory only explains the production of characters really beneficial to the race, though these may be fatal to individuals.* But more broadly and philosophically conceived, Darwinian evolution is evolution by the operation of chance, and the destruction of bad results, while Lamarckian evolution is evolution by the effect of habit and effort.

A third theory of evolution is that of Clarence King. The testimony of monuments and of rocks is that species are unmodified or scarcely modified, under ordinary circumstances, but are rapidly altered after cataclysms or rapid geological changes. Under novel circumstances, we often see animals and plants sporting excessively in reproduction, and sometimes even undergoing transformations during individual life, phenomena no doubt due partly to the enfeeblement of vitality from the breaking up of habitual modes of life, partly to changed food, partly to direct specific influence of the element in which the organism is immersed. If evolution has been brought about in this way, not only have its single steps not been insensible, as both Darwinians and Lamarckians suppose, but they are furthermore neither haphazard on the one hand, nor yet determined by an inward striving on the other, but on the contrary are effects of the changed environment, and have a positive general tendency to adapt the organism to that environment, since variation will particularly affect organs at once enfeebled and stimulated. This mode of evolution, by external forces and the breaking up of habits, seems to be called for by some of the broadest and most important facts of biology and paleontology; while it certainly has been the chief factor in the historical evolution of institutions as in that of ideas; and cannot possibly be refused a very prominent place in the process of evolution of the universe in general.

Passing to psychology, we find the elementary phenomena of mind fall into three categories. First, we have feelings, comprising all that is immediately present, such as pain, blue, cheerfulness, the feeling that

*The neo-Darwinian, August Weismann, has shown that mortality would almost necessarily result from the action of the Darwinian principle.

arises when we contemplate a consistent theory, etc. A feeling is a state of mind having its own living quality, independent of any other state of mind. Or, a feeling is an element of consciousness that might conceivably override every other state until it monopolized the mind, although such a rudimentary state cannot actually be realized, and would not properly be consciousness. Still, it is conceivable, or supposable, that the quality of blue should usurp the whole mind, to the exclusion of the ideas of shape, extension, contrast, commencement, and cessation, and all other ideas, whatsoever. A feeling is necessarily perfectly simple, *in itself,* for if it had parts these would also be in the mind., whenever the whole was present, and thus the whole could not monopolize the mind.*

Besides feelings, we have sensations of reaction; as when a person blindfolded suddenly runs against a post, when we make a muscular effort, or when any feeling gives way to a new feeling. Suppose I had nothing in my mind but a feeling of blue, which were suddenly to give place to a feeling of red; then, at the instant of transition there would be a shock, a sense of reaction, my blue life being transmuted into red life. If I were further endowed with a memory, that sense would continue for some time, and there would also be a peculiar feeling or sentiment connected with it. This last feeling might endure (conceivably, I mean) after the memory of the occurrence and the feelings of blue and red had passed away. But the *sensation* of reaction cannot exist except in the actual presence of the two feelings blue and red to which it relates. Wherever we have two feelings and pay attention to a relation between them of whatever kind, there is the sensation of which I am speaking. But the sense of action and reaction has two types: it may either be a perception of relation between feeling and something out of feeling. And this sense of external reaction again has two forms; for it is either a sense of something happening to us, by no act of ours, we being passive in the matter, or it is a sense of resistance, that is, of our expending feeling upon something without. The sense of reaction is thus a sense of connection or comparison between feelings, either, *a*, between one feeling and another, or *b*, between feeling and its absence or lower

---

*A feeling may certainly be compound, but only in virtue of a perception that is not that feeling nor any feeling at all.

degree; and under *b* we have, first, the sense of the access of feeling, and second, the sense of remission of feeling.

Very different both from feelings and from reaction-sensations or disturbances of feeling are general conceptions. When we think, we are conscious that a connection between feelings is determined by a general rule, we are aware of being governed by a habit. Intellectual power is nothing but facility in taking habits and in following them in cases essentially analogous to, but in nonessentials widely remote from, the normal cases of connections of feelings under which those habits were formed.

The one primary and fundamental law of mental action consists in a tendency to generalization. Feeling tends to spread, connections between feelings awaken feelings; neighboring feelings become assimilated; ideas are apt to reproduce themselves. These are so many formulations of the one law of the growth of mind. When a disturbance of feeling takes place, we have a consciousness of gain, the gain of experience; and a new disturbance will be apt to assimilate itself to the one that preceded it. Feelings, by being excited, become more easily excited, especially in the ways in which they have previously been excited. The consciousness of such a habit constitutes a general conception.

The cloudiness of psychological notions may be corrected by connecting them with physiological conceptions. Feeling may be supposed to exist, wherever a nerve cell is in an excited condition. The disturbance of feeling, or sense of reaction, accompanies the transmission of disturbance between nerve cells or from a nerve cell to a muscle cell or the external stimulation of a nerve cell. General conceptions arise upon the formation of habits in the nerve matter, which are molecular changes consequent upon its activity and probably connected with its nutrition.

The law of habit exhibits a striking constrast to all physical laws in the character of its commands. A physical law is absolute. What it requires is an exact relation. Thus, a physical force introduces into a motion a component motion to be combined with the rest by the parallelogram of forces; but the component motion must actually take place exactly as required by the law of force. On the other hand, no exact conformity is required by the mental law. Nay, exact conformity would be in downright conflict with the law; since it would instantly crystallize thought and prevent all further formation of habit. The law of mind only makes a given feeling *more likely* to arise. It thus resembles the "non-conservative" forces of physics, such as viscosity and the like, which are due to statistical uniformities in the chance encounters of trillions of molecules.

The old dualistic notion of mind and matter, so prominent in Cartesianism, as two radically different kinds of substance, will hardly find defenders today. Rejecting this, we are driven to some form of hylopathy, otherwise called monism. Then the question arises whether physical laws on the one hand, and the psychical law on the other are to be taken—

(A) as independent, a doctrine often called *monism*, but which I would name *neutralism*; or,

(B) the psychical law as derived and special, the physical law alone as primordial, which is *materialism*; or,

(C) the physical law as derived and special, the psychical law alone as primordial, which is *idealism*.

The materialistic doctrine seems to me quite as repugnant to scientific logic as to common sense; since it requires us to suppose that a certain kind of mechanism will feel, which would be a hypothesis absolutely irreducible to reason—an ultimate, inexplicable regularity; while the only possible justification of any theory is that it should make things clear and reasonable.

Neutralism is sufficiently condemned by the logical maxim known as Ockham's razor, i.e., that not more independent elements are to be supposed than necessary. By placing the inward and outward aspects of substance on a par, it seems to render both primordial.

The one intelligible theory of the universe is that of objective idealism, that matter is effete mind, inveterate habits becoming physical laws. But before this can be accepted it must show itself capable of explaining the tridimensionality of space, the laws of motion, and the general characteristics of the universe, with mathematical clearness and precision; for no less should be demanded of every philosophy.

Modern mathematics is replete with ideas that may be applied to philosophy. I can only notice one or two. The manner in which mathematicians generalize is very instructive. Thus, painters are accustomed to think of a picture as consisting geometrically of the intersections of its plane by rays of light from the natural objects to the eye. But geometers use a generalized perspective. For instance, in the figure let O be the eye, let A B C D E be the edgewise view of any plane, and let a f e D c be the edgewise view of another plane. The geometers draw rays through O cutting both these planes, and treat the points of intersection of each ray with one plane as representing the point of intersection of the same ray with the other plane. Thus, e represents E, in the painter's way. D represents itself. C is represented by c, which is further from the eye; and A is represented by a which is on the other side of the eye. Such generalization is not bound down to sensuous images. Further, according to this mode of representation every point on one plane represents a point on the other, and every point on the latter is represented by a point on the former. But how about the point f that is in a direction from O parallel to the represented plane, and how about the point B that is in a direction parallel to the representing plane? Some will say that these are exceptions; but modern mathematics does not allow exceptions that can be annulled by generalization. As a point moves from C to D and thence to E and off toward infinity, the corresponding point on the other plane moves from c to D and thence to e and toward f. But this second point can pass through f to a; and when it is there the first point has arrived at A. We therefore say that the first point has passed *through infinity*, and that every line joins in to itself somewhat like an oval. Geometers talk of the parts of lines at an infinite distance as points. This is a kind of generalization very efficient in mathematics.

Modern views of measurement have a philosophical aspect. There is an indefinite number of systems of measuring along a line; thus, a perspective representation of a scale on one line may be taken to measure another, although of course such measurements will not agree with what we call the distances of points on the latter line. To establish a system of measurement on a line we must assign a distinct number to each point of it, and for this purpose we shall plainly have to suppose

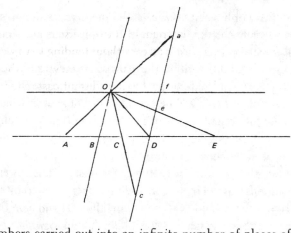

the numbers carried out into an infinite number of places of decimals. These numbers must be ranged along the line in unbroken sequence. Further, in order that such a scale of numbers should be of any use, it must be capable of being shifted into new positions, each number continuing to be attached to a single distinct point. Now it is found that if this is true for "imaginary" as well as for real points (an expression that I cannot stop to elucidate), any such shifting will necessarily leave two numbers attached to the same points as before. So that when the scale is moved over the line by any continuous series of shiftings of one kind, there are two points which no numbers on the scale can ever reach, except the numbers fixed there. This pair of points, thus unattainable in measurement, is called the absolute. These two points may be distinct and real, or they may coincide, or they may be both imaginary. As an example of a linear quantity with a double absolute we may take probability, which ranges from an unattainable absolute certainty *against* a proposition to an equally unattainable absolute certainty *for* it. A line, according to ordinary notions, we have seen is a linear quantity, where the two points at infinity coincide. A velocity is another example. A train going with infinite velocity from Chicago to New York would be at all the points on the line at the very same instant, and if the time of transit were reduced to less than nothing it would be moving in the other direction. An angle is a familiar example of a mode of magnitude with no real immeasurable values. One of the questions philosophy has to consider is whether the development of the universe is like the increase of an angle, so that it proceeds forever without tending toward anything unattained, which I take to be the Epicurean view, or whether the universe sprang from a chaos in the infinitely distant past to tend toward something different in the infinitely distant future, or whether the universe sprang from nothing in the past to go on indefinitely toward a point in the infinitely distant future, which, were it attained, would be the mere nothing from which is set out.

The doctrine of the absolute applied to space comes to this, that either—

First, space is, as Euclid teaches, both *unlimited* and *immeasurable*, so that the infinitely distant parts of any plane seen in perspective appear as a straight line, in which case the sum of the three angles of a triangle amounts to 180°; or,

Second, space is *immeasurable* but *limited*, so that the infinitely distant parts of any plane seen in perspective appear as a circle, beyond which all is blackness, and in this case the sum of the three angles of a triangle is less than 180° by any amount proportional to the area of the triangle; or,

Third, space is *unlimited* but *finite* (like the surface of a sphere), so that it has no infinitely distant parts; but a finite journey along any straight line would bring one back to his original position, and looking off with an unobstructed view one would see the back of his own head enormously magnified, in which case the sum of the three angles of a triangle exceeds 180° by an amount proportional to the area.

Which of these three hypotheses is true we know not. The largest triangles we can measure are such as have the earth's orbit for base, and the distance of a fixed star for altitude. The angular magnitude resulting from subtracting the sum of the two angles at the base of such a triangle from 180° is called the star's *parallax*. The parallaxes of only about forty stars have been measured as yet. Two of them come out negative, that of Arided (α Cycni), a star of magnitude 1½, which is − 0."082, according to C. A. F. Peters, and that of a star of magnitude 7¾, known as Piazzi III 422, which is −0."045 according to R. S. Ball. But these negative parallaxes are undoubtedly to be attributed to errors of observation; for the probable error of such a determination is about $\pm 0.''075$, and it would be strange indeed if we were to be able to see, as it were, more than half way around space, without being able to see stars with larger negative parallaxes. Indeed, the very fact that of all the parallaxes measured only two come out negative would be a strong argument that the smallest parallaxes really amount to $+0.''1$, were it not for the reflection that the publication of other negative parallaxes may have been suppressed. I think we may feel confident that the parallax of the furthest star lies somewhere between $-0.''05$ and $+0.''15$, and within another century our grandchildren will surely know whether the three angles of a triangle are greater or less than 180°—that they are *exactly* that amount is what nobody ever can be justified in concluding. It is true that according to the axioms of geometry the sum of the three sides of a triangle are precisely 180°; but these axioms are now exploded, and geometers confess that they, as geometers, know not the slightest reason for supposing them to be precisely true. They are expressions of our inborn conception of space, and as such are entitled to credit, so far as their truth could have influenced the formation of the mind. But that affords not the slightest reason for supposing them exact.

Now, metaphysics has always been the ape of mathematics. Geometry suggested the idea of a demonstrative system of absolutely certain philosophical principles; and the ideas of the metaphysicians have at all times been in large part drawn from mathematics. The metaphysical axioms are imitations of the geometrical axioms; and now that the latter have been thrown overboard, without doubt the former will be sent after them. It is evident, for instance, that we can have no reason to think that every phenomenon in all its minutest details is precisely determined by law. That there is an arbitrary element in the universe we see— namely, its variety. This variety must be attributed to spontaneity in some form.

Had I more space, I now ought to show how important for philosophy is the mathematical conception of continuity. Most of what is true in Hegel is a darkling glimmer of a conception that the mathematicians

had long before made pretty clear, and that recent researches have still
further illustrated.

Among the many principles of logic that find their application in
philosophy, I can here only mention one. Three conceptions are perpetually turning up at every point in every theory of logic, and in the
most rounded systems they occur in connection with one another. They
are conceptions so very broad and consequently indefinite that they are
hard to seize and may be easily overlooked. I call them the conceptions
of First, Second, Third. First is the conception of being or existing
independent of anything else. Second is the conception of being relative
to, the conception of reaction with, something else. Third is the conception of mediation, whereby a first and second are brought into relation.
To illustrate these ideas, I will show how they enter into those we have
been considering. The origin of things, considered not as leading to
anything, but in itself, contains the idea of First, the end of things that
of Second, the process mediating between them that of Third. A philosophy that emphasizes the idea of the One, is generally a dualistic philosophy in which the conception of Second receives exaggerated attention;
for this One (though of course involving the idea of First) is always the
other of a manifold that is not one. The idea of the Many, because
variety is arbitrariness and arbitrariness is repudiation of any Secondness, has for its principal component the conception of First. In psychology Feeling is First, Sense of reaction Second, General conception
Third, or mediation. In biology, the idea of arbitrary sporting is First,
heredity is Second, the process whereby the accidental characters become fixed is Third. Chance is First, Law is Second, the tendency to
take habits is Third. Mind is First, Matter is Second, Evolution is Third.

Such are the materials out of which chiefly a philosophical theory
ought to be built, in order to represent the state of knowledge to which
the nineteenth century has brought us. Without going into other important questions of philosophical architectonic, we can readily foresee
what sort of a metaphysics would appropriately be constructed from
those conceptions. Like some of the most ancient and some of the most
recent speculations it would be a Cosmogonic Philosophy. It would
suppose that in the beginning—infinitely remote—there was a chaos of

unpersonalized feeling, which being without connection or regularity would properly be without existence. This feeling, sporting here and there in pure arbitrariness, would have started the germ of a generalizing tendency. Its other sportings would be evanescent, but this would have a growing virtue. Thus, the tendency to habit would be started; and from this with the other principles of evolution all the regularities of the universe would be evolved. At any time, however, an element of pure chance survives and will remain until the world becomes an absolutely perfect, rational, and symmetrical system, in which mind is at last crystallized in the infinitely distant future.

That idea has been worked out by me with elaboration. It accounts for the main features of the universe as we know it—the characters of time, space, matter, force, gravitation, electricity, etc. It predicts many more things that new observations can alone bring to the test. May some future student go over this ground again, and have the leisure to give his results to the world.

2. The Doctrine of Necessity Examined

In *The Monist* for January, 1891, I endeavored to show what elementary ideas ought to enter into our view of the universe. I may mention that on these considerations I had already grounded a cosmical theory, and from it had deduced a considerable number of consequences capable of being compared with experience. This comparison is now in progress, but under existing circumstances must occupy many years.

I propose here to examine the common belief that every single fact in the universe is precisely determined by law. It must not be supposed that this is a doctrine accepted everywhere and at all times by all rational men. Its first advocate appears to have been Democritus the atomist, who was led to it, as we are informed, by reflecting upon the "impenetrability, translation, and impact of matter (ἀντιτυπία καὶ φορὰ καὶ πληγὴ τῆς ὕλης)." That is to say, having restricted his attention to a field where no influence other than mechanical constraint could possibly come

before his notice, he straightway jumped to the conclusion that throughout the universe that was the sole principle of action—a style of reasoning so usual in our day with men not unreflecting as to be more than
excusable in the infancy of thought. But Epicurus, in revising the atomic
doctrine and repairing its defenses, found himself obliged to suppose
that atoms swerve from their courses by spontaneous chance; and
thereby he conferred upon the theory life and entelechy. For we now
see clearly that the peculiar function of the molecular hypothesis in
physics is to open an entry for the calculus of probabilities. Already, the
prince of philosophers had repeatedly and emphatically condemned the
dictum of Democritus (especially in the "Physics," Book II, chapters iv,
v, vi), holding that events come to pass in three ways, namely, (1) by
external compulsion, or the action of efficient causes, (2) by virtue of an
inward nature, or the influence of final causes, and (3) irregularly without
definite cause, but just by absolute chance; and this doctrine is of the
inmost essence of Aristotelianism. It affords, at any rate, a valuable
enumeration of the possible ways in which anything can be supposed to
have come about. The freedom of the will, too, was admitted both by
Aristotle and by Epicurus. But the Stoa, which in every department
seized upon the most tangible, hard, and lifeless element, and blindly
denied the existence of every other, which, for example, impugned the
validity of the inductive method and wished to fill its place with the
reductio ad absurdum, very naturally became the one school of ancient
philosophy to stand by a strict necessitarianism, thus returning to the
single principle of Democritus that Epicurus had been unable to swal-
low. Necessitarianism and materialism with the Stoics went hand in
hand, as by affinity they should. At the revival of learning, Stoicism met
with considerable favor, partly because it departed just enough from
Aristotle to give it the spice of novelty, and partly because its superficiali-
ties well adapted it for acceptance by students of literature and art who
wanted their philosophy drawn mild. Afterwards, the great discoveries
in mechanics inspired the hope that mechanical principles might suffice
to explain the universe; and though without logical justification, this
hope has since been continually stimulated by subsequent advances in
physics. Nevertheless, the doctrine was in too evident conflict with the

freedom of the will and with miracles to be generally acceptable, at first. But meantime there arose that most widely spread of philosophical blunders, the notion that associationalism belongs intrinsically to the materialistic family of doctrines; and thus was evolved the theory of motives; and libertarianism became weakened. At present, historical criticism has almost exploded the miracles, great and small; so that the doctrine of necessity has never been in so great vogue as now.

The proposition in question is that the state of things existing at any time, together with certain immutable laws, completely determine the state of things at every other time (for a limitation to *future* time is indefensible). Thus, given the state of the universe in the original nebula, and given the laws of mechanics, a sufficiently powerful mind could deduce from these data the precise form of every curlicue of every letter I am now writing.

Whoever holds that every act of the will as well as every idea of the mind is under the rigid governance of a necessity coordinated with that of the physical world, will logically be carried to the proposition that minds are part of the physical world in such a sense that the laws of mechanics determine everything that happens according to immutable attractions and repulsions. In that case, that instantaneous state of things from which every other state of things is calculable consists in the positions and velocities of all the particles at any instant. This, the usual and most logical form of necessitarianism, is called the mechanical philosophy.

When I have asked thinking men what reason they had to believe that every fact in the universe is precisely determined by law, the first answer has usually been that the proposition is a "presupposition" or postulate of scientific reasoning. Well, if that is the best that can be said for it, the belief is doomed. Suppose it be "postulated": that does not make it true, nor so much as afford the slightest rational motive for yielding it any credence. It is as if a man should come to borrow money, and when asked for his security, should reply he "postulated" the loan. To "postulate" a proposition is no more than to hope it is true. There are, indeed, practical emergencies in which we act upon assumptions of certain propositions as true, because if they are not so, it can make no difference how we act. But all such propositions I take to be hypotheses of individual facts. For it is manifest that no universal principle can in its universality be compromised in a special case or can be requisite for the validity of any ordinary inference. To say, for instance, that the demonstration by Archimedes of the property of the lever would fall to the ground if men were endowed with free will, is extravagant; yet this is implied by those who make a proposition incompatible with the freedom of the will the postulate of all inference. Considering, too, that the conclusions of science make no pretence to being more than probable, and considering that a probable inference can at most only suppose something to be most frequently, or otherwise approximately, true, but never that anything is precisely true without exception throughout the universe, we see how far this proposition in truth is from being so postulated.

But the whole notion of a postulate being involved in reasoning appertains to a bygone and false conception of logic. Nondeductive, or ampliative inference is of three kinds: induction, hypothesis, and analogy. If there be any other modes, they must be extremely unusual and highly complicated, and may be assumed with little doubt to be of the same nature as those enumerated. For induction, hypothesis, and analogy, as far as their ampliative character goes, that is, so far as they conclude something not implied in the premises, depend upon one principle and involve the same procedure. All are essentially inferences from sampling. Suppose a ship arrives in Liverpool laden with wheat in bulk. Suppose that by some machinery the whole cargo be stirred up with great thoroughness. Suppose that twenty-seven thimblefuls be taken equally from the forward, midships, and aft parts, from the starboard, center, and larboard parts, and from the top, half depth, and lower parts of her hold, and that these being mixed and the grains counted, four-fifths of the latter are found to be of quality A. Then we infer, experientially and provisionally, that approximately four-fifths of all the grain in the cargo is of the same quality. I say we infer this *experientially* and *provisionally*. By saying that we infer it *experientially*, I mean that our conclusion makes no pretension to knowledge of wheat-in-itself, our ἀλήθεια, as the derivation of that word implies, has nothing to do with *latent* wheat. We are dealing only with the matter of possible experience—experience in the full acceptation of the term as something not merely affecting the senses but also as the subject of thought. If there be any wheat hidden on the ship, so that it can neither turn up in the sample nor be heard of subsequently from purchasers—or if it be half-hidden, so that it may, indeed, turn up, but is less likely to do so than the rest—or if it can affect our senses and our pockets, but from some strange cause or causelessness cannot be reasoned about—all such wheat is to be excluded (or have only its proportional weight) in calculating that true proportion of quality A, to which our inference seeks to approximate. By saying that we draw the inference *provisionally*, I mean that we do not hold that we have reached any assigned degree of approximation as yet, but only hold that if our experience be indefinitely extended, and if every fact of whatever nature, as fast as it presents itself, be duly applied, according to the inductive method, in correcting the inferred ratio, then our approximation will become indefinitely close in the long run; that is to say, close to the experience *to come* (not merely close by the exhaustion of a finite collection) so that if experience in general is to fluctuate irregularly to and fro, in a manner to deprive the ratio sought of all definite value, we shall be able to find out approximately within what limits it fluctuates, and if, after having one definite value, it changes and assumes another, we shall be able to find that out, and in short, whatever may be the variations of this ratio in experience, experience indefinitely extended will enable us to detect them, so as to predict rightly, at last, what its ultimate value may be, if it have any ultimate value, or what the ultimate law of succession of values may be, if there be any such ultimate law, or that it ultimately fluctuates irregularly within certain limits, if it do so ultimately fluctuate. Now our inference, claiming to be no more than thus experiential and provisional, manifestly involves no postulate whatever.

For what is a postulate? It is the formulation of a material fact that we are not entitled to assume as a premise, but the truth of which is requisite to the validity of an inference. Any fact, then, that might be supposed postulated, must either be such that it would ultimately present itself in experience, or not. If it will present itself, we need not postulate it now in our provisional inference, since we shall ultimately be entitled to use it as a premise. But if it never would present itself in experience, our conclusion is valid but for the possibility of this fact being otherwise than assumed, that is, it is valid as far as possible experience goes, and that is all that we claim. Thus, every postulate is cut off, either by the provisionality or by the experientiality of our inference. For instance, it has been said that induction postulates that, if an indefinite succession of samples be drawn, examined, and thrown back each before the next is drawn, then in the long run every grain will be drawn as often as any other, that is to say postulates that the ratio of the numbers of times in which any two are drawn will indefinitely approximate to unity. But no such postulate is made; for if, on the one hand, we are to have no other experience of the wheat than from such drawings, it is the ratio that presents itself in those drawings and not the ratio that belongs to the wheat in its latent existence that we are endeavoring to determine; while if, on the other hand, there is some other mode by which the wheat is to come under our knowledge, equivalent to another kind of sampling, so that after all our care in stirring up the wheat, some experiential grains will present themselves in the first sampling operation more often than others in the long run, this very singular fact will be sure to get discovered by the inductive method, which must avail itself of every sort of experience; and our inference, which was only provisional, corrects itself at last. Again, it has been said, that induction postulates that under like circumstances like events will happen, and that this postulate is at bottom the same as the principle of universal causation. But this is a blunder, or *bevue*, due to thinking exclusively of inductions where the concluded ratio is either 1 or 0. If any such proposition were postulated, it would be that under like circumstances (the circumstances of drawing the different samples) different events occur in the same proportions in all the different sets— a proposition that is false and even absurd. But in truth no such thing is postulated, the experiential character of the inference reducing the condition of validity to this, that if a certain result does not occur, the opposite result will be manifested, a condition assured by the provisionality of the inference. But it may be asked whether it is not conceivable that every instance of a certain class destined to be ever employed as a datum of induction should have one character, while every instance destined not to be so employed should have the opposite character. The answer is that in that case, the instances excluded from being subjects of reasoning would not be experienced in the full sense of the word, but would be among these *latent* individuals of which our conclusion does not pretend to speak.

To this account of the rationale of induction I know of but one objection worth mentioning: it is that I thus fail to deduce the full degree of force that this mode of inference in fact possesses; that according to my view, no matter how thorough and elaborate the stirring and mixing process had been, the examination of a single handul of grain would not give me any assurance, sufficient to risk money upon, that the next handful would not greatly modify the concluded value of the ratio under inquiry, while, in fact, the assurance would be very high that this ratio was not greatly in error. If the true ratio of grains of quality A were 0·80 and the handful contained a thousand grains, nine such handfuls out of every ten would contain from 780 to 820 grains of quality A. The answer to this is that the calculation given is correct when we know that the units of this handful and the quality inquired into have the normal independence of one another, if for instance the stirring has been complete and the character sampled for has been settled upon in advance of the examination of the sample. But in so far as these conditions are not known to be complied with, the above figures cease to be applicable. Random sampling and predesignation of the character sampled for should always be striven after in inductive reasoning, but when they cannot be attained, so long as it is conducted honestly, the inference retains some value. When we cannot ascertain how the sampling has been done or the sample-character selected, induction still has the essential validity that my present account of it shows it to have.

I do not think a man who combines a willingness to be convinced with a power of appreciating an argument upon a difficult subject can resist the reasons that have been given to show that the principle of universal necessity cannot be defended as being a postulate of reasoning. But then the question immediately arises whether it is not proved to be true, or at least rendered highly probable, by observation of nature.

Still, this question ought not long to arrest a person accustomed to reflect upon the force of scientific reasoning. For the essence of the necessitarian position is that certain continuous quantities have certain exact values. Now, how can observation determine the value of such a quantity with a probable error absolutely *nil?* To one who is behind the scenes, and knows that the most refined comparisons of masses, lengths, and angles, far surpassing in precision all other measurements, yet fall behind the accuracy of bank accounts, and that the ordinary determinations of physical constants, such as appear from month to month in the journals, are about on a par with an upholsterer's measurements of carpets and curtains, the idea of mathematical exactitude being demonstrated in the laboratory will appear simply ridiculous. There is a recognized method of estimating the probable magnitudes of errors in physics —the method of least squares. It is universally admitted that this method makes the errors smaller than they really are; yet even according to that theory an error indefinitely small is indefinitely improbable; so that any statement to the effect that a certain continuous quantity has a certain exact value, if well-founded at all, must be founded on something other than observation.

Still, I am obliged to admit that this rule is subject to a certain qualification. Namely, it only applies to continuous* quantity. Now, certain kinds of continuous quantity are discontinuous at one or at two limits, and for such limits the rule must be modified. Thus, the length of a line cannot be less than zero. Suppose, then, the question arises how long a line a certain person had drawn from a marked point on a piece of paper. If no line at all can be seen, the observed length is zero; and the only conclusion this observation warrants is that the length of the line is less than the smallest length visible with the optical power employed. But indirect observations—for example, that the person supposed to have drawn the line was never within fifty feet of the paper— may make it probable that no line at all was made, so that the concluded length will be strictly zero. In like manner, experience no doubt would

---

Continuous is not exactly the right word, but I let it go to avoid a long and irrelevant discussion.

warrant the conclusion that there is absolutely *no* indigo in a given ear of wheat, and absolutely *no* attar in a given lichen. But such inferences can only be rendered valid by positive experiential evidence, direct or remote, and cannot rest upon a mere inability to detect the quantity in question. We have reason to think there is no indigo in the wheat because we have remarked that wherever indigo is produced it is produced in considerable quantities, to mention only one argument. We have reason to think there is no attar in the lichen, because essential oils seem to be in general peculiar to single species. If the question had been whether there was iron in the wheat or the lichen, though chemical analysis should fail to detect its presence, we should think some of it probably was there, since iron is almost everywhere. Without any such information, one way or the other, we could only abstain from any opinion as to the presence of the substance in question. It cannot, I conceive, be maintained that we are in any *better* position than this in regard to the presence of the element of chance or spontaneous departures from law in nature.

Those observations which are generally adduced in favor of mechanical causation simply prove that there is an element of regularity in nature, and have no bearing whatever upon the question of whether such regularity is exact and universal, or not. Nay, in regard to this *exactitude*, all observation is directly *opposed* to it; and the most that can be said is that a good deal of this observation can be explained away. Try to verify any law of nature, and you will find that the more precise your observations, the more certain they will be to show irregular departures from the law. We are accustomed to ascribe these, and I do not say wrongly, to errors of observation; yet we cannot usually account for such errors in any antecedently probable way. Trace their causes back far enough, and you will be forced to admit they are always due to arbitrary determination, or chance.

But it may be asked whether if there were an element of real chance in the universe it must not occasionally be productive of signal effects such as could not pass unobserved. In answer to this question, without stopping to point out that there is an abundance of great events that one might be tempted to suppose were of that nature, it will be simplest to remark that physicists hold that the particles of gases are moving about irregularly, substantially as if by real chance, and that by the principles of probabilities there must occasionally happen to be concentrations of heat in the gases contrary to the second law of thermodynamics, and these concentrations, occurring in explosive mixtures, must sometimes have tremendous effects. Here, then, is in substance the very situation supposed; yet no phenomena ever have resulted that we are forced to attribute to such chance concentration of heat, or that anybody, wise or foolish, has ever dreamed of accounting for in that manner.

In view of all these considerations, I do not believe that anybody, not in a state of case-hardened ignorance respecting the logic of science, can maintain that the precise and universal conformity of facts to law is clearly proved, or even rendered particularly probable, by any observations hitherto made. In this way, the determined advocate of exact regularity will soon find himself driven to a priori reasons to support his thesis. These received such a socdolager from Stuart Mill in his Examination of Hamilton, that holding to them now seems to me to denote a high degree of imperviousness to reason; so that I shall pass them by with little notice.

To say that we cannot help believing a given proposition is no argument, but it is a conclusive fact if it be true; and with the substitution of "I" for "we," it is true in the mouths of several classes of minds, the blindly passionate, the unreflecting and ignorant, and the person who has overwhelming evidence before his eyes. But that which has been inconceivable today has often turned out indisputable on the morrow. Inability to conceive is only a stage through which every man must pass in regard to a number of beliefs—unless endowed with extraordinary obstinacy and obtuseness. His understanding is enslaved to some blind compulsion that a vigorous mind is pretty sure soon to cast off.

Some seek to back up the a priori postion with empirical arguments. They say that the exact regularity of the world is a natural belief, and that natural beliefs have generally been confirmed by experience. There is some reason in this. Natural beliefs, however, if they generally have a foundation of truth, also require correction and purification from natural illusions. The principles of mechanics are undoubtedly natural beliefs; but, for all that, the early formulations of them were exceedingly erroneous. The general approximation to truth in natural beliefs is, in fact, a case of the general adaptation of genetic products to recognizable utilities or ends. Now, the adaptations of nature, beautiful and often marvelous as they verily are, are never found to be quite perfect; so that the argument is quite *against* the absolute exactitude of any natural belief, including that of the principle of causation.

Another argument, or convenient commonplace, is that absolute chance is *inconceivable.* This word has eight current significations. The Century Dictionary enumerates six. Those who talk like this will hardly be persuaded to say in what sense they mean that chance is inconceivable. Should they do so, it would easily be shown either that they have no sufficient reason for the statement or that the inconceivability is of a kind that does not prove that chance is nonexistent.

Another *a priori* argument is that chance is unintelligible; that is to say, while it may perhaps be conceivable, it does not disclose to the eye of reason the how or why of things; and since a hypothesis can only be justified so far as it renders some phenomenon intelligible, we never can have any right to suppose absolute chance to enter into the production of anything in nature. This argument may be considered in connection with two others. Namely, instead of going so far as to say that the supposition of chance can *never* properly be used to explain any observed fact, it may be alleged merely that no facts are known that such a supposition could in any way help in explaining. Or again, the allegation being still further weakened, it may be said that since departures from law are not unmistakably observed, chance is not a *vera causa*, and ought not unnecessarily to be introduced into a hypothesis.

These are no mean arguments, and require us to examine the matter a little more closely. Come, my superior opponent, let me learn from your wisdom. It seems to me that every throw of sixes with a pair of dice is a manifest instance of chance.

"While you would hold a throw of deuce-ace to be brought about by necessity?" [The opponent's supposed remarks are placed in quotation marks.]

Clearly one throw is as much chance as another.

"Do you think throws of dice are of a different nature from other events?"

I see that I must say that *all* the diversity and specificalness of events is attributable to chance.

"Would you, then, deny that there is any regularity in the world?"

That is clearly undeniable. I must acknowledge there is an approximate regularity, and that every event is influenced by it. But the diversifications, specificalness, and irregularity of things I suppose is chance. A throw of sixes appears to me a case in which this element is particularly obtrusive.

"If you reflect more deeply, you will come to see that *chance* is only a name for a cause that is unknown to us."

Do you mean that we have no idea whatever what kind of causes could bring about a throw of sixes?

"On the contrary, each die moves under the influence of precise mechanical laws."

But it appears to me that it is not these *laws* that made the dice turn up sixes; for these laws act just the same when other throws come up. The chance lies in the diversity of throws; and this diversity cannot be due to laws that are immutable.

"The diversity is due to the diverse circumstances under which the laws act. The dice lie differently in the box, and the motion given to the box is different. These are the unknown causes that produce the throws, and to which we give the name of chance; not the mechanical law that regulates the operation of these causes. You see you are already beginning to think more clearly about this subject."

Does the operation of mechanical law not increase the diversity?

"Properly not. You must know that the instantaneous state of a system of particles is defined by six times as many numbers as there are particles, three for the coordinates of each particle's position, and three more for the components of its velocity. This number of numbers, which expresses the amount of diversity in the system, remains the same at all times. There may be, to be sure, some kind of relation between the coordinates and component velocities of the different particles, by means of which the state of the system might be expressed by a smaller number of numbers. But, if this is the case, a precisely corresponding relationship must exist between the coordinates and component velocities at any other time, though it may doubtless be a relation less obvious to us. Thus, the intrinsic complexity of the system is the same at all times."

Very well, my obliging opponent, we have now reached an issue. You think all the arbitrary specifications of the universe were introduced in one dose, in the beginning, if there was a beginning, and that the variety and complication of nature has always been just as much as it is now. But I, for my part, think that the diversification, the specification, has been continually taking place. Should you condescend to ask me why I so think, I should give my reasons as follows:

1) Question any science that deals with the course of time. Consider the life of an individual animal or plant, or of a mind. Glance at the history of states, of institutions, of language, of ideas. Examine the successions of forms shown by paleontology, the history of the globe as set forth in geology, of what the astronomer is able to make out concerning the changes of stellar systems. Everywhere the main fact is growth and increasing complexity. Death and corruption are mere accidents or secondary phenomena. Among some of the lower organisms, it is a moot point with biologists whether there be anything that ought to be called death. Races, at any rate, do not die out except under unfavorable circumstances. From these broad and ubiquitous facts we may fairly infer, by the most unexceptionable logic, that there is probably in nature some agency by which the complexity and diversity of things can be increased; and that consequently the rule of mechanical necessity meets in some way with interference.

2) By thus admitting pure spontaneity or life as a character of the universe, acting always and everywhere though restrained within narrow bounds by law, producing infinitesimal departures from law continually, and great ones with infinite infrequency, I account for all the variety and diversity of the universe, in the only sense in which the really *sui generis* and new can be said to be accounted for. The ordinary view has to admit the inexhaustible multitudinous variety of the world, has to admit that its mechanical law cannot account for this in the least, that variety can

spring only from spontaneity, and yet denies without any evidence or reason the existence of this spontaneity, or else shoves it back to the beginning of time and supposes it dead ever since. The superior logic of my view appears to me not easily controverted.

3) When I ask the necessitarian how he would explain the diversity and irregularity of the universe, he replies to me out of the treasury of his wisdom that irregularity is something that from the nature of things we must not seek to explain. Abashed at this, I seek to cover my confusion by asking how he would explain the uniformity and regularity of the universe, whereupon he tells me that the laws of nature are immutable and ultimate facts, and no account is to be given of them. But my hypothesis of spontaneity does explain irregularity, in a certain sense; that is, it explains the general fact of irregularity, though not, of course, what each lawless event is to be. At the same time, by thus loosening the bond of necessity, it gives room for the influence of another kind of causation, such as seems to be operative in the mind in the formation of associations, and enables us to understand how the uniformity of nature could have been brought about. That single events should be hard and unintelligible, logic will permit without difficulty: we do not expect to make the shock of a personally experienced earthquake appear natural and reasonable by any amount of cogitation. But logic does expect things *general* to be understandable. To say that there is a universal law, and that it is a hard, ultimate, unintelligible fact, the why and wherefore of which can never be inquired into, at this a sound logic will revolt; and will pass over at once to a method of philosophizing that does not thus barricade the road of discovery.

4) Necessitarianism cannot logically stop short of making the whole action of the mind a part of the physical universe. Our notion that we decide what we are going to do, if as the necessitarian says, it has been calculable since the earliest times, is reduced to illusion. Indeed, consciousness in general thus becomes a mere illusory aspect of a material system. What we call red, green, and violet are in reality only different rates of vibration. The sole reality is the distribution of qualities of matter in space and time. Brain-matter is protoplasm in a certain degree and kind of complication—a certain arrangement of mechanical parti-

cles. Its feeling is but an inward aspect, a phantom. For, from the positions and velocities of the particles at any one instant, and the knowledge of the immutable forces, the positions at all other times are calculable; so that the universe of space, time, and matter is a rounded system uninterfered with from elsewhere. But from the state of feeling at any instant there is no reason to suppose the states of feeling at all other instants are thus exactly calculable; so that feeling is, as I said, a mere fragmentary and illusive aspect of the universe. This is the way, then, that necessitarianism has to make up its accounts. It enters consciousness under the head of sundries, as a forgotten trifle; its scheme of the universe would be more satisfactory if this little fact could be dropped out of sight. On the other hand, by supposing the rigid exactitude of causation to yield, I care not how little—be it but by a strictly infinitesimal amount—we gain room to insert mind into our scheme, and to put it into the place where it is needed, into the position which, as the sole self-intelligible thing, it is entitled to occupy, that of the fountain of existence; and in so doing we resolve the problem of the connection of soul and body.

5) But I must leave undeveloped the chief of my reasons, and can only adumbrate it. The hypothesis of chance-spontaneity is one whose inevitable consequences are capable of being traced out with mathematical precision into considerable detail. Much of this I have done and find the consequences to agree with observed facts to an extent that seems to me remarkable. But the matter and methods of reasoning are novel, and I have no right to promise that other mathematicians shall find my deductions as satisfactory as I myself do, so that the strongest reason for my belief must for the present remain a private reason of my own, and cannot influence others. I mention it to explain my own position; and partly to indicate to future mathematical speculators a veritable goldmine, should time and circumstances and the abridger of all joys prevent my opening it to the world.

If now I, in my turn, inquire of the necessitarian why he prefers to suppose that all specification goes back to the beginning of things, he will answer me with one of those last three arguments that I left unanswered.

First, he may say that chance is a thing absolutely unintelligible, and therefore that we never can be entitled to make such a supposition. But does not this objection smack of naive impudence? It is not mine, it is his own conception of the universe that leads abruptly up to hard, ultimate, inexplicable, immutable law, on the one hand, and to inexplicable specification and diversification of circumstances on the other. My view, on the contrary, hypothesizes nothing at all, unless it be hypothesis to say that all specification came about in some sense, and is not to be accepted as unaccountable. To undertake to account for anything by saying boldly that it is due to chance would, indeed, be futile. But this I do not do. I make use of chance chiefly to make room for a principle of generalization, or tendency to form habits, which I hold has produced all regularities. The mechanical philosopher leaves the whole specification of the world utterly unaccounted for, which is pretty nearly as bad as to boldly attribute it to chance. I attribute it altogether to chance, it is true, but to chance in the form of a spontaneity that is to some degree regular. It seems to me clear at any rate that one of these two positions must be taken, or else specification must be supposed due to a spontaneity that develops itself in a certain and not in a chance way, by an objective logic like that of Hegel. This last way I leave as an open possibility for the present; for it is as much opposed to the necessitarian scheme of existence as my own theory is.

Secondly, the necessitarian may say there are, at any rate, no observed phenomena that the hypothesis of chance could aid in explaining. In reply, I point first to the phenomenon of growth and developing complexity, which appears to be universal, and which though it may possibly be an affair of mechanism perhaps, certainly presents all the appearance of increasing diversification. Then, there is variety itself, beyond comparison the most obtrusive character of the universe: no mechanism can account for this. Then, there is the very fact the necessitarian most insists upon, the regularity of the universe that for him serves only to block the road of inquiry. Then, there are the regular relationships between the laws of nature—similarities and comparative characters, that appeal to our intelligence as its cousins, and call upon us for a reason. Finally, there is consciousness, feeling, a patent fact enough, but a very inconvenient one to the mechanical philosopher.

Thirdly, the necessitarian may say that chance is not a *vera causa*, that we cannot know positively there is any such element in the universe. But the doctrine of the *vera causa* has nothing to do with elementary conceptions. Pushed to that extreme, it at once cuts off belief in the existence of a material universe; and without that necessitarianism could hardly maintain its ground. Besides, variety is a fact that must be admitted; and the theory of chance merely consists in supposing this diversification does not antedate all time. Moreover, the avoidance of hypotheses involving causes nowhere positively known to act—is only a recommendation of logic, not a positive command. It cannot be formulated in any precise terms without at once betraying its untenable character—I mean as rigid rule, for as a recommendation it is wholesome enough.

I believe I have thus subjected to fair examination all the important reasons for adhering to the theory of universal necessity, and have shown their nullity. I earnestly beg that whoever may detect any flaw in my reasoning will point it out to me, either privately or publicly; for if I am wrong, it much concerns me to be set right speedily. If my argument remains unrefuted, it will be time, I think, to doubt the absolute truth of the principle of universal law; and when once such a doubt has obtained a living root in any man's mind, my cause with him, I am persuaded, is gained.

3. The Law of Mind

In an article published in *The Monist* for January, 1891, I endeavored to show what ideas ought to form the warp of a system of philosophy, and particularly emphasized that of absolute chance. In the number of April, 1892, I argued further in favor of that way of thinking, which it will be convenient to christen *tychism* (from τύχη, chance). A serious student of philosophy will be in no haste to accept or reject this doctrine; but he will see in it one of the chief attitudes that speculative thought may take, feeling that it is not for an individual, nor for an age, to pronounce upon a fundamental question of philosophy. That is a task for a whole era to work out. I have begun by showing that *tychism* must give birth to an evolutionary cosmology, in which all the regularities of nature and of mind are regarded as products of growth, and to a Schelling-fashioned idealism that holds matter to be mere specialized and partially deadened mind. I may mention, for the benefit of those who are curious in studying mental biographies, that I was born and reared in the neighborhood of Concord—I mean in Cambridge—at the time when Emerson, Hedge, and their friends were disseminating the ideas that they had caught from Schelling, and Schelling from Plotinus, from Boehm, or from God-knows-what minds stricken with the monstrous mysticism of the East. But the atmosphere of Cambridge held many an antiseptic against Concord transcendentalism; and I am not conscious of having contracted any of that virus. Nevertheless, it is probable that some cultured bacilli, some benignant form of the disease was implanted in my soul, unawares, and that now, after long incubation, it comes to the surface, modified by mathematical conceptions and by training in physical investigations.

The next step in the study of cosmology must be to examine the general law of mental action. In doing this, I shall for the time drop my tychism out of view, in order to allow a free and independent expansion to another conception signalized in my first *Monist* paper as one of the most indispensable to philosophy, though it was not there dwelt upon: I mean the idea of continuity. The tendency to regard continuity, in the sense in which I shall define it, as an idea of prime importance in philosophy may conveniently be termed *synechism*. The present paper is intended chiefly to show what synechism is, and what it leads to. I attempted, a good many years ago, to develop this doctrine in the *Journal of Speculative Philosophy* (Vol. III.); but I am able now to improve upon that exposition, in which I was a little blinded by nominalistic prepossessions. I refer to it, because students may possibly find that some points not sufficiently explained in the present paper are cleared up in those earlier ones.

WHAT THE LAW IS

Logical analysis applied to mental phenomena shows that there is but one law of mind, namely, that ideas tend to spread continuously and to affect certain others that stand to them in a peculiar relation of affectibility. In this spreading they lose intensity, and especially the power of affecting others, but gain generality and become welded with other ideas.

I set down this formula at the beginning, for convenience; and now proceed to comment upon it.

INDIVIDUALITY OF IDEAS

We are accustomed to speak of ideas as reproduced, as passed from mind to mind, as similar or dissimilar to one another, and, in short, as if they were substantial things; nor can any reasonable objection be raised to such expressions. But taking the word "idea" in the sense of an event in an individual consciousness, it is clear that an idea once past is gone forever, and any supposed recurrence of it is another idea. These two ideas are not present in the same state of consciousness, and therefore cannot possibly be compared. To say, therefore, that they are similar can only mean that an occult power from the depths of the soul forces us to connect them in our thoughts after they are both no more. We may note, here, in passing that of the two generally recognized principles of association, contiguity and similarity, the former is a connection due to a power without, the latter a connection due to a power within.

But what can it mean to say that ideas wholly past are thought of at all, any longer? They are utterly unknowable. What distinct meaning can attach to saying that an idea in the past in any way affects an idea in the future, from which it is completely detached? A phrase between the assertion and the denial of which there can in no case be any sensible difference is mere gibberish.

I will not dwell further upon this point, because it is a commonplace of philosophy.

CONTINUITY OF IDEAS

We have here before us a question of difficulty, analogous to the question of nominalism and realism. But when once it has been clearly formulated, logic leaves room for one answer only. How can a past idea be present? Can it be present vicariously? To a certain extent, perhaps, but not merely so, for then the question would arise how the past idea can be related to its vicarious representation. The relation, being between ideas, can only exist in some consciousness: now that past idea was in no consciousness but that past consciousness that alone contained it, and that did not embrace the vicarious idea.

Some minds will here jump to the conclusion that a past idea cannot in any sense be present. But that is hasty and illogical. How extravagant, too, to pronounce our whole knowledge of the past to be mere delusion! Yet it would seem that the past is as completely beyond the bonds of possible experience as a Kantian thing-in-itself.

How can a past idea be present? Not vicariously. Then, only by direct perception. In other words, to be present, it must be *ipso facto* present. That is, it cannot be wholly past; it can only be going, infinitesimally past, less past than any assignable past date. We are thus brought to the conclusion that the present is connected with the past by a series of real infinitesimal steps.

It has already been suggested by psychologists that consciousness necessarily embraces an interval of time. But if a finite time be meant, the opinion is not tenable. If the sensation that precedes the present by half a second were still immediately before me, then, on the same principle the sensation preceding that would be immediately present, and so on *ad infinitum*. Now, since there is a time, say a year, at the end of which an idea is no longer *ipso facto* present, it follows that this is true of any finite interval, however short.

But yet consciousness must essentially cover an interval of time; for if it did not, we could gain no knowledge of time, and not merely no veracious cognition of it, but no conception whatever. We are, therefore, forced to say that we are immediately conscious through an infinitesimal interval of time.

This is all that is requisite. For, in this infinitesimal interval, not only is consciousness continuous in a subjective sense, that is, considered as a subject or substance having the attribute of duration; but also, because it is immediate consciousness, its object is *ipso facto* continuous. In fact, this infinitesimally spread-out consciousness is a direct feeling of its contents as spread out. This will be further elucidated below. In an infinitesimal interval we directly perceive the temporal sequence of its beginning, middle, and end—not, of course, in the way of recognition, for recognition is only of the past, but in the way of immediate feeling. Now upon this interval follows another, whose beginning is the middle of the former, and whose middle is the end of the former. Here, we have an immediate perception of the temporal sequence of its beginning, middle, and end, or say of the second, third, and fourth instants. From these two immediate perceptions, we gain a mediate, or inferential, perception of the relation of all four instants. This mediate perception is objectively, or as to the object represented, spread over the four instants; but subjectively, or as itself the subject of duration, it is completely embraced in the second moment. [The reader will observe that I use the word *instant* to mean a point of time, and *moment* to mean an infinitesimal duration.] If it is objected that, upon the theory proposed, we must have more than a mediate perception of the succession of the four instants, I grant it; for the sum of the two infinitesimal intervals is itself infinitesimal, so that it is immediately perceived. It is immediately perceived in the whole interval, but only mediately perceived in the last two thirds of the interval. Now, let there be an indefinite succession of these inferential acts of comparative perception; and it is plain that the last moment will contain objectively the whole series. Let there be not merely an indefinite succession, but a continuous flow of inference through a finite time, and the result will be a mediate objective consciousness of the whole time in the last moment. In this last moment the whole series will be recognized, or known as known before, except only the last moment, which of course will be absolutely unrecognizable to itself. Indeed, even this last moment will be recognized like the rest, or, at least be just beginning to be so. There is a little *elenchus,* or appearance of contradiction, here, which the ordinary logic of reflection quite suffices to resolve.

INFINITY AND CONTINUITY IN GENERAL

Most of the mathematicians who during the last two generations have treated the differential calculus have been of the opinion that an infinitesimal quantity is an absurdity; although, with their habitual caution, they have often added "or, at any rate, the conception of an infinitesimal is so difficult, that we practically cannot reason about it with confidence and security." Accordingly, the doctrine of limits has been invented to evade the difficulty, or, as some say, to explain the signification of the word "infinitesimal." This doctrine, in one form or another, is taught in all the textbooks, though in some of them only as an alternative view of the matter; it answers well enough the purposes of calculation, though even in that application it has its difficulties.

The illumination of the subject by a strict notation for the logic of relatives had shown me clearly and evidently that the idea of an infinitesimal involves no contradiction, before I became acquainted with the writings of Dr. Georg Cantor (though many of these had already appeared in the *Mathematische Annalen* and in *Borchardt's Journal,* if not yet in the *Acta Mathematica,* all mathematical journals of the first distinction), in which the same view is defended with extraordinary genius and penetrating logic.

The prevalent opinion is that finite numbers are the only ones that we can reason about, at least, in any ordinary mode of reasoning, or, as some authors express it, they are the only numbers that can be reasoned about mathematically. But this is an irrational prejudice. I long ago showed that finite collections are distinguished from infinite ones only by one circumstance and its consequences, namely, that to them is applicable a peculiar and unusual mode of reasoning called by its discoverer, Augustus De Morgan, the "syllogism of transposed quantity."

Balzac, in the introduction of his *Physiologie du marriage,* remarks that every young Frenchman boasts of having seduced some French-woman. Now, as a woman can only be seduced once, and there are no more Frenchwomen than Frenchmen, it follows, if these boasts are true, that no French women escape seduction. If their number be finite, the reasoning holds. But since the population is continually increasing, and the seduced are on the average younger than the seducers, the conclusion need not be true. In like manner, De Morgan, as an actuary, might have argued that if an insurance company pays to its insured on an average more than they have ever paid it, including interest, it must lose money. But every modern actuary would see a fallacy in that, since the business is continually on the increase. But should war, or other cataclysm, cause the class of insured to be a finite one, the conclusion would turn out painfully correct, after all. The above two reasonings are examples of the syllogism of transposed quantity.

The proposition that finite and infinite collections are distinguished by the applicability to the former of the syllogism of transposed quantity ought to be regarded as the basal one of scientific arithmetic.

If a person does not know how to reason logically, and I must say that a great many fairly good mathematicians—yea, distinguished ones—fall under this category, but simply uses a rule of thumb in blindly drawing inferences like other inferences that have turned out well, he will, of course, be continually falling into error about infinite numbers. The truth is such people do not reason, at all. But for the few who do reason, reasoning about infinite numbers is easier than about finite numbers, because the complicated syllogism of transposed quantity is not called for. For example, that the whole is greater than its part is not an axiom, as that eminently bad reasoner, Euclid, made it to be. It is a theorem readily proved by r. . .ns of a syllogism of transposed quantity, but not otherwise. Of finite collections it is true, of infinite collections false. Thus, a part of the whole numbers are even numbers. Yet the even numbers are no fewer than all the numbers; an evident proposition since if every number in the whole series of whole numbers be doubled, the result will be the series of even numbers.

1, 2, 3, 4, 5, 6, etc.

2, 4, 6, 8, 10, 12, etc.

So for every number there is a distinct even number. In fact, there are as many distinct doubles of numbers as there are of distinct numbers.

But the doubles of numbers are all even numbers.

In truth, of infinite collections there are but two grades of magnitude, the *endless* and the *innumerable.* Just as a finite collection is distinguished from an infinite one by the applicability to it of a special mode of reasoning, the syllogism of transposed quantity, so, as I showed in the paper last referred to, a numerable collection is distinguished from an innumerable one by the applicability to it of a certain mode of reasoning, the Fermatian inference, or, as it is sometimes improperly termed, "mathematical induction."

As an example of this reasoning, Leonhard Euler's demonstration of the binomial theorem for integral powers may be given. The theorem is that $(x + y)^n$, where n is a whole number, may be expanded into the sum of a series of terms of which the first is $x^n y^o$ and each of the others is derived from the next preceding by diminishing the exponent of x by 1 and multiplying by that exponent and at the same time increasing the exponent of y by 1 and dividing by that increased exponent. Now, suppose this proposition to be true for a certain exponent, $n = M$, then it must also be true for $n = M + 1$. For let one of the terms in the expansion of $(x + y)^M$ be written $Ax^p y^q$. Then, this term with the two following will be

$$Ax^p y^q + A\frac{p}{q+1}x^{p-1}y^{q+1} + A\frac{p}{q+1}\frac{p-1}{q+2}x^{p-2}y^{q+2}$$

Now, when $(x + y)^M$ is multiplied by $x + y$ to give $(x + y)^{M+1}$, we multiply first by x and then by y instead of by x and add the two results. When we multiply by x, the second of the above three terms will be the only one giving a term involving $x^p y^{q+1}$ and the third will be the only one giving a term in $x^{p-1}y^{q+2}$; and when we multiply by y the first will be the only term giving a term in $x^p y^{q+1}$, and the second will be the only term giving a term in $x^{p-1}y^{q+2}$. Hence, adding like terms, we find that the coefficient of $x^p y^{q+1}$ in the expansion of $(x + y)^{M+1}$ will be the sum of the coefficients of the first two of the above three terms, and that the coefficient of $x^{p-1}y^{q+2}$ will be the sum of the coefficients of the last two terms. Hence, two successive terms in the expansion of $(x + y)^{M+1}$ will be

$$A \left[1 + \frac{p}{q-1} \right] x^p y^{q+1} + A \frac{p}{q+1} \left[1 + \frac{p-1}{q+2} \right] x^{p-1} y^{q+2}$$

$$= A \frac{p+q+1}{q-1} x^p y^{q+1} + A \frac{p+q+1}{q-1} \cdot \frac{p}{q-2} x^{p-1} y^{q+2}.$$

It is, thus, seen that the succession of terms follows the rule. Thus if any integral power follows the rule, so also does the next higher power. But the first power obviously follows the rule. Hence, all powers do so.

Such reasoning holds good of any collection of objects capable of being ranged in a series that though it may be endless, can be numbered so that each member of it receives a definite integral number. For instance, all the whole numbers constitute such a numerable collection. Again, all numbers resulting from operating according to any definite rule with any finite number of whole numbers form such a collection. For they may be arranged in a series thus. Let F be the symbol of operation. First operate on 1, giving F (1). Then, operate on a second 1, giving F(1, 1). Next, introduce 2, giving 3rd, F(2); 4th, F(2,1); 5th, F(1, 2); 6th, F (2, 2). Next use a third variable giving 7th, F (1, 1, 1); 8th, F (2, 1, 1); 9th, F (1, 2, 1); 10th, F (2, 2, 1); 11th, F (1, 1, 2); 12th, F (2, 1, 2); 13th, F (1, 2, 2); 14th, F (2, 2, 2). Next introduce 3, and so on, alternately introducing new variables and new figures; and in this way it is plain that every arrangement of integral values of the variables will receive a numbered place in the series.*

The class of endless but numerable collections (so called because they can be so ranged that to each one corresponds a distinct whole number) is very large. But there are collections that are certainly innumerable. Such is the collection of all numbers to which endless series of decimals are capable of approximating. It has been recognized since the time of Euclid that certain numbers are surd or incommensurable, and are not exactly expressible by any finite series of decimals, nor by a circulating decimal. Such is the ratio of the circumference of a circle to its diameter, which we know is nearly 3.1415926. The calculation of this number has been carried to over 700 figures without the slightest appearance of

---

*This proposition is substantially the same as a theorem of Cantor, though it is enunciated in a much more general form.

regularity in their sequence. The demonstrations that this and many other numbers are incommensurable are perfect. That the entire collection of incommensurable numbers is innumerable has been clearly proved by Georg Cantor. I omit the demonstration; but it is easy to see that to discriminate one from some other would, in general, require the use of an endless series of numbers. Now if they cannot be exactly expressed and discriminated, clearly they cannot be ranged in a linear series.

It is evident that there are as many points on a line or in an interval of time as there are of real numbers in all. These are, therefore, innumerable collections. Many mathematicians have incautiously assumed that the points on a surface or in a solid are more than those on a line. But this has been refuted by Cantor. Indeed, it is obvious that for every set of values of coordinates there is a single distinct number. Suppose, for instance, the values of the coordinates all lie between 0 and + 1. Then if we compose a number by putting in the first decimal place the first figure of the first coordinate, in the second the first figure of the second coordinate, and so on, and when the first figures are all dealt out go on to the second figures in like manner, it is plain that the values of the coordinates can be read off from the single resulting number, so that a triad or tetrad of numbers, each having innumerable values, has no more values than a single incommensurable number.

Were the number of dimensions infinite, this would fail; and the collection of infinite sets of numbers having each innumerable variations, might, therefore, be greater than the simple innumerable collection, and might be called *endlessly infinite*. The single individuals of such a collection could not, however, be designated, even approximately, so that this is indeed a magnitude concerning which it would be possible to reason only in the most general way, if at all.

Although there are but two grades of magnitudes of infinite collections, yet when certain conditions are imposed upon the order in which individuals are taken, distinctions of magnitude arise from that cause. Thus, if a simply endless series be doubled by separating each unit into two parts, the successive first parts and also the second parts being taken in the same order as the units from which they are derived, this double endless series will, so long as it is taken in that order, appear as twice as large as the original series. In like manner the product of two innumerable collections, that is, the collection of possible pairs composed of one individual of each, if the order of continuity is to be maintained, is, by virtue of that order, infinitely greater than either of the component collections.

We now come to the difficult question, What is continuity? Kant confounds it with infinite divisibility, saying that the essential character of a continuous series is that between any two members of it a third can always be found. This is an analysis beautifully clear and definite; but unfortunately, it breaks down under the first test. For according to this, the entire series of rational fractions arranged in the order of their magnitude, would be an infinite series, although the rational fractions are numerable, while the points of a line are innumerable. Nay, worse yet, if from that series of fractions any two with all that lie between them be excised, and any number of such finite gaps he made, Kant's definition is still true of the series, though it has lost all appearance of continuity.

Cantor defines a continuous series as one that is *concatenated* and *perfect*. By a concatenated series, he means such a one that if any two points are given in it, and any finite distance, however small, it is possible to proceed from the first point to the second through a succession of points of the series each at a distance from the preceding one less than the given distance. This is true of the series of rational fractions ranged in the order of their magnitude. By a perfect series he means one that contains every point such that there is no distance so small that this point has not an infinity of points of the series within that distance of it. This is true of the series of numbers between 0 and 1 capable of being expressed by decimals in which only the digits 0 and 1 occur.

It must be granted that Cantor's definition includes every series that is continuous; nor can it be objected that it includes any important or indubitable case of a series not continuous. Nevertheless, it has some serious defects. In the first place, it turns upon metrical considerations; while the distinction between a continuous and a discontinuous series is manifestly nonmetrical. In the next place, a perfect series is defined as one containing "every point" of a certain description. But no positive idea is conveyed of what all the points are: that is definition by negation, and cannot be admitted. If that sort of thing were allowed, it would be very easy to say, at once, that the continuous linear series of points is one which contains every point of the line between its extremities. Finally, Cantor's definition does not convey a distinct notion of what the components of the conception of continuity are. It ingeniously wraps up its properties in two separate parcels, but does not display them to our intelligence.

Kant's definition expresses one simple property of a continuum; but it allows of gaps in the series. To mend the definition, it is only necessary to notice how these gaps can occur. Let us suppose, then, a linear series of points extending from a point, A, to a point, B, having a gap from B to a third point, C, and thence extending to a final limit, D; and let us suppose this series conforms to Kant's definition. Then, of the two points, B and C, one or both must be excluded from the series; for otherwise, by the definition, there would be points between them. That is, if the series contains C, though it contains all the points up to B, it cannot contain B. What is required, therefore, is to state in nonmetrical terms that if a series of points up to a limit is included in a continuum the limit is included. It may be remarked that this is the property of a continuum to which Aristotle's attention seems to have been directed when he defines a continuum as something whose parts have a common limit. The property may be exactly stated as follows: If a linear series of points is continuous between two points, A and D, and if an endless series of points be taken, the first of them between A and D and each of the others between the last preceding one and D, then there is a point of the continuous series between all that endless series of points and D, and such that every other point of which this is true lies between this point and D. For example, take any number between 0 and 1, as 0.1; then, any number between 0.1 and 1, as 0.11; then any number between 0.11 and 1, as 0.111; and so on, without end. Then, because the series of real numbers between 0 and 1 is continuous, there must be a *least* real number, greater than every number of that endless series. This property, which may be called the Aristotelicity of the series, together with Kant's property, or its Kanticity, completes the definition of a continuous series.

The property of Aristotelicity may be roughly stated thus: A continuum contains the end point belonging to every endless series of points that it contains. An obvious corollary is that every continuum contains its limits. But in using this principle it is necessary to observe that a series may be continuous except in this, that it omits one or both of the limits.

Our ideas will find expression more conveniently if, instead of points upon a line, we speak of real numbers. Every real number is, in one sense, the limit of a series, for it can be indefinitely approximated to. Whether every real number is a limit of a *regular* series may perhaps be open to doubt. But the series referred to in the definition of Aristotelicity must be understood as including all series whether regular or not. Consequently, it is implied that between any two points an innumerable series of points can be taken.

Every number whose expression in decimals requires but a finite number of places of decimals is commensurable. Therefore, incommensurable numbers suppose an infinitieth place of decimals. The word infinitesimal is simply the Latin form of infinitieth; that is, it is an ordinal formed from *infinitum*, as centesimal from *centum*. Thus, continuity supposes infinitesimal quantities. There is nothing contradictory about the idea of such quantities. In adding and multiplying them the continuity must not be broken up, and consequently they are precisely like any other quantities, except that neither the syllogism of transposed quantity, nor the Fermatian inference applies to them.

If A is a finite quantity and i an infinitesimal, then in a certain sense we may write $A + i = A$. That is to say, this is so for all purposes of measurement. But this principle must not be applied except to get rid of *all* the terms in the highest order of infinitesimals present. As a mathematician, I prefer the method of infinitesimals to that of limits, as far easier and less infested with snares. Indeed, the latter, as stated in some books, involves propositions that are false; but this is not the case with the forms of the method used by Cauchy, Duhamel, and others. As they understand the doctrine of limits, it involves the notion of continuity, and therefore contains in another shape the very same ideas as the doctrine of infinitesimals.

Let us now consider an aspect of the Aristotelical principle that is particularly important in philosophy. Suppose a surface to be part red and part blue; so that every point on it is either red or blue, and, of course, no part can be both red and blue. What, then, is the color of the boundary line between the red and the blue? The answer is that red or blue, to exist at all, must be spread over a surface; and the color of the surface is the color of the surface in the immediate neighborhood of the point. I purposely use a vague form of expression. Now, as the parts of the surface in the immediate neighborhood of any ordinary point upon a curved boundary are half of them red and half blue, it follows that the boundary is half red and half blue. In like manner, we find it necessary to hold that consciousness essentially occupies time; and what is present to the mind at any ordinary instant, is what is present during a moment in which that instant occurs. Thus, the present is half past and half to come. Again, the color of the parts of a surface at any finite distance from a point, has nothing to do with its color just at that point; and, in the parallel, the feeling at any finite interval from the present has nothing to do with the present feeling, except vicariously. Take another case: the velocity of a particle at any instant of time is its mean velocity during an infinitesimal instant in which that time is contained. Just so my immediate feeling is my feeling through an infinitesimal duration containing the present instant.

ANALYSIS OF TIME

One of the most marked features about the law of mind is that it makes time have a definite direction of flow from past to future. The relation of past to future is, in reference to the law of mind, different from the relation of future to past. This makes one of the great contrasts between the law of mind and the law of physical force, where there is no more distinction between the two opposite directions in time than between moving northward and moving southward.

In order therefore, to analyze the law of mind, we must begin by asking what the flow of time consists in. Now, we find that in reference to any individual state of feeling, all others are of two classes, those that affect this one (or have a tendency to affect it, and what this means we shall inquire shortly), and those that do not. The present is affectible by the past but not by the future.

Moreover, if state A is affected by state B, and state B by state C, then A is affected by state C, though not so much so. It follows, that if A is affectible by B, B is not affectible by A.

If, of two states, each is absolutely unaffectible by the other, they are to be regarded as parts of the same state. They are contemporaneous.

To say that a state is *between* two states means that it affects one and is affected by the other. Between any two states in this sense lies an innumerable series of states affecting one another; and if a state lies between a given state and any other state which can be reached by inserting states between this state and any third state, these inserted states not immediately affecting or being affected by either, then the second state mentioned immediately affects or is affected by the first, in the sense that in the one the other is *ipso facto* present in a reduced degree.

These propositions involve a definition of time and of its flow. Over and above this definition they involve a doctrine, namely, that every state of feeling is affectible by every earlier stage.

THAT FEELINGS HAVE INTENSIVE CONTINUITY

Time with its continuity logically involves some other kind of continuity than its own. Time, as the universal form of change, cannot exist unless there is something to undergo change, and to undergo a change continuous in time, there must be a continuity of changeable qualities. Of the continuity of intrinsic qualities of feeling we can now form but a feeble conception. The development of the human mind has practically extinguished all feelings, except a few sporadic kinds, sound, colors, smells, warmth, etc., which now appear to be disconnected and disparate. In the case of colors, there is a tridimensional spread of feelings. Originally, all feelings may have been connected in the same way, and the presumption is that the number of dimensions were endless. For development essentially involves a limitation of possibilities. But given a number of dimensions of feeling, all possible varieties are obtainable by varying the intensities of the different elements. Accordingly, time logically supposes a continuous range of intensity in feeling. It follows, then, from the definition of continuity, that when any particular kind of feeling is present, an infinitesimal continuum of all feelings differing infinitesimally from that is present.

THAT FEELINGS HAVE SPATIAL EXTENSION

Consider a gob of protoplasm, say an amoeba or a slime mould. It does not differ in any radical way from the contents of a nerve cell, though its functions may be less specialized. There is no doubt that this slime mould, or this amoeba, or at any rate some similar mass of protoplasm, feels. That is to say, it feels when it is in its excited condition. But note how it behaves. When the whole is quiescent and rigid, a place upon it is irritated. Just at this point, an active motion is set up, and this gradually spreads to other parts. In this action, no unity nor relation to a nucleus, or other unitary organ can be discerned. It is a mere amorphous continuum of protoplasm, with feeling passing from one part to another. Nor is there anything like a wavemotion. The activity does not advance to new parts, just as fast as it leaves old parts. Rather, in the beginning, it dies out at a slower rate than that at which it spreads. And while the process is going on, by exciting the mass at another point, a second quite independent state of excitation will be set up. In some places neither excitation will exist, in others each separately, in still other places both effects will be added together. Whatever there is in the whole phenomenon to make us think there is feeling in such a mass of protoplasm—*feeling*, but plainly no *personality*—goes logically to show that that feeling has a subjective, or substantial, spatial extension, as the excited state has. This is, no doubt, a difficult idea to seize, for the reason that it is a subjective, not an objective, extension. It is not that we have a feeling of bigness; though Professor William James, perhaps rightly, teaches that we have. It is that the feeling, as a subject of inhesion, is big. Moreover, our own feelings are focused in attention to such a degree that we are not aware that ideas are not brought to an absolute unity;

just as nobody not instructed by special experiment has any idea how very, very little of the field of vision is distinct. Still, we all know how the attention wanders about among our feelings; and this fact shows that those feelings that are not coordinated in attention have a reciprocal externality, although they are present at the same time. But we must not tax introspection to make a phenomenon manifest which essentially involves externality.

Since space is continuous, it follows that there must be an immediate community of feeling between parts of mind infinitesimally near together. Without this, I believe it would have been impossible for minds external to one another, ever to become coordinated, and equally impossible for any coordination to be established in the action of the nerve matter of one brain.

AFFECTIONS OF IDEAS

But we are met by the question what is meant by saying that one idea affects another. The unravelment of this problem requires us to trace out phenomena a little further.

Three elements go to make up an idea. The first is its intrinsic quality as a feeling. The second is the energy with which it affects other ideas, an energy that is infinite in the here-and-nowness of immediate sensation, finite and relative in the recency of the past. The third element is the tendency of an idea to bring along other ideas with it.

As an idea spreads, its power of affecting other ideas gets rapidly reduced; but its intrinsic quality remains nearly unchanged. It is long years now since I last saw a cardinal in his robes; and my memory of their color has become much dimmed. The color itself, however, is not remembered as dim. I have no inclination to call it a dull red. Thus, the intrinsic quality remains little changed; yet more accurate observation will show a slight reduction of it. The third element, on the other hand, has increased. As well as I can recollect, it seems to me the cardinals I used to see wore robes more scarlet than vermilion is, and highly luminous. Still, I know the color commonly called cardinal is on the crimson side of vermilion and of quite moderate luminosity, and the original idea calls up so many other hues with it, and asserts itself so feebly, that I am unable any longer to isolate it.

A finite interval of time generally contains an innumerable series of feelings; and when these become welded together in association, the result is a general idea. For we have just seen how by continuous spreading an idea becomes generalized.

The first character of a general idea so resulting is that it is living feeling. A continuum of this feeling, infinitesimal in duration, but still embracing innumerable parts, and also, though infinitesimal, entirely unlimited, is immediately present. And in its absence of boundedness a vague possibility of more than is present is directly felt.

Second, in the presence of this continuity of feeling, nominalistic maxims appear futile. There is no doubt about one idea affecting another, when we can directly perceive the one gradually modified and shaping itself into the other. Nor can there any longer be any difficulty about one idea resembling another, when we can pass along the continuous field of quality from one to the other and back again to the point that we had marked.

Third, consider the insistency of an idea. The insistency of a past idea with reference to the present is a quantity that is less the further back that past idea is, and rises to infinity as the past idea is brought up into coincidence with the present. Here we must make one of those inductive applications of the law of continuity that have produced such great results in all the positive sciences. We must extend the law of insistency into the future. Plainly, the insistency of a future idea with reference to the present is a quantity affected by the minus sign; for it is the present that affects the future, if there be any effect, not the future that affects the present. Accordingly, the curve of insistency is a sort of equilateral hyperbola. [See the figure.] Such a conception is none the less mathematical, that its quantification cannot now be exactly specified.

Now consider the induction that we have here been led into. This curve says that feeling that has not yet emerged into immediate consciousness is already affectible and already affected. In fact, this is habit, by virtue of which an idea is brought up into present consciousness by

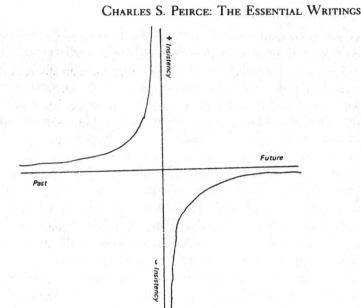

a bond that had already been established between it, and another idea while it was still *in futuro*.

We can now see what the affection of one idea by another consists in. It is that the affected idea is attached as a logical predicate to the affecting idea as subject. So when a feeling emerges into immediate consciousness, it always appears as a modification of a more or less general object already in the mind. The word suggestion is well adapted to expressing this relation. The future is suggested by or rather is influenced by the suggestions of, the past.

IDEAS CANNOT BE CONNECTED EXCEPT BY CONTINUITY

That ideas can no wise be connected without continuity is sufficiently evident to one who reflects upon the matter. But still the opinion may be entertained that after continuity has once made the connection of ideas possible, then they may get to be connected in other modes than through continuity. Certainly, I cannot see how anyone can deny that the infinite diversity of the universe, which we call chance, may bring ideas into proximity that are not associated in one general idea. It may do this many times. But then the law of continuous spreading will produce a mental association; and this I suppose is an abridged statement of the way the universe has been evolved. But if I am asked whether a blind ἀνάγκη cannot bring ideas together, first I point out that it would not remain blind. There being a continuous connection between the ideas, they would infallibly become associated in a living, feeling, and perceiving general idea. Next, I cannot see what the mustness or necessity of this ἀνάγκη would consist in. In the absolute uniformity of the phenomenon, says the nominalist. Absolute is well put in; for if it merely happened so three times in succession, or three million times in succession, in the absence of any reason, the coincidence could only be attributed to chance. But absolute uniformity must extend over the whole infinite future; and it is idle to talk of that except as an idea. No; I think we can only hold that wherever ideas come together they tend to weld into general ideas; and wherever they are generally connected, general ideas govern the connection; and these general ideas are living feelings spread out.

MENTAL LAW FOLLOWS THE FORMS OF LOGIC

The three main classes of logical inference are deduction, induction, and hypothesis. These correspond to three chief modes of action of the human soul. In deduction the mind is under the dominion of a habit or association by virtue of which a general idea suggests in each case a corresponding reaction. But a certain sensation is seen to involve that idea. Consequently, that sensation is followed by that reaction. That is the way the hind legs of a frog, separated from the rest of the body, reason, when you pinch them. It is the lowest form of psychical manifestation.

By induction, a habit becomes established. Certain sensations, all involving one general idea, are followed each by the same reaction; and an association becomes established, whereby that general idea gets to be followed uniformly by that reaction.

Habit is that specialization of the law of mind whereby a general idea gains the power of exciting reactions. But in order that the general idea should attain all its functionality, it is necessary, also, that it should become suggestible by sensations. That is accomplished by a psychical process having the form of hypothetic inference. By hypothetic inference, I mean, as I have explained in other writings, an induction from qualities. For example, I know that the kind of man known and classed as a "mugwump" has certain characteristics. He has a high self-respect and places great value upon social distinction. He laments the great part that rowdyism and unrefined good-fellowship play in the dealings of American politicians with their constituency. He thinks that the reform that would follow from the abandonment of the system by which the distribution of offices is made to strengthen party organizations and a return to the original and essential conception of officefilling would be found an unmixed good. He holds that monetary considerations should usually be the decisive ones in questions of public policy. He respects the principle of individualism and of *laissez-faire* as the greatest agency of civilization. These views, among others, I know to be obtrusive marks of a "mugwump." Now, suppose I casually meet a man in a railway train, and falling into conversation find that he holds opinions of this sort; I am naturally led to suppose that he is a "mugwump." That is hypothetic inference. That is to say, a number of readily verifiable marks of a mugwump being selected, I find this man has these, and infer that he has all the other characters that go to make a thinker of that stripe. Or let us suppose that I meet a man of a semiclerical appearance and a subpharisaical sniff, who appears to look at things from the point of view of a rather wooden dualism. He cites several texts of scripture and always with particular attention to their logical implications; and he exhibits a sternness, almost amounting to vindictiveness, toward evil-doers, in general. I readily conclude that he is a minister of a certain denomination. Now the mind acts in a way similar to this, every time we acquire a power of coordinating reactions in a peculiar way, as in performing any act requiring skill. Thus, most persons have a difficulty in moving the two hands simultaneously and in opposite directions through two parallel circles nearly in the medial plane of the body. To learn to do this, it is necessary to attend, first, to the different actions in different parts of the motion, when suddenly a general conception of the action springs up and it becomes perfectly easy. We think the motion we are trying to do involves this action, and this, and this. Then, the general idea comes that unites all those actions, and thereupon the desire to perform the motion calls up the general idea. The same mental process is many times employed whenever we are learning to speak a language or are acquiring any sort of skill.

Thus, by induction, a number of sensations followed by one reaction become united under one general idea followed by the same reaction; while by the hypothetic process, a number of reactions called for by one occasion get united in a general idea that is called out by the same occasion. By deduction, the habit fulfills its function of calling out certain reactions on certain occasions.

UNCERTAINTY OF MENTAL ACTION

The inductive and hypothetic forms of inference are essentially probable inferences, not necessary; while deduction may be either necessary or probable.

But no mental action seems to be necessary or invariable in its character. In whatever manner the mind has reacted under a given sensation, in that manner it is the more likely to react again; were this, however, an absolute necessity, habits would become wooden and ineradicable, and no room being left for the formation of new habits, intellectual life would come to a speedy close. Thus, the uncertainty of the mental law is no mere defect of it, but is on the contrary, of its essence. The truth is, the mind is not subject to "law," in the same rigid sense that matter is. It only experiences gentle forces that merely render it more likely to act in a given way than it otherwise would. There always remains a certain amount of arbitrary spontaneity in its action, without which it would be dead.

Some psychologists think to reconcile the uncertainty of reactions with the principle of necessary causation by means of the law of fatigue. Truly for a *law*, this law of fatigue is a little lawless. I think it is merely a case of the general principle that an idea in spreading loses its insistency. Put me tarragon into my salad, when I have not tasted it for years, and I exclaim "What nectar is this!" But add it to every dish I taste for week after week, and a habit of expectation has been created; and in thus spreading into habit, the sensation makes hardly any more impression upon me; or, if it be noticed, it is on a new side from which it appears as rather a bore. The doctrine that fatigue is one of the primordial phenomena of mind I am much disposed to doubt. It seems a somewhat little thing to be allowed as an exception to the great principle of mental uniformization. For this reason, I prefer to explain it in the manner here indicated, as a special case of that great principle. To consider it as something distinct in its nature, certainly somewhat strengthens the necessitarian position; but even if it be distinct, the hypothesis that all the variety and apparent arbitrariness of mental action ought to be explained away in favor of absolute determinism does not seem to me to recommend itself to a sober and sound judgment, which seeks the guidance of observed facts and not that of prepossessions.

RESTATEMENT OF THE LAW

Let me now try to gather up all these odds and ends of commentary and restate the law of mind, in a unitary way.

First, then, we find that when we regard ideas from a nominalistic, individualistic, sensualistic way, the simplest facts of mind become utterly meaningless. That one idea should resemble another or influence another, or that one state of mind should so much as be thought of in another is, from that standpoint, sheer nonsense.

Second, by this and other means we are driven to perceive, what is quite evident of itself, that instantaneous feelings flow together into a continuum of feeling, that has in a modified degree the peculiar vivacity of feeling and has gained generality. And in reference to such general ideas, or continua of feeling, the difficulties about resemblance and suggestion and reference to the external, cease to have any force.

Third, these general ideas are not mere words, nor do they consist in this, that certain concrete facts will every time happen under certain descriptions of conditions; but they are just as much, or rather far more,

living realities than the feelings themselves out of which they are con-
creted. And to say that mental phenomena are governed by law does not
mean merely that they are describable by a general formula; but that
there is a living idea, a conscious continuum of feeling, which pervades
them, and to which they are docile.

Fourth, this supreme law, which is the celestial and living harmony,
does not so much as demand that the special ideas shall surrender their
peculiar arbitrariness and caprice entirely; for that would be self-destruc-
tive. It only requires that they shall influence and be influenced by one
another.

Fifth, in what measure this unification acts, seems to be regulated
only by special rules; or, at least, we cannot in our present knowledge
say how far it goes. But it may be said that, judging by appearances, the
amount of arbitrariness in the phenomena of human minds is neither
altogether trifling nor very prominent.

PERSONALITY

Having thus endeavored to state the law of mind, in general, I de-
scend to the consideration of a particular phenomenon that is remarkably prominent in our own consciousnesses, that of personality. A strong
light is thrown upon this subject by recent observations of double and
multiple personality. The theory that at one time seemed plausible that
two persons in one body corresponded to the two halves of the brain will,
I take it, now be universally acknowledged to be insufficient. But that
which these cases make quite manifest is that personality is some kind
of coordination or connection of ideas. Not much to say, this, perhaps.
Yet when we consider that, according to the principle that we are
tracing out, a connection between ideas is itself a general idea, and that
a general idea is a living feeling, it is plain that we have at least taken
an appreciable step toward the understanding of personality. This personality, like any general idea, is not a thing to be apprehended in an
instant. It has to be lived in time; nor can any finite time embrace it
in all its fullness. Yet in each infinitesimal interval it is present and living,
though specially colored by the immediate feelings of that moment.

Personality, so far as it is apprehended in a moment, is immediate self-consciousness.

But the word coordination implies somewhat more than this; it implies a teleological harmony in ideas, and in the case of personality this teleology is more than a mere purposive pursuit of a predeterminate end; it is a developmental teleology. This is personal character. A general idea, living and conscious now, it is already determinative of acts in the future to an extent to which it is not now conscious. This reference to the future is an essential element of personality. Were the ends of a person already explicit, there would be no room for development, for growth, for life; and consequently there would be no personality. The mere carrying out of predetermined purposes is mechanical. This remark has an application to the philosophy of religion. It is that a genuine evolutionary philosophy, that is, one that makes the principle of growth a primordial element of the universe, is so far from being antagonistic to the idea of a personal creator, that it is really inseparable from that idea; while a necessitarian religion is in an altogether false position and is destined to become disintegrated. But a pseudo-evolutionism that enthrones mechanical law above the principle of growth, is at once scientifically unsatisfactory, as giving no possible hint of how the universe has come about, and hostile to all hopes of personal relations to God.

COMMUNICATION

Consistently with the doctrine laid down in the beginning of this paper, I am bound to maintain that an idea can only be affected by an idea in continuous connection with it. By anything but an idea, it cannot be affected at all. This obliges me to say, as I do say, on other grounds, that what we call matter is not completely dead, but is merely mind hide-bound with habits. It still retains the element of diversification; and in that diversification there is life. When an idea is conveyed from one mind to another, it is by forms of combination of the diverse elements of nature, say by some curious symmetry, or by some union of a tender color with a refined odor. To such forms the law of mechanical energy has no application. If they are eternal, it is in the spirit they embody;

and their origin cannot be accounted for by any mechanical necessity. They are embodied ideas; and so only can they convey ideas. Precisely how primary sensations, as colors and tones, are excited, we cannot tell, in the present state of psychology. But in our ignorance, I think that we are at liberty to suppose that they arise in essentially the same manner as the other feelings, called secondary. As far as sight and hearing are in question, we know that they are only excited by vibrations of inconceivable complexity; and the chemical senses are probably not more simple. Even the least psychical of peripheral sensations, that of pressure, has in its excitation conditions that, though apparently simple, are seen to be complicated enough when we consider the molecules and their attractions. The principle with which I set out requires me to maintain that these feelings are communicated to the nerves by continuity, so that there must be something like them in the excitants themselves. If this seems extravagant, it is to be remembered that it is the sole possible way of reaching any explanation of sensation, which otherwise must be pronounced a general fact absolutely inexplicable and ultimate. Now absolute inexplicability is a hypothesis that sound logic refuses under any circumstances to justify.

I may be asked whether my theory would be favorable or otherwise to telepathy. I have no decided answer to give to this. At first sight, it seems unfavorable. Yet there may be other modes of continuous connection between minds other than those of time and space.

The recognition by one person of another's personality takes place by means to some extent identical with the means by which he is conscious of his own personality. The idea of the second personality, which is as much as to say that second personality itself, enters within the field of direct consciousness of the first person, and is as immediately perceived as his ego, though less strongly. At the same time, the opposition between the two persons is perceived, so that the externality of the second is recognized.

The psychological phenomena of intercommunication between two minds have been unfortunately little studied. So that it is impossible to say, for certain, whether they are favorable to this theory or not. But the very extraordinary insight that some persons are able to gain of others from indications so slight that it is difficult to ascertain what they are, is certainly rendered more comprehensible by the view here taken.

A difficulty that confronts the synechistic philosophy is this. In considering personality, that philosophy is forced to accept the doctrine of a personal God; but in considering communication, it cannot but admit that if there is a personal God, we must have a direct perception of that person and indeed be in personal communication with him. Now, if that be the case, the question arises how it is possible that the existence of this being should ever have been doubted by anybody. The only answer that I can at present make is that facts that stand before our face and eyes and stare us in the face are far from being, in all cases, the ones most easily discerned. That has been remarked from time immemorial.

CONCLUSION

I have thus developed as well as I could in a little space the *synechistic* philosophy, as applied to mind. I think that I have succeeded in making it clear that this doctrine gives room for explanations of many facts that without it are absolutely and hopelessly inexplicable; and further that it carries along with it the following doctrines: first, a logical realism of the most pronounced type; second, objective idealism; third, tychism, with its consequent thoroughgoing evolutionism. We also notice that the doctrine presents no hindrances to spiritual influences, such as some philosophies are felt to do.

4.   Man's Glassy Essence

In *The Monist* for January, 1891, I tried to show what conceptions ought to form the brick and mortar of a philosophical system. Chief among these was that of absolute chance for which I argued again in last April's number.* In July, I applied another fundamental idea, that

---

*I am rejoiced to find, since my last paper was printed, that a philosopher as subtle and profound as Dr. Edmund Montgomery has long been arguing for the same element in the universe. Other world-renowned thinkers, as Renouvier and Delboeuf, appear to share this opinion.

of continuity, to the law of mind. Next in order, I have to elucidate, from the point of view chosen, the relation between the psychical and physical aspects of a substance.

The first step towards this ought, I think, to be the framing of a molecular theory of protoplasm. But before doing that, it seems indispensable to glance at the constitution of matter, in general. We shall, thus, unavoidably make a long detour; but, after all, our pains will not be wasted, for the problems of the papers that are to follow in the series will call for the consideration of the same question.

All physicists are rightly agreed the evidence is overwhelming that shows all sensible matter is composed of molecules in swift motion and exerting enormous mutual attractions, and perhaps repulsions, too. Even Sir William Thomson, Lord Kelvin, who wishes to explode action at a distance and return to the doctrine of a plenum, not only speaks of molecules, but undertakes to assign definite magnitudes to them. The brilliant Judge Stallo, a man who did not always rightly estimate his own qualities in accepting tasks for himself, declared war upon the atomic theory in a book well worth careful perusal. To the old arguments in favor of atoms that he found in Gustar Fechner's monograph, he was able to make replies of considerable force, though they were not sufficient to destroy those arguments. But against modern proofs he made no headway at all. These set out from the mechanical theory of heat. Benjamin Rumford's experiments showed that heat is not a substance. Jamie Joule demonstrated that it was a form of energy. The heating of gases under constant volume, and other facts instanced by Rankine, proved that it could not be an energy of strain. This drove physicists to the conclusion that it was a mode of motion. Then it was remembered that John Bernoulli had shown that the pressure of gases could be accounted for by assuming their molecules to be moving uniformly in rectilinear paths. The same hypothesis was now seen to account for Avogadro's law, that in equal volumes of different kinds of gases exposed to the same pressure and temperature are contained equal numbers of molecules. Shortly after, it was found to account for the laws of diffusion and viscosity of gases, and for the numerical relation between these properties. Finally, Crookes's radiometer furnished the last link in the strongest chain of evidence that supports any physical hypothesis.

Such being the constitution of gases, liquids must clearly be bodies in which the molecules wander in curvilinear paths, while in solids they move in orbits or quasi-orbits. (See my definition *solid* II, I, in the "Century Dictionary.")

We see that the resistance to compression and to interpenetration between sensible bodies is, by one of the prime propositions of the molecular theory, due in large measure to the kinetical energy of the particles, which must be supposed to be quite remote from one another, on the average, even in solids. This resistance is no doubt influenced by finite attractions and repulsions between the molecules. All the impenetrability of bodies that we can observe is, therefore, a limited impenetrability due to kinetic and positional energy. This being the case, we have no logical right to suppose that absolute impenetrability, or the exclusive occupancy of space, belongs to molecules or to atoms. It is an unwarranted hypothesis, not a *vera causa*.* Unless we are to give up the theory of energy, finite positional attractions and repulsions between molecules must be admitted. Absolute impenetrability would amount to an infinite repulsion at a certain distance. No analogy of known phenomena exists to excuse such a wanton violation of the principle of continuity as such a hypothesis is. In short, we are logically bound to adopt the Boscovichian idea that an atom is simply a distribution of component potential energy throughout space (this distribution being absolutely rigid), combined with inertia. The potential energy belongs to two molecules, and is to be conceived as different between molecules *A* and *B* from what it is between molecules *A* and *C*. The distribution of energy is not necessarily spherical. Nay, a molecule may conceivably have more than one center; it may even have a central curve, returning into itself. But I do not think there are any observed facts pointing to such multiple or linear centers. On the other hand, many facts relating to crystals, especially those observed by Voigt,† go to show that the distribution of

---

*By a *vera causa*, in the logic of science, is meant a state of things known to exist in some cases and supposed to exist in other cases, because it would account for observed phenomena.
†Wiedemann, *Annalen*, 1887–1889.

energy is harmonical but not concentric. We can easily calculate the forces that such atoms must exert upon one another by considering* that they are equivalent to aggregations of pairs of electrically positive and negative points infinitely near to one another. About such an atom there would be regions of positive and of negative potential, and the number and distribution of such regions would determine the valency of the atom, a number that it is easy to see would in many cases be somewhat indeterminate. I must not dwell further upon this hypothesis, at present. In another paper, its consequences will be further considered.

I cannot assume that the students of philosophy who read this magazine are thoroughly versed in modern molecular physics, and therefore it is proper to mention that the governing principle in this branch of science is Clausius's law of the virial. I will first state the law, and then explain the peculiar terms of the statement. This statement is that the total kinetic energy of the particles of a system in stationary motion is equal to the total virial. By a *system* is here meant a number of particles acting upon one another.† Stationary motion is a quasi-orbital motion among a system of particles so that none of them are removed to indefinitely great distances nor acquire indefinitely great velocities. The kinetic energy of a particle is the work that would be required to bring it to rest, independently of any forces that may be acting upon it. The virial of a pair of particles is half the work that the force that actually operates between them would do if, being independent of the distance, it were to bring them together. The equation of the virial is

$$\tfrac{1}{2} \Sigma mv^2 = \tfrac{1}{2} \Sigma\Sigma Rr.$$

Here m is the mass of a particle, v its velocity, R is the attraction between two particles, and r is the distance between them. The sign

---

*See Maxwell on Spherical Harmonics, in his *Electricity and Magnetism.*
†The word *system* has three peculiar meanings in mathematics. *(A)* It means an orderly exposition of the truths of astronomy, and hence a theory of the motions of the stars; as the Ptolemaic *system*, the Copernican *system*. This is much like the sense in which we speak of the Calvinistic *system* of theology, the Kantian *system* of philosophy, etc. *(B)* It means the aggregate of the planets considered as all moving in somewhat the same way, as the solar *system*; and hence any aggregate of particles moving under mutual forces. *(C)* It means a number of forces acting simultaneously upon a number of particles.

Σ on the left hand side signifies that the values of mv^2 are to be summed for all the particles, and $\Sigma\Sigma$ on the right hand side signifies that the values of Rr are to be summed for all the pairs of particles. If there is an external pressure P (as from the atmosphere) upon the system, and the volume of vacant space within the boundary of that pressure is V, then the virial must be understood as including $\frac{3}{2}$ PV, so that the equation is

$$\frac{1}{2}\Sigma mv^2 = \frac{3}{2}PV + \frac{1}{2}\Sigma\Sigma Rr.$$

There is strong (if not demonstrative) reason for thinking that the temperature of any body above the absolute zero ($-273°$ C.), is proportional to the average kinetic energy of its molecules, or say $a\theta$ where a is a constant and θ is the absolute temperature. Hence, we may write the equation

$$a\theta = \frac{1}{2}\overline{mv^2} = \frac{3}{2}\overline{PV} + \frac{1}{2}\overline{\Sigma Rr}$$

where the heavy lines above the different expressions signify that the average values for single molecules are to be taken. In 1872, a student in the University of Leyden, J. D. Van der Waals, propounded in his thesis for the doctorate a specialization of the equation of the virial that has since attracted great attention. Namely, he writes it

$$a\theta = \left(P + \frac{c}{V^2}\right)(V - b).$$

The quantity b is the volume of a molecule, which he supposes to be an impenetrable body, and all the virtue of the equation lies in this term which makes the equation a cubic in V, which is required to account for the shape of certain isothermal curves.* But if the idea of an impenetrable atom is illogical, that of an impenetrable molecule is almost absurd. For the kinetical theory of matter teaches us that a molecule is like a solar system of star-cluster in miniature. Unless we suppose that

---

*But, in fact, an inspection of these curves is sufficient to show that they are of a higher degree than the third. For they have the line $V = 0$, or some line V a constant for an asymptote, while for small values of P, the values of $d^2P/(dV)^2$ are positive.

in all heating of gases and vapors internal work is performed upon the molecules, implying that their atoms are at considerable distances, the whole kinetical theory of gases falls to the ground. As for the term added to P, there is no more than a partial and roughly approximative justification for it. Namely, let us imagine two spheres described around a particle as their center, the radius of the larger being so great as to include all the particles whose action upon the center is sensible, while the radius of the smaller is so large that a good many molecules are included within it. The possibility of describing such a sphere as the outer one implies that the attraction of the particles varies at some distances inversely as some higher power of the distance than the cube, or, to speak more clearly, that the attraction multiplied by the cube of the distance diminishes as the distance increases; for the number of particles at a given distance from any one particle is proportionate to the square of that distance and each of these gives a term of the virial which is the product of the attraction into the distance. Consequently unless the attraction multiplied by the cube of the distance diminished so rapidly with the distance as soon to become insensible, no such outer sphere as is supposed could be described. However, ordinary experience shows that such a sphere is possible; and consequently there must be distances at which the attraction does thus rapidly diminish as the distance increases. The two spheres, then, being so drawn, consider the virial of the central particle due to the particles between them. Let the density of the substance be increased, say, N times. Then, for every term, Rr, of the virial before the condensation, there will be N terms of the same magnitude after the condensation. Hence, the virial of each particle will be proportional to the density, and the equation of the virial becomes

$$a\theta = P\overline{V} + \frac{c}{\overline{V}}.$$

This omits the virial within the inner sphere, the radius of which is so taken that within that distance the number of particles is not proportional to the number in a large sphere. For Van der Waals this radius is the diameter of his hard molecules, which assumption gives his equation. But it is plain that the attraction between the molecules must to a certain extent modify their distribution, unless some peculiar conditions are fulfilled. The equation of Van der Waals can be approximately true therefore only for a gas. In a solid or liquid condition, in which the removal of a small amount of pressure has little effect on the volume, and where consequently the virial must be much greater than $P\overline{V}$, the virial must increase with the volume. For suppose we had a substance in a critical condition in which an increase of the volume would diminish the virial more than it would increase $\frac{3}{2}P\overline{V}$. If we were forcibly to diminish the volume of such a substance, when the temperature became equalized, the pressure that it could withstand would be less than before, and it would be still further condensed, and this would go on indefinitely until a condition were reached in which an increase of volume would increase $\frac{3}{2}P\overline{V}$ more than it would decrease the virial. In the case of solids, at least, P may be zero; so that the state reached would be one in which the virial increases with the volume, or the attraction between the particles does not increase so fast with a diminution of their distance as it would if the attraction were inversely as the distance.

Almost contemporaneously with Van der Waals's paper, another remarkable thesis for the doctorate was presented at Paris by Amagat. It related to the elasticity and expansion of gases, and to this subject the superb experimenter, its author, has devoted his whole subsequent life. Especially interesting are his observations of the volumes of ethylene and of carbonic acid at temperatures from 20° to 100° and at pressures ranging from an ounce to 5000 pounds to the square inch. As soon as Amagat had obtained these results, he remarked that the "coefficient of expansion at constant volume," as it is absurdly called, that is, the rate of variation of the pressure with the temperature, was very nearly constant for each volume. This accords with the equation of the virial, which gives

$$\frac{dp}{d\theta} = \frac{a}{\overline{V}} - \frac{d\Sigma\overline{R}r}{d\theta}$$

Now, the virial must be nearly independent of the temperature, and therefore the last term almost disappears. The virial would not be quite independent of the temperature, because if the temperature (i.e., the square of the velocity of the molecules) is lowered, and the pressure correspondingly lowered, so as to make the volume the same, the attractions of the molecules will have more time to produce their effects, and consequently, the pairs of molecules the closest together will be held together longer and closer; so that the virial will generally be increased by a decrease of temperature. Now, Amagat's experiments do show an excessively minute effect of this sort, at least, when the volumes are not too small. However, the observations are well enough satisfied by assuming the "coefficient of expansion at constant volume" to consist wholly of the first term, $a/\overline{V}$. Thus, Amagat's experiments enable us to determine the values of a and thence to calculate the virial; and this we find varies for carbonic acid gas nearly inversely to $\overline{V}^{0.9}$. There is, thus, a rough approximation to satisfying Van der Waals's equation. But the most interesting result of Amagat's experiments, for our purpose at any rate, is that the quantity a, though nearly constant for any one volume, differs considerably with the volume, nearly doubling when the volume is reduced fivefold. This can only indicate that the mean kinetic energy of a given mass of the gas for a given temperature is greater the more the gas is compressed. But the laws of mechanics appear to enjoin that the mean kinetic energy of a moving particle shall be constant at any given temperature. The only escape from contradiction, then, is to suppose that the mean mass of a moving particle diminishes upon the condensation of the gas. In other words, many of the molecules are dissociated, or broken up into atoms or submolecules. The idea that dissociation should be favored by diminishing the volume will be pronounced by physicists, at first blush, as contrary to all our experience. But it must be remembered that the circumstances we are speaking of, that of a gas under fifty or more atmospheres pressure, are also unusual. That the "coefficient of expansion under constant volume" when multiplied by the volumes should increase with a decrement of the volume is also quite contrary to ordinary experience; yet it undoubtedly takes place in all gases under great pressure. Again, the doctrine of Arrhenius[*] is now generally accepted, that the molecular conductivity of an elec-

---

[*]Anticipated by Clausius as long ago as 1857; and by Alexander Williamson in 1851.

trolyte is proportional to the dissociation of ions. Now the molecular conductivity of a fused electrolyte is usually superior to that of a solution. Here is a case, then, in which diminution of volume is accompanied by increased dissociation.

The truth is that several different kinds of dissociation have to be distinguished. In the first place, there is the dissociation of a chemical molecule to form chemical molecules under the regular action of chemical laws. This may be a double decomposition, as when iodhydric acid is dissociated, according to the formula

$$HI + HI = HH + II;$$

or, it may be a simple decomposition, as when pentachloride of phosphorus is dissociated according to the formula

$$PCl_5 = PCl_3 + ClCl.$$

All these dissociations require, according to the laws of thermochemistry, an elevated temperature. In the second place, there is the dissociation of a physically polymerous molecule, that is, of several chemical molecules joined by physical attractions. This I am inclined to suppose is a common concomitant of the heating of solids and liquids; for in these bodies there is no increase of compressibility with the temperature at all comparable with the increase of the expansibility. But, in the third place, there is the dissociation with which we are now concerned, which must be supposed to be a throwing off of unsaturated submolecules or atoms from the molecule. The molecule may, as I have said, be roughly likened to a solar system. As such, molecules are able to produce perturbations of one another's internal motions; and in this way a planet, i.e., a submolecule, will occasionally get thrown off and wander about by itself, till it finds another unsaturated submolecule with which it can unite. Such dissociation by perturbation will naturally be favored by the proximity of the molecules to one another.

Let us now pass to the consideration of that special substance, or rather class of substances, whose properties form the chief subject of botany and of zoology, as truly as those of the silicates form the chief subject of mineralogy: I mean the life-slimes, or protoplasm. Let us begin by cataloguing the general characters of these slimes. They one and all exist in two states of aggregation, a solid or nearly solid state and a liquid or nearly liquid state; but they do not pass from the former to the latter by ordinary fusion. They are readily decomposed by heat, especially in the liquid state; nor will they bear any considerable degree of cold. All their vital actions take place at temperatures very little below the point of decomposition. This extreme instability is one of numerous facts that demonstrate the chemical complexity of protoplasm. Every chemist will agree that they are far more complicated than the albumens. Now, albumen is estimated to contain in each molecule about a thousand atoms; so that it is natural to suppose that the protoplasms contain several thousands. We know that while they are chiefly composed of oxygen, hydrogen, carbon, and nitrogen, a large number of other elements enter into living bodies in small proportions; and it is likely that most of these enter into the composition of protoplasms. Now, since the numbers of chemical varieties increase at an enormous rate with the number of atoms per molecule, so that there are certainly hundreds of thousands of substances whose molecules contain twenty atoms or fewer, we may well suppose that the number of protoplasmic substances runs into the billions or trillions. Professor Arthur Cayley has given a mathematical theory of "trees," with a view of throwing a light upon such questions; and in that light the estimate of trillions (in the English senses) seems immoderately moderate. It is true that an opinion has been emitted, and defended among biologists, that there is but one kind of protoplasm; but the observations of biologists, themselves, have almost exploded that hypothesis, which from a chemical standpoint appears utterly incredible. The anticipation of the chemist would decidedly be that enough different chemical substances having protoplasmic characters might be formed to account, not only for the differences between nerve-slime and muscle-slime, between whale-slime and lion-slime, but also for those minuter pervasive variations that characterize different breeds and single individuals.

Protoplasm, when quiescent, is, broadly speaking, solid; but when it is disturbed in an appropriate way, or sometimes even spontaneously without external disturbance, it becomes, broadly speaking, liquid. A moner in this state is seen under the microscope to have streams within its matter; a slime-mould slowly flows by force of gravity. The liquefaction starts from the point of disturbance and spreads through the mass. This spreading, however, is not uniform in all directions; on the contrary it takes at one time one course, at another another, through the homogeneous mass, in a manner that seems a little mysterious. The cause of disturbance being removed, these motions gradually (with higher kinds of protoplasm, quickly) cease, and the slime returns to its solid condition.

The liquefaction of protoplasm is accompanied by a mechanical phenomenon. Namely, some kinds exhibit a tendency to draw themselves up into a globular form. This happens particularly with the contents of muscle cells. The prevalent opinion, founded on some of the most exquisite experimental investigations that the history of science can show, is undoubtedly that the contraction of muscle cells is due to osmotic pressure; and it must be allowed that that is a factor in producing the effect. But it does not seem to me that it satisfactorily accounts even for the phenomena of muscular contraction; and besides, even naked slimes often draw up in the same way. In this case, we seem to recognize an increase of the surface tension. In some cases, too, the reverse action takes place, extraordinary pseudopodia being put forth, as if the surface tension were diminished in spots. Indeed, such a slime always has a sort of skin, due no doubt to surface tension, and this seems to give way at the point where a pseudopodium is put forth.

Long-continued or frequently repeated liquefaction of the protoplasm results in an obstinate retention of the solid state, which we call fatigue. On the other hand repose in this state, if not too much prolonged, restores the liquefiability. These are both important functions.

The life-slimes have, further, the peculiar property of growing. Crystals also grow; their growth, however, consists merely in attracting matter like their own from the circumambient fluid. To suppose the growth of protoplasm of the same nature, would be to suppose this substance to be spontaneously generated in copious supplies wherever food is in solution. Certainly, it must be granted that protoplasm is but a chemical substance, and that there is no reason why it should not be formed synthetically like any other chemical substance. Indeed, William K. Clifford had clearly shown that we have overwhelming evidence that it is so formed. But to say that such formation is as regular and frequent as the assimilation of food is quite another matter. It is more consonant with the facts of observation to suppose that assimilated protoplasm is formed at the instant of assimilation, under the influence of the protoplasm already present. For each slime in its growth preserves its distinctive characters with wonderful truth, nerve-slime growing nerve-slime and muscle-slime muscle-slime, lion-slime growing lion-slime, and all the varieties of breeds and even individual characters being preserved in the growth. Now it is too much to suppose there are billions of different kinds of protoplasm floating about wherever there is food.

The frequent liquefaction of protoplasm increases its power of assimilating food; so much so, indeed, that it is questionable whether in the solid form it possesses this power.

The life-slime wastes as well as grows; and this too takes place chiefly if not exclusively in its liquid phases.

Closely connected with growth is reproduction; and though in higher forms this is a specialized function, it is universally true that wherever there is protoplasm, there is, will be, or has been a power of reproducing that same kind of protoplasm in a separated organism. Reproduction seems to involve the union of two sexes; though it is not demonstrable that this is always requisite.

Another physical property of protoplasm is that of taking habits. The course that the spread of liquefaction has taken in the past is rendered thereby more likely to be taken in the future; although there is no absolute certainty that the same path will be followed again.

Very extraordinary, certainly, are all these properties of protoplasm; as extraordinary as indubitable. But the one that has next to be mentioned, while equally undeniable, is infinitely more wonderful. It is that protoplasm feels. We have no direct evidence that this is true of protoplasm universally, and certainly some kinds feel far more than others. But there is a fair analogical inference that all protoplasm feels. It not only feels but exercises all the functions of mind.

Such are the properties of protoplasm. The Problem is to find a hypothesis of the molecular constitution of this compound that will account for these properties, one and all.

Some of them are obvious results of the excessively complicated constitution of the protoplasm molecule. All very complicated substances are unstable; and plainly a molecule of several thousand atoms may be separated in many ways into two parts in each of which the polar chemical forces are very nearly saturated. In the solid protoplasm, as in other solids, the molecules must be supposed to be moving, as it were, in orbits, or, at least, so as not to wander indefinitely. But this solid cannot be melted, for the same reason that starch cannot be melted; because an amount of heat insufficient to make the entire molecules wander is sufficient to break them up completely and cause them to form new and simpler molecules. But when one of the molecules is disturbed, even if it be not quite thrown out of its orbit at first, submolecules of perhaps several hundred atoms each are thrown off from it. These will soon acquire the same mean kinetic energy as the others, and therefore velocities several times as great. They will naturally begin to wander, and in wandering will perturb a great many other molecules and cause them in their turn to behave like the one originally deranged. So many molecules will thus be broken up, that even those that are intact will no longer be restrained within orbits, but will wander about freely. This is the usual condition of a liquid, as modern chemists understand it; for in all electrolytic liquids there is considerable dissociation.

But this process necessarily chills the substance, not merely on account of the heat of chemical combination, but still more because the number of separate particles being greatly increased, the mean kinetic energy must be less. The substance being a bad conductor, this heat is not at once restored. Now the particles moving more slowly, the attractions between them have time to take effect, and they approach the condition of equilibrium. But their dynamic equilibrium is found in the restoration of the solid condition, which therefore takes place, if the disturbance is not kept up.

When a body is in the solid condition, most of its molecules must be moving at the same rate, or, at least, at certain regular sets of rates;

otherwise the orbital motion would not be preserved. The distances of neighboring molecules must always be kept between a certain maximum and a certain minimum value. But if, without absorption of heat, the body be thrown into a liquid condition, the distances of neighboring molecules will be far more unequally distributed, and an effect upon the virial will result. The chilling of protoplasm upon its liquefaction must also be taken into account. The ordinary effect will no doubt be to increase the cohesion and with that the surface tension, so that the mass will tend to draw itself up. But in special cases, the virial will be increased so much that the surface tension will be diminished at points where the temperature is first restored. In that case, the outer film will give way and the tension at other places will aid in causing the general fluid to be poured out at those points, forming pseudopodia.

When the protoplasm is in a liquid state, and then only, a solution of food is able to penetrate its mass by diffusion. The protoplasm is then considerably dissociated; and so is the food, like all dissolved matter. If then the separated and unsaturated submolecules of the food happen to be of the same chemical species as submolecules of the protoplasm, they may unite with other submolecules of the protoplasm to form new molecules, in such a fashion that when the solid state is resumed, there may be more molecules of protoplasm than there were at the beginning. It is like the jack-knife whose blade and handle, after having been severally lost and replaced, were found and put together to make a new knife.

We have seen that protoplasm is chilled by liquefaction, and that this brings it back to the solid state, when the heat is recovered. This series of operations must be very rapid in the case of nerve-slime and even of muscle-slime, and may account for the unsteady or vibratory character of their action. Of course, if assimilation takes place, the heat of combination, which is probably trifling, is gained. On the other hand, if work is done, whether by nerve or by muscle, loss of energy must take place. In the case of the muscle, the mode by which the instantaneous part of the fatigue is brought about is easily traced out. If when the muscle contracts it be under stress, it will contract less than it otherwise would do, and there will be a loss of heat. It is like an engine that should work by dissolving salt in water and using the contraction during the solution to lift a weight, the salt being recovered afterwards by distillation. But the major part of fatigue has nothing to do with the correlation of forces. A man must labor hard to do in a quarter of an hour the work that draws from him enough heat to cool his body by a single degree. Meantime, he will be getting heated, he will be pouring out extra products of combustion, perspiration, etc., and he will be driving the blood at an accelerated rate through minute tubes at great expense. Yet all this will have little to do with his fatigue. He may sit quietly at his table writing, doing practically no physical work at all, and yet in a few hours be terribly fagged. This seems to be owing to the deranged submolecules of the nerve-slime not having had time to settle back into their proper combinations. When such submolecules are thrown out, as they must be from time to time, there is so much waste of material.

In order that a submolecule of food may be thoroughly and firmly assimilated into a broken molecule of protoplasm, it is necessary not only that it should have precisely the right chemical composition, but also that it should be at precisely the right spot at the right time and should be moving in precisely the right direction with precisely the right velocity. If all these conditions are not fulfilled, it will be more loosely retained than the other parts of the molecule; and every time it comes around into the situation in which it was drawn in, relatively to the other parts of that molecule and to such others as were near enough to be factors in the action, it will be in special danger of being thrown out again. Thus, when a partial liquefaction of the protoplasm takes place many times to about the same extent, it will, each time, be pretty nearly the same molecules that were last drawn in that are now thrown out. They will be thrown out, too, in about the same way, as to position, direction of motion, and velocity, in which they were drawn in; and this will be in about the same course that the ones last before them were thrown out. Not exactly, however; for the very cause of their being thrown off so easily is their not having fulfilled precisely the conditions of stable retention. Thus, the law of habit is accounted for, and with it its perculiar characteristic of not acting with exactitude.

It seems to me that this explanation of habit, aside from the question of its truth or falsity, has a certain value as an addition to our little store of mechanical examples of actions analogous to habit. All the others, so far as I know, are either statical or else involve forces which, taking only the sensible motions into account, violate the law of energy. It is so with the stream that wears its own bed. Here, the sand is carried to its most stable situation and left there. The law of energy forbids this; for when anything reaches a position of stable equilibrium, its momentum will be at a maximum, so that it can according to this law only be left at rest in an unstable situation. In all the statical illustrations, too, things are brought into certain states and left there. A garment receives folds and keeps them; that is, its limit of elasticity is exceeded. This failure to spring back is again an apparent violation of the law of energy; for the substance will not only not spring back of itself (which might be due to an unstable equilibrium being reached) but will not even do so when an impulse that way is applied to it. Accordingly, Professor James says "the phenomena of habit . . . are due to the plasticity of the . . . materials." Now, plasticity of materials means the having of a low limit of elasticity. (See the "Century Dictionary," under *solid*.) But the hypothetical constitution of protoplasm here proposed involves no forces but attractions and repulsions strictly following the law of energy. The action here, that is, the throwing of an atom out of its orbit in a molecule, and the entering of a new atom into nearly, but not quite the same orbit, is somewhat similar to the molecular actions that may be supposed to take place in a solid strained beyond its limit of elasticity. Namely, in that case certain molecules must be thrown out of their orbits, to settle down again shortly after into new orbits. In short, the plastic solid resembles protoplasm in being partially and temporarily liquefied by a slight mechanical force. But the taking of a set by a solid body has but a moderate resemblance to the taking of a habit, inasmuch as the characteristic feature of the latter, its inexactitude and want of complete determinacy, is not so marked in the former, if it can be said to be present there, at all.

The truth is that though the molecular explanation of habit is pretty vague on the mathematical side, there can be no doubt that systems of atoms having polar forces would act substantially in that manner, and the explanation is even too satisfactory to suit the convenience of an advocate of tychism. For it may fairly be urged that since the phenomena of habit may thus result from a purely mechanical arrangement, it is unnecessary to suppose that habit-taking is a primordial principle of the universe. But one fact remains unexplained mechanically, which concerns not only the facts of habit, but all cases of actions apparently violating the law of energy; it is that all these phenomena depend upon aggregations of trillions of molecules in one and the same condition and neighborhood; and it is by no means clear how they could have all been brought and left in the same place and state by any conservative forces. But let the mechanical explanation be as perfect as it may, the state of things that it supposes presents evidence of a primordial habit-taking tendency. For it shows us like things acting in like ways because they are alike. Now, those who insist on the doctrine of necessity will for the most part insist that the physical world is entirely individual. Yet law involves an element of generality. Now to say that generality is primordial, but generalization not, is like saying that diversity is primordial but diversification not. It turns logic upside down. At any rate, it is clear that nothing but a principle of habit, itself due to the growth by habit of an infinitesimal chance tendency toward habit-taking, is the only bridge that can span the chasm between the chance medley of chaos and the cosmos of order and law.

I shall not attempt a molecular explanation of the phenomena of reproduction, because that would require a subsidiary hypothesis, and carry me away from my main object. Such phenomena, universally diffused though they be, appear to depend upon special conditions; and we do not find that all protoplasm has reproductive powers.

But what is to be said of the property of feeling? If consciousness belongs to all protoplasm, by what mechanical constitution is this to be accounted for? The slime is nothing but a chemical compound. There is no inherent impossibility in its being formed synthetically in the laboratory, out of its chemical elements; and if it were so made, it would present all the characters of natural protoplasm. No doubt, then, it would feel. To hesitate to admit this would be puerile and ultrapuerile. By what element of the molecular arrangement, then, would that feeling be caused? This question cannot be evaded or pooh-poohed. Protoplasm certainly does feel; and unless we are to accept a weak dualism, the property must be shown to arise from some peculiarity of the mechanical system. Yet the attempt to deduce it from the three laws of mechanics, applied to never so ingenious a mechanical contrivance, would obviously be futile. It can never be explained, unless we admit that physical events are but degraded or undeveloped forms of psychical events. But once grant that the phenomena of matter are but the result of the sensibly complete sway of habits upon mind, and it only remains to explain why in the protoplasm these habits are to some slight extent broken up, so that according to the law of mind, in that special clause of it sometimes called the principle of accommodation,* feeling becomes intensified. Now the manner in which habits generally get broken up is this: Reactions usually terminate in the removal of a stimulus; for the excitation continues as long as the stimulus is present. Accordingly, habits are general ways of behavior that are associated with the removal of stimuli. But when the expected removal of the stimulus fails to occur, the excitation continues and increases, and nonhabitual reactions take place; and these tend to weaken the habit. If, then, we suppose that matter never does obey its ideal laws with absolute precision, but that there are almost insensible fortuitous departures from regularity, these will produce, in general, equally minute effects. But protoplasm is in an excessively unstable condition; and it is the characteristic of unstable equilibrium, that near that point excessively minute causes may produce startlingly large effects. Here then, the usual departures from regularity will be followed by others that are very great; and the large fortuitous departures from law so produced, will tend still further to break up the laws, supposing that these are of the nature of habits. Now, this breaking up of habit and renewed fortuitous spontaneity will, according to the law of mind, be accompanied by an intensification of feeling. The nerve-protoplasm is, without doubt, in the most unstable condition of any kind

*"Physiologically, ... accommodation means the breaking up a habit. .... Psychologically, it means reviving consciousness." Baldwin, *Psychology*, Part III, ch. i., § 5.

of matter; and consequently, there the resulting feeling is the most manifest.

Thus we see that the idealist has no need to dread a mechanical theory of life. On the contrary, such a theory, fully developed, is bound to call in a tychistic idealism as its indispensable adjunct. Wherever chance-spontaneity is found, there, in the same proportion, feeling exists. In fact, chance is but the outward aspect of that which within itself is feeling. I long ago showed that real existence, or thing-ness, consists in regularities. So, that primeval chaos in which there was no regularity was mere nothing, from a physical aspect. Yet it was not a blank zero; for there was an intensity of consciousness there in comparison with which all that we ever feel is but as the struggling of a molecule or two to throw off a little of the force of law to an endless and innumerable diversity of chance utterly unlimited.

But after some atoms of the protoplasm have thus become partially emancipated from law, what happens next to them? To understand this, we have to remember that no mental tendency is so easily strengthened by the action of habit as is the tendency to take habits. Now, in the higher kinds of protoplasm, especially, the atoms in question have not only long belonged to one molecule or another of the particular mass of slime of which they are parts; but before that, they were constituents of food of a protoplasmic constitution. During all this time, they have been liable to lose habits and to recover them again; so that now, when the stimulus is removed, and the foregone habits tend to reassert themselves, they do so in the case of such atoms with great promptness. Indeed, the return is so prompt that there is nothing but the feeling to show conclusively that the bonds of law have ever been relaxed.

In short, diversification is the vestige of chance-spontaneity; and wherever diversity is increasing, there chance must be operative. On the other hand, wherever uniformity is increasing, habit must be operative. But wherever actions take place under an established uniformity, there so much feeling as there may be takes the mode of a sense of reaction. That is the manner in which I am led to define the relation between the fundamental elements of consciousness and their physical equivalents.

It remains to consider the physical relations of general ideas. It may be well here to reflect that if matter has no existence except as a specialization of mind, it follows that whatever affects matter according to regular laws is itself matter. But all mind is directly or indirectly connected with all matter, and acts in a more or less regular way; so that all mind more or less partakes of the nature of matter. Hence, it would be a mistake to conceive of the psychical and the physical aspects of matter as two aspects absolutely distinct. Viewing a thing from the outside, considering its relations of action and reaction with other things, it appears as matter. Viewing it from the inside, looking at its immediate character as feeling, it appears as consciousness. These two views are combined when we remember that mechanical laws are nothing but acquired habits, like all the regularities of mind, including the tendency to take habits, itself; and that this action of habit is nothing but generalization, and generalization is nothing but the spreading of feelings. But the question is, how do general ideas appear in the molecular theory of protoplasm?

The consciousness of a habit involves a general idea. In each action of that habit certain atoms get thrown out of their orbit, and replaced by others. Upon all the different occasions it is different atoms that are thrown off, but they are analogous from a physical point of view, and there is an inward sense of their being analogous. Every time one of the associated feelings recurs, there is a more or less vague sense that there are others, that it has a general character, and of about what this general character is. We ought not, I think, to hold that in protoplasm habit never acts in any other than the particular way suggested above. On the contrary, if habit be a primary property of mind, it must be equally so of matter, as a kind of mind. We can hardly refuse to admit that wherever chance motions have general characters, there is a tendency for this generality to spread and to perfect itself. In that case, a general idea is a certain modification of consciousness that accompanies any regularity or general relation between chance actions.

The consciousness of a general idea has a certain "unity of the ego," in it, which is identical when it passes from one mind to another. It is, therefore, quite analogous to a person; and, indeed, a person is only a particular kind of general idea. Long ago, in the *Journal of Speculative Philosophy* (Vol. III, p. 156), I pointed out that a person is nothing but a symbol involving a general idea; but my views were, then, too nominalistic to enable me to see that every general idea has the unified living feeling of a person.

All that is necessary, upon this theory, to the existence of a person is that the feelings out of which he is constructed should be in close enough connection to influence one another. Here we can draw a consequence that it may be possible to submit to experimental test. Namely, if this be the case, there should be something like personal consciousness in bodies of men who are in intimate and intensely sympathetic communion. It is true that when the generalization of feeling has been carried so far as to include all within a person, a stopping place, in a certain sense, has been attained; and further generalization will have a less lively character. But we must not think it will cease. *Esprit de corps*, national sentiment, sympathy, are no mere metaphors. None of us can fully realize what the minds of corporations are, any more than one of my brain cells can know what the whole brain is thinking. But the law of mind clearly points to the existence of such personalities, and there are many ordinary observations that, if they were critically examined and supplemented by special experiments, might, as first appearances promise, give evidence of the influence of such greater persons upon individuals. It is often remarked that on one day half a dozen people, strangers to one another, will take it into their heads to do one and the same strange deed, whether it be a physical experiment, a crime, or an act of virtue. When the thirty thousand young people of the Society for Christian Endeavor were in New York, there seemed to me to be some mysterious diffusion of sweetness and light. If such a fact is capable of being made out anywhere, it should be in the church. The Christians have always been ready to risk their lives for the sake of having prayers in common, of getting together and praying simultaneously with great energy, and especially for their common body, for "the whole state of Christ's church militant here in earth," as one of the missals has it. This practice they have been keeping up everywhere, weekly, for many centuries. Surely, a personality ought to have developed in that church, in that "bride of Christ," as they call it, or else there is a strange break in the action of mind, and I shall have to acknowledge my views are much mistaken. Would not the societies for psychical research be more likely to break through the clouds, in seeking evidences of such corporate personality, than in seeking evidences of telepathy, which, upon the same theory, should be a far weaker phenomenon?

5. Evolutionary Love

AT FIRST BLUSH: COUNTER GOSPELS

Philosophy, when just escaping from its golden pupa-skin, mythology, proclaimed the great evolutionary agency of the universe to be Love. Or, since this pirate lingo, English, is poor in suchlike words, let us say Eros, the exuberance-love. Afterwards, Empedocles set up passionate-love and hate as the two coordinate powers of the universe. In some passages, kindness is the word. But certainly, in any sense in which it has an opposite, to be senior partner of that opposite, is the highest position that love can attain. Nevertheless, the ontological gospeller, in whose days those views were familiar topics, made the One Supreme Being, by whom all things have been made out of nothing, to be cherishing-love. What, then, can he say to hate? Never mind at this time, what the scribe of the apocalypse, if he were John, stung at length by persecution into a rage unable to distinguish suggestions of evil from visions of heaven, and so become the Slanderer of God to men, may have dreamed. The question is rather what the sane John thought, or ought to have thought, in order to carry out his idea consistently. His statement that God is love seems aimed at that saying of Ecclesiastes that we cannot tell whether God bears us love or hatred. "Nay," says John, "we can tell, and very simply! We know and have trusted the love which God hath in us. God is love." There is no logic in this, unless it means that God loves all men. In the preceding paragraph, he had said, "God is light and in him is no darkness at all." We are to understand, then, that as darkness is merely the defect of light, so hatred and evil are mere imperfect stages of ἀγάπη and ἀγαθόν, love and loveliness. This concords with that utterance reported in John's Gospel: "God sent not the Son into the world to judge the world; but that the world should through him be saved. He that believeth on him is not judged: he that believeth not hath been judged already . . . And this is the judgment, that the light is come into the world, and that men loved darkness rather than the light." That is to say, God visits no punishment on them; they punish themselves, by their natural affinity for the defective. Thus, the love that God is, is not a love of which hatred is the contrary; otherwise Satan would be a coordinate power; but it is a love which embraces hatred as an imperfect stage of it, an Anteros—yea, even needs hatred and hatefulness as its object. For self-love is no love; so if God's self is love, that which he loves must be defect of love; just as a luminary can light up only that which otherwise would be dark. Henry James, the Swedenborgian, says: "It is no doubt very tolerable finite or creaturely love to love one's own in another, to love another for his conformity to one's self: but nothing can be in more flagrant contrast with the creative Love, all whose tenderness *ex vi termini* must be reserved only for what intrinsically is most bitterly hostile and negative to itself." This is from "Substance and Shadow: an Essay on the Physics of Creation." It is a pity he had not filled his pages with things like this, as he was able easily to do, instead of scolding at his reader and at people generally, until the physics of creation was well nigh forgot. I must deduct, however, from what I just wrote: obviously no genius could make his every sentence as sublime as one that discloses for the problem of evil its everlasting solution.

The movement of love is circular, at one and the same impulse projecting creations into independency and drawing them into harmony. This seems complicated when stated so; but it is fully summed up in the simple formula we call the Golden Rule. This does not, of course, say, Do everything possible to gratify the egoistic impulses of others, but it says, Sacrifice your own perfection to the perfectionment of your neighbor. Nor must it for a moment be confounded with the Benthamite, or Helvetian, or Beccarian motto, Act for the greatest good of the greatest number. Love is not directed to abstractions but to persons; not to persons we do not know, nor to numbers of people but to our own dear ones, our family and neighbors. "Our neighbor," we remember, is one whom we live near, not locally perhaps, but in life and feeling.

Everybody can see that the statement of St. John is the formula of an evolutionary philosophy, which teaches that growth comes only from love, from—I will not say self-*sacrifice*, but from the ardent impulse to fulfill another's highest impulse. Suppose, for example, that I have an idea that interests me. It is my creation. It is my creature; for as shown in last July's *Monist*, it is a little person. I love it; and I will sink myself in perfecting it. It is not by dealing out cold justice to the circle of my ideas that I can make them grow, but by cherishing and tending them as I would the flowers in my garden. The philosophy we draw from John's gospel is that this is the way mind develops; and as for the cosmos, only so far as it yet is mind, and so has life, is it capable of further evolution. Love, recognizing germs of loveliness in the hateful, gradually warms it into life, and makes it lovely. That is the sort of evolution that every careful student of my essay "The Law of Mind" must see that *synechism* calls for.

The nineteenth century is now fast sinking into the grave, and we all begin to review its doings and to think what character it is destined to bear as compared with other centuries in the minds of future historians. It will be called, I guess, the Economical Century; for political economy has more direct relations with all the branches of its activity than has any other science. Well, political economy has its formula of redemption, too. It is this: Intelligence in the service of greed ensures the justest prices, the fairest contracts, the most enlightened conduct of all the dealings between men, and leads to the *summum bonum*, food in plenty and perfect comfort. Food for whom? Why, for the greedy master of intelligence. I do not mean to say that this is one of the legitimate conclusions of political economy, the scientific character of which I fully acknowledge. But the study of doctrines, themselves true, will often temporarily encourage generalizations extremely false, as the study of physics has encouraged necessitarianism. What I say, then, is that the great attention paid to economical questions during our century has induced an exaggeration of the beneficial effects of greed and of the unfortunate results of sentiment, until there has resulted a philosophy that comes unwittingly to this, that greed is the great agent in the elevation of the human race and in the evolution of the universe.

I open a handbook of political economy—the most typical and middling one I have at hand—and there find some remarks of which I will here make a brief analysis. I omit qualifications, sops thrown to Cerberus, phrases to placate Christian prejudice, trappings that serve to hide from author and reader alike the ugly nakedness of the greedgod. But I have surveyed my position. The author enumerates "three motives to human action:

The love of self;

The love of a limited class having common interests and feelings with one's self;

The love of mankind at large."

Remark, at the outset, what obsequious title is bestowed on greed— "the love of self." Love! The second motive *is* love. In place of "a limited class" put "certain persons," and you have a fair description. Taking "class" in the old-fashioned sense, a weak kind of love is described. In the sequel, there seems to be some haziness as to the delimitation of this motive. By the love of mankind at large, the author does not mean that deep, subconscious passion that is properly so called; but merely public spirit, perhaps little more than a fidget about pushing ideas. The author proceeds to a comparative estimate of the worth of these motives. Greed, says he, but using, of course, another word, "is not so great an evil as is commonly supposed. . . . Every man can promote his own interests a great deal more effectively than he can promote any one else's, or than any one else can promote his." Besides, as he remarks on another page, the more miserly a man is, the more good he does. The second motive "is the most dangerous one to which society is exposed." Love is all very pretty: "no higher or purer source of human happiness exists." (Ahem!) But it is a "source of enduring injury," and, in short, should be overruled by something wiser. What is this wise motive? We shall see.

As for public spirit, it is rendered nugatory by the "difficulties in the way of its effective operation." For example, it might suggest putting checks upon the fecundity of the poor and the vicious; and "no measure of repression would be too severe," in the case of criminals. The hint is broad. But unfortunately, you cannot induce legislatures to take such measures, owing to the pestiferous "tender sentiments of man towards man." It thus appears, that public spirit, or Benthamism, is not strong enough to be the effective tutor of love (I am skipping to another page), which must therefore be handed over to "the motives which animate men in the pursuit of wealth," in which alone we can confide, and which "are in the highest degree beneficent."* Yes, in the "highest degree" without exception are they beneficent to the being upon whom all their blessings are poured out, namely, the Self, whose "sole object," says the writer in accumulating wealth is his individual "sustenance and enjoyment." Plainly, the author holds the notion that some other motive might be in a higher degree beneficent even for the man's self to be a paradox wanting in good sense. He seeks to gloze and modify his doctrine; but he lets the perspicacious reader see what his animating principle is; and when, holding the opinions I have repeated, he at the same time acknowledges that society could not exist upon a basis of intelligent greed alone, he simply pigeon-holes himself as one of the eclectics of inharmonious opinions. He wants his mammon flavored with a *soupçon* of god.

The economists accuse those to whom the enunciation of their atrocious villainies communicates a thrill of horror of being *sentimentalists*. It may be so: I willingly confess to having some tincture of sentimentalism in me, God be thanked! Ever since the French Revolution brought this leaning of thought into ill-repute—and not altogether undeservedly, I must admit, true, beautiful, and good as that great movement was—it has been the tradition to picture sentimentalists as persons incapable of logical thought and unwilling to look facts in the eyes. This tradition may be classed with the French tradition that an Englishman says *godam* at every second sentence, the English tradition that an American

---

* How can a writer have any respect for science, as such, who is capable of confounding with the scientific propositions of political economy, which have nothing to say concerning what is "beneficent," such brummagem generalizations as this?

talks about "Britishers," and the American tradition that a Frenchman carries forms of etiquette to an inconvenient extreme, in short with all those traditions that survive simply because the men who use their eyes and ears are few and far between. Doubtless some excuse there was for all those opinions in days gone by; and sentimentalism, when it was the fashionable amusement to spend one's evening in a flood of tears over a woeful performance on a candle-lit stage, sometimes made itself a little ridiculous. But what after all is sentimentalism? It is an *ism*, a doctrine, namely, the doctrine that great respect should be paid to the natural judgments of the sensible heart. This is what sentimentalism precisely is; and I entreat the reader to consider whether to condemn it is not of all blasphemies the most degrading. Yet the nineteenth century has steadily condemned it, because it brought about the Reign of Terror. That it did so is true. Still, the whole question is one of *how much*. The reign of terror was very bad; but now the Gradgrind banner has been this century long flaunting in the face of heaven, with an insolence to provoke the very skies to scowl and rumble. Soon a flash and quick peal will shake economists quite out of their complacency, too late. The twentieth century, in its latter half, shall surely see the deluge-tempest burst upon the social order—to clear upon a world as deep in ruin as that greed-philosophy has long plunged it into guilt. No postthermidorian highjinks then!

So a miser is a beneficent power in a community, is he? With the same reason precisely, only in a much higher degree, you might pronounce the Wall Street sharp to be a good angel, who takes money from heedless persons not likely to guard it properly, who wrecks feeble enterprises better stopped, and who administers wholesome lessons to unwary scientific men, by passing worthless checks upon them—as you did, the other day, to me, my millionaire master in glomery, when you thought you saw your way to using my process without paying for it, and of so bequeathing to your children something to boast of their father about—and who by a thousand wiles puts money at the service of intelligent greed, in his own person. Bernard Mandeville, in his "Fable of the Bees," maintains that private vices of all descriptions are public benefits, and proves it, too, quite as cogently as the economist proves his point concerning the miser. He even argues, with no slight force, that but for vice civilization would never have existed. In the same spirit, it has been strongly maintained and is today widely believed that all acts of charity and benevolence, private and public, go seriously to degrade the human race.

The "Origin of Species" of Darwin merely extends politico-economical views of progress to the entire realm of animal and vegetable life. The vast majority of our contemporary naturalists hold the opinion that the true cause of those exquisite and marvelous adaptations of nature for which, when I was a boy, men used to extol the divine wisdom, is that creatures are so crowded together that those of them that happen to have the slightest advantage force those less pushing into situations unfavorable to multiplication or even kill them before they reach the age of reproduction. Among animals, the mere mechanical individualism is vastly reinforced as a power making for good by the animal's ruthless greed. As Darwin puts it on his title page, it is the struggle for existence; and he should have added for his motto: Every individual for himself, and the Devil take the hindmost! Jesus, in his sermon on the Mount, expressed a different opinion.

Here, then, is the issue. The Gospel of Christ says that progress comes from every individual merging his individuality in sympathy with his neighbors. On the other side, the conviction of the nineteenth century is that progress takes place by virtue of every individual's striving for himself with all his might and trampling his neighbor under foot whenever he gets a chance to do so. This may accurately be called the Gospel of Greed.

Much is to be said on both sides. I have not concealed, I could not conceal, my own passionate predilection. Such a confession will probably shock my scientific brethren. Yet the strong feeling is in itself, I think, an argument of some weight in favor of the agapastic theory of evolution —so far as it may be presumed to bespeak the normal judgment of the Sensible Heart. Certainly, if it were possible to believe in agapasm without believing it warmly, that fact would be an argument against the truth of the doctrine. At any rate, since the warmth of feeling exists, it should on every account be candidly confessed; especially since it creates a liability to onesidedness on my part against which it behooves my readers and me to be severally on our guard.

SECOND THOUGHTS: IRENICA

Let us try to define the logical affinities of the different theories of evolution. Natural selection, as conceived by Darwin, is a mode of evolution in which the only positive agent of change in the whole passage from moner to man is fortuitous variation. To secure advance in a definite direction chance has to be seconded by some action that shall hinder the propagation of some varieties or stimulate that of others. In natural selection, strictly so called, it is the crowding out of the weak. In sexual selection, it is the attraction of beauty, mainly.

The "Origin of Species" was published toward the end of the year 1859. The preceding years since 1846 had been one of the most productive seasons—or if extended so as to cover the great book we are considering, *the* most productive period of equal length in the entire history of science from its beginnings until now. The idea that chance begets order, which is one of the cornerstones of modern physics (although Dr. Paul Carus considers it "the weakest point in Mr. Peirce's system,") was at that time put into its clearest light. L. A. J. Quetelet had opened the discussion by his "Letters on the Application of Probabilities to the Moral and Political Sciences," a work that deeply impressed the best minds of that day, and to which Sir John Herschel had drawn general attention in Great Britain. In 1857, the first volume of Henry Buckle's "History of Civilization" had created a tremendous sensation, owing to the use he made of this same idea. Meantime, the "statistical method" had, under that very name, been applied with brilliant success to molecular physics. Dr. John Herapath, an English chemist, had in 1847 outlined the kinetical theory of gases in his "Mathematical Physics"; and the interest the theory excited had been refreshed in 1856 by notable memoirs by R. J. E. Clausius and Krönig. In the very summer preceding Darwin's publication, James Clerk Maxwell had read before the British Association the first and most important of his researches on this subject. The consequence was that the idea that fortuitous events may result in a physical law, and further that this is the way in which those laws that appear to conflict with the principle of the conservation of energy are to be explained, had taken a strong hold upon the minds of all who were abreast of the leaders of thought. By such minds, it was inevitable that the "Origin of Species," whose teaching was simply the application of the same principle to the explanation of another "nonconservative" action, that of organic development, should be hailed and welcomed. The sublime discovery of the conservation of energy by H. L. F. Helmholtz in 1847, and that of the mechanical theory of heat by Clausius and by W. J. Rankine, independently, in 1850, had decidedly overawed all those who might have been inclined to sneer at physical science. Thereafter a belated poet still harping upon "science peddling with the names of things" would fail of his effect. Mechanism was now known to be all, or very nearly so. All this time, utilitarianism—that improved substitute for the Gospel—was in its fullest feather; and was a natural ally of an individualistic theory. Dean Mansell's injudicious advocacy had led to mutiny among the bondsmen of Sir William Hamilton, and the nominalism of John Stuart Mill had profited accordingly; and although the real science that Darwin was leading men to was sure some day to give a death blow to the sham science of Mill, yet there were several elements of the Darwinian theory that were sure to charm the followers of Mill. Another thing: anaesthetics had been in use for thirteen years. Already, people's acquaintance with suffering had dropped off very much; and as a consequence, that unlovely hardness by which our times are so contrasted with those that immediately preceded them, had already set in, and inclined people to relish a ruthless theory. The reader would quite mistake the drift of what I am saying if he were to understand me as wishing to suggest that any of those things (except perhaps Malthus) influenced Darwin himself. What I mean is that his hypothesis, while without dispute one of the most ingenious and pretty ever devised, and while argued with a wealth of knowledge, a strength of logic, a charm of rhetoric, and above all with a certain magnetic genuineness that was almost irresistible, did not appear, at first, at all near to being proved; and to a sober mind its case looks less hopeful now than it did twenty years ago; but the extraordinarily favorable reception it met with was plainly owing, in large measure, to its ideas being those toward which the age was favorably disposed, especially, because of the encouragement it gave to the greed philosophy.

Diametrically opposed to evolution by chance, are those theories that attribute all progress to an inward necessary principle, or other form of necessity. Many naturalists have thought that if an egg is destined to go through a certain series of embryological transformations, from which it is pefectly certain not to deviate, and if in geological time almost exactly the same forms appear successively, one replacing another in the same order, the strong presumption is that this latter succession was as predeterminate and certain to take place as the former. So, Nägeli, for instance, conceives that it somehow follows from the first law of motion and the peculiar, but unknown, molecular constitution of protoplasm, that forms must complicate themselves more and more. Albert von Kölliker makes one form generate another after a certain maturation has been accomplished. Weismann, too, though he calls himself a Darwinian, holds that nothing is due to chance, but that all forms are simple mechanical resultants of the heredity from two parents.* It is very noticeable that all these different sectaries seek to import into their science a mechanical necessity to which the facts that come under their observation do not point. Those geologists who think that the variation of species is due to cataclysmic alterations of climate or of the chemical constitution of the air and water are also making mechanical necessity the chief factor of evolution.

Evolution by sporting and evolution by mechanical necessity are conceptions warring against one another. A third method, that supersedes their strife, lies enwrapped in the theory of Lamarck. According to his view, all that distinguishes the highest organic forms from the most rudimentary has been brought about by little hypertrophies or atrophies that have affected individuals early in their lives, and have been transmitted to their offspring. Such a transmission of acquired characters is of the general nature of habit-taking, and this is the representative and derivative within the physiological domain of the law of mind. Its action is essentially dissimilar to that of a physical force; and that is the secret of the repugnance of such necessitarians as Weismann to admitting its existence. The Lamarckians further suppose that although some of the modifications of form so transmitted were originally

* I am happy to find that Dr. Carus, too, ranks Weismann among the opponents of Darwin, notwithstanding his flying that flag.

due to mechanical causes, yet the chief factors of their first production were the straining of endeavor and the overgrowth superinduced by exercise, together with the opposite actions. Now, endeavor, since it is directed toward an end, is essentially psychical, even though it be sometimes unconscious; and the growth due to exercise, as I argued in my last paper, follows a law of a character quite contrary to that of mechanics.

Lamarckian evolution is thus evolution by the force of habit.—That sentence slipped off my pen while one of those neighbors whose function in the social cosmos seems to be that of an Interrupter, was asking me a question. Of course, it is nonsense. Habit is mere inertia, a resting on one's oars, not a propulsion. Now it is energetic projaculation (lucky there is such a word, or this untried hand might have been put to inventing one) by which in the typical instances of Lamarckian evolution the new elements of form are first created. Habit, however, forces them to take practical shapes, compatible with the structures they affect, and in the form of heredity and otherwise, gradually replaces the spontaneous energy that sustains them. Thus, habit plays a double part; it serves to establish the new features, and also to bring them into harmony with the general morphology and function of the animals and plants to which they belong. But if the reader will now kindly give himself the trouble of turning back a page or two, he will see that this account of Lamarckian evolution coincides with the general description of the action of love, to which, I suppose, he yielded his assent.

Remembering that all matter is really mind, remembering, too, the continuity of mind, let us ask what aspect Lamarckian evolution takes on within the domain of consciousness. Direct endeavor can achieve almost nothing. It is as easy by taking thought to add a cubit to one's stature, as it is to produce an idea acceptable to any of the Muses by merely straining for it, before it is ready to come. We haunt in vain the sacred well and throne of Mnemosyne; the deeper workings of the spirit take place in their own slow way, without our connivance. Let but their bugle sound, and we may then make our effort, sure of an oblation for the altar of whatsoever divinity its savor gratifies. Besides this inward process, there is the operation of the environment, which goes to break up habits destined to be broken up and so to render the mind lively. Everybody knows that the long continuance of a routine of habit makes us lethargic, while a succession of surprises wonderfully brightens the ideas. Where there is a motion, where history is amaking, there is the focus of mental activity, and it has been said that the arts and sciences reside within the temple of Janus, waking when that is open, but slumbering when it is closed. Few psychologists have perceived how fundamental a fact this is. A portion of mind abundantly commissured to other portions works almost mechanically. It sinks to the condition of a railway junction. But a portion of mind almost isolated, a spiritual peninsula, or *cul-de-sac*, is like a railway terminus. Now mental commissures are habits. Where they abound, originality is not needed and is not found; but where they are in defect, spontaneity is set free. Thus, the first step in the Lamarckian evolution of mind is the putting of sundry thoughts into situations in which they are free to play. As to growth by exercise, I have already shown, in discussing "Man's Glassy Essence," in last October's *Monist*, what its *modus operandi* must be conceived to be, at least, until a second equally definite hypothesis shall have been offered. Namely, it consists of the flying asunder of molecules, and the reparation of the parts by new matter. It is, thus, a sort of reproduction. It takes place only during exercise, because the activity of protoplasm consists in the molecular disturbance which is its necessary condition. Growth by exercise takes place also in the mind. Indeed, that is what it is to *learn*. But the most perfect illustration is the development of a philosophical idea by being put into practice. The conception that appeared, at first, as unitary, splits up into special cases; and into each of these new thought must enter to make a practicable idea. This new thought, however, follows pretty closely the model of the parent conception; and thus a homogeneous development takes place. The parallel between this and the course of molecular occurrences is apparent. Patient attention will be able to trace all these elements in the transaction called learning.

Three modes of evolution have thus been brought before us; evolution by fortuitous variation, evolution by mechanical necessity, and evolution by creative love. We may term them *tychastic* evolution, or *tychasm*, *anancastic* evolution, or *anancasm*, and *agapastic* evolution, or *agapasm*. The doctrines that represent these as severally of principal importance, we may term *tychasticism*, *anancasticism*, and *agapasticism*. On the other hand the mere propositions that absolute chance, mechanical necessity, and the law of love are severally operative in the cosmos, may receive the names of *tychism*, *anancism*, and *agapism*.

All three modes of evolution are composed of the same general elements. Agapasm exhibits them the most clearly. The good result is here brought to pass, first, by the bestowal of spontaneous energy by the parent upon the offspring, and, second, by the disposition of the latter to catch the general idea of those about it and thus to subserve the general purpose. In order to express the relation that tychasm and anancasm bear to agapasm, let me borrow a word from geometry. An ellipse crossed by a straight line is a sort of cubic curve; for a cubic is a curve that is cut thrice by a straight line; now a straight line might cut the ellipse twice and its associated straight line a third time. Still the ellipse with the straight line across it would not have the characteristics of a cubic. It would have, for instance, no contrary flexure, which no true cubic wants; and it would have two nodes, which no true cubic has. The geometers say that it is a *degenerate* cubic. Just so, tychasm and anancasm are degenerate forms of agapasm.

Men who seek to reconcile the Darwinian idea with Christianity will remark that tychastic evolution, like the agapastic, depends upon a reproductive creation, the forms preserved being those that use the spontaneity conferred upon them in such ways as to be drawn into harmony with their original, quite after the Christian scheme. Very good! This only shows that just as love cannot have a contrary, but must embrace what is most opposed to it, as a degenerate case of it, so tychasm is a kind of agapasm. Only, in the tychastic evolution progress is solely owing to the distribution of the napkin-hidden talent of the rejected servant among those not rejected, just as ruined gamesters leave their money on the table to make those not yet ruined so much the richer. It makes the felicity of the lambs just the damnation of the goats, transposed to the other side of the equation. In genuine agapasm, on the other hand, advance takes place by virtue of a positive sympathy among the created springing from continuity of mind. This is the idea which tychasticism knows not how to manage.

The anancasticist might here interpose, claiming that the mode of evolution for which he contends agrees with agapasm at the point at which tychasm departs from it. For it makes development go through certain phases, having its inevitable ebbs and flows, yet tending on the whole to a foreordained perfection. Bare existence by this its destiny betrays an intrinsic affinity for the good. Herein, it must be admitted, anancasm shows itself to be in a broad acception a species of agapasm. Some forms of it might easily be mistaken for the genuine agapasm. The Hegelian philosophy is such an anancasticism. With its revelatory religion, with its synechism (however imperfectly set forth), with its "reflection," the whole idea of the theory is superb, almost sublime. Yet, after all, living freedom is practically omitted from its method. The whole movement is that of a vast engine, impelled by a *vis a tergo*, with a blind and mysterious fate of arriving at a lofty goal. I mean that such an engine it *would* be, if it really worked; but in point of fact, it is a Keely motor. Grant that it really acts as it professes to act, and there is nothing to do but accept the philosophy. But never was there seen such an example of a long chain of reasoning—shall I say with a flaw in every link?—no, with every link a handful of sand, squeezed into shape in a dream. Or say, it is a pasteboard model of a philosophy that in reality does not exist. If we use the one precious thing it contains, the idea of it, introducing the tychism that the arbitrariness of its every step suggests, and make that the support of a vital freedom that is the breath of the spirit of love, we may be able to produce that genuine agapasticism, at which Hegel was aiming.

A THIRD ASPECT: DISCRIMINATION

In the very nature of things, the line of demarcation between the three modes of evolution is not perfectly sharp. That does not prevent its being quite real; perhaps it is rather a mark of its reality. There is in the nature of things no sharp line of demarcation between the three fundamental colors, red, green, and violet. But for all that they are really different. The main question is whether three radically different evolutionary elements have been operative; and the second question is what are the most striking characteristics of whatever elements have been operative.

I propose to devote a few pages to a very slight examination of these questions in their relation to the historical development of human thought. I first formulate for the reader's convenience the briefest possible definitions of the three conceivable modes of development of thought, distinguishing also two varieties of anancasm and three of agapasm. The tychastic development of thought, then, will consist in slight departures from habitual ideas in different directions indifferently, quite purposeless and quite unconstrained whether by outward circumstances or by force of logic, these new departures being followed by unforeseen results that tend to fix some of them as habits more than others. The anancastic development of thought will consist of new ideas adopted without foreseeing whither they tend, but having a character determined by causes either external to the mind, such as changed circumstances of life, or internal to the mind as logical developments of ideas already accepted, such as generalizations. The agapastic development of thought is the adoption of certain mental tendencies, not altogether heedlessly, as in tychasm, nor quite blindly by the mere force of circumstances or of logic, as in anancasm, but by an immediate attraction for the idea itself, whose nature is divined before the mind possesses it, by the power of sympathy, that is, by virtue of the continuity of mind; and this mental tendency may be of three varieties, as follows. First, it may affect a whole people or community in its collective personality, and be thence communicated to such individuals as are in powerfully sympathetic connection with the collective people, although they may be intellectually incapable of attaining the idea by their private understandings or even perhaps of consciously apprehending it. Second, it may affect a private person directly, yet so that he is only enabled to apprehend the idea, or to appreciate its attractiveness, by virtue of his sympathy with his neighbors, under the influence of a striking experience or development of thought. The conversion of St. Paul may be taken as an example of what is meant. Third, it may affect an individual, independently of his human affections, by virtue of an attraction it exercises upon his mind, even before he has comprehended it. This is the phenomenon which has been well called the *divination* of genius; for it is due to the continuity between the man's mind and the Most High.

Let us next consider by means of what tests we can discriminate between these different categories of evolution. No absolute criterion is possible in the nature of things, since in the nature of things there is no sharp line of demarcation between the different classes. Nevertheless, quantitative symptoms may be found by which a sagacious and sympathetic judge of human nature may be able to estimate the approximate proportions in which the different kinds of influence are commingled.

So far as the historical evolution of human thought has been tychastic, it should have proceeded by insensible or minute steps; for such is the nature of chances when so multiplied as to show phenomena of regularity. For example, assume that of the nativeborn white adult males of the United States in 1880, one fourth part were below 5 feet 4 inches in stature and one fourth part above 5 feet 8 inches. Then by the principles of probability, among the whole population, we should expect

216	under 4 feet 6 inches			216	above 6 feet 6 inches		
48	"	4	" 5 "	48	"	6	" 7 "
9	"	4	" 4 "	9	"	6	" 8 "
less than 2	"	4	" 3 "	less than 2	"	6	" 9 "

I set down these figures to show how insignificantly few are the cases in which anything very far out of the common run presents itself by chance. Though the stature of only every second man is included within the four inches between 5 feet 4 inches and 5 feet 8 inches, yet if this interval be extended by thrice four inches above and below, it will embrace all our 8 millions odd of nativeborn adult white males (of 1880), except only 9 taller and 9 shorter.

The test of minute variation, if *not* satisfied, absolutely negatives tychasm. If it *is* satisfied, we shall find that it negatives anancasm but not agapasm. We want a positive test, satisfied by tychasm, only. Now wherever we find men's thought taking by imperceptible degrees a turn contrary to the purposes that animate them, in spite of their highest impulses, there, we may safely conclude, there has been a tychastic action.

Students of the history of mind there be of an erudition to fill an imperfect scholar like me with envy edulcorated by joyous admiration, who maintain that ideas when just started are and can be little more than freaks, since they cannot yet have been critically examined, and further that everywhere and at all times progress has been so gradual that it is difficult to make out distinctly what original step any given man has taken. It would follow that tychasm has been the sole method of intellectual development. I have to confess I cannot read history so; I cannot help thinking that while tychasm has sometimes been operative, at others great steps covering nearly the same ground and made by different men independently, have been mistaken for a succession of small steps, and further that students have been reluctant to admit a real entitative "spirit" of an age or of a people, under the mistaken and unscrutinized impression that they should thus be opening the door to wild and unnatural hypotheses. I find, on the contrary, that, however it may be with the education of individual minds, the historical development of thought has seldom been of a tychastic nature, and exclusively in backward and barbarising movements. I desire to speak with the extreme modesty that befits a student of logic who is required to survey so very wide a field of human thought that he can cover it only by a reconnaisance, to which only the greatest skill and most adroit methods can impart any value at all; but, after all, I can only express my own opinions and not those of anybody else; and in my humble judgment, the largest example of tychasm is afforded by the history of Christianity, from about its establishment by Constantine, to, say, the time of the Irish monasteries, an era or eon of about 500 years. Undoubtedly the external circumstance that more than all others at first inclined men to accept Christianity in its loveliness and tenderness, was the fearful extent to which society was broken up into units by the unmitigated greed and hard-heartedness into which the Romans had seduced the world. And yet it was that very same fact, more than any other external circumstance, that fostered that bitterness against the wicked world of which the primitive Gospel of Mark contains not a single trace. At least, I do not detect it in the remark about the blasphemy against the Holy Ghost, where nothing is said about vengeance, nor even in that speech where the closing lines of Isaiah are quoted, about the worm and the fire that feed upon the "carcasses of the men that have transgressed against me." But little by little the bitterness increases until in the last book of the New Testament, its poor distracted author represents that all the time Christ was talking about having come to save the world, the secret design was to catch the entire human race, with the exception of a paltry 144,000, and souse them all in a brimstone lake, and as the smoke of their torment went up for ever and ever, to turn and remark, "There is no curse any more." Would it be an insensible smirk or a fiendish grin that should accompany such an utterance? I wish I could believe St. John did not write it; but it is his gospel that tells about the "resurrection unto condemnation,"—that is, of men's being resuscitated just for the sake of torturing them;—and, at any rate, the Revelation is a very ancient composition. One can understand that the early Christians were like men trying with all their might to climb a steep declivity of smooth wet clay; the deepest and truest element of their life, animating both heart and head, was universal love; but they were continually, and against their wills, slipping into a party spirit, every slip serving as a precedent, in a fashion but too familiar to every man. This party feeling insensibly grew until by about A.D. 330 the lusture of the pristine integrity that in St. Mark reflects the white spirit of light was so far tarnished that Eusebius, (the Jared Sparks of that day), in the preface to his History, could announce his intention of exaggerating everything that tended to the glory of the church and of suppressing whatever might disgrace it. His Latin contemporary Lactantius is worse, still; and so the darkling went on increasing until before the end of the century the great library of Alexandria was destroyed by Theophilus,* until Gregory the Great, two centuries later, burned the great library of Rome, proclaiming that "Ignorance is the mother of devotion," (which

*See J. W. Draper, *History of Intellectual Development of Europe*, chap. x, 2nd ed., New York, 1876.

is true, just as oppression and injustice is the mother of spirituality), until a sober description of the state of the church would be a thing our not too nice newspapers would treat as "unfit for publication." All this movement is shown by the application of the test given above to have been tychastic. Another very much like it on a small scale, only a hundred times swifter, for the study of which there are documents by the library-full, is to be found in the history of the French Revolution.

Anancastic evolution advances by successive strides with pauses between. The reason is that in this process a habit of thought having been overthrown is supplanted by the next strongest. Now this next strongest is sure to be widely disparate from the first, and as often as not is its direct contrary. It reminds one of our old rule of making the second candidate vice-president. This character, therefore, clearly distinguishes anancasm from tychasm. The character that distinguishes it from agapasm is its purposelessness. But external and internal anancasm have to be examined separately. Development under the pressure of external circumstances, or cataclasmic evolution, is in most cases unmistakable enough. It has numberless degrees of intensity, from the brute force, the plain war, which has more than once turned the current of the world's thought, down to the hard fact of evidence, or what has been taken for it, which has been known to convince men by hordes. The only hesitation that can subsist in the presence of such a history is a quantitative one. Never are external influences the only ones that affect the mind, and therefore it must be a matter of judgment for which it would scarcely be worthwhile to attempt to set rules, whether a given movement is to be regarded as principally governed from without or not. In the rise of medieval thought, I mean scholasticism and the synchronistic art developments, undoubtedly the crusades and the discovery of the writings of Aristotle were powerful influences. The development of scholasticism from Roscellin to Albertus Magnus closely follows the successive steps in the knowledge of Aristotle. Carl Prantl thinks that that is the whole story, and few men have thumbed more books than Prantl. He has done good solid work, notwithstanding his slap-dash judgments. But we shall never make so much as a good beginning of comprehending scholasticism until the whole has been systematically explored and digested by a company of students regularly organized and held under the rule for that purpose. But as for the period we are now specially considering, that which synchronized the Romanesque architecture, the literature is easily mastered. It does not quite justify Prantl's dicta as to the slavish dependence of these authors upon their authorities. Moreover, they kept a definite purpose steadily before their minds, throughout all their studies. I am, therefore, unable to offer this period of scholasticism as an example of pure external anancasm, which seems to be the fluorine of the intellectual elements. Perhaps the recent Japanese reception of western ideas is the purest instance of it in history. Yet in combination with other elements, nothing is commoner. If the development of ideas under the influence of the study of external facts be considered as external anancasm—it is on the border between the external and the internal forms—it is, of course, the principal thing in modern learning. But Whewell, whose masterly comprehension of the history of science critics have been too ignorant properly to appreciate, clearly shows that it is far from being the overwhelmingly preponderant influence, even there.

Internal anancasm, or logical groping, which advances upon a predestined line without being able to foresee whither it is to be carried nor to steer its course, this is the rule of development of philosophy. Hegel first made the world understand this; and he seeks to make logic not merely the subjective guide and monitor of thought, which was all it had been ambitioning before, but to be the very mainspring of thinking, and not merely of individual thinking but of discussion, of the history of the development of thought, of all history, of all development. This involves a positive, clearly demonstrable error. Let the logic in question be of whatever kind it may, a logic of necessary inference or a logic of probable inference (the theory might perhaps be shaped to fit), in any case it supposes that logic is sufficient of itself to determine what conclusion follows from given premises; for unless it will do so much, it will not suffice to explain why an individual train of reasoning should take just the course it does take, to say nothing of other kinds of development. It thus supposes that from given premises only one conclusion can logically be drawn, and that there is no scope at all for free choice. That

from given premises only one conclusion can logically be drawn is one
of the false notions that have come from logicians' confining their
attention to that Nantucket of thought, the logic of nonrelative terms.
In the logic of relatives it does not hold good.

One remark occurs to me. If the evolution of history is in considerable
part of the nature of internal anancasm, it resembles the development
of individual men; and just as thirty-three years is a rough but natural
unit of time for individuals, being the average at which man has issue,
so there should be an approximate period at the end of which one great
historical movement ought to be likely to be supplanted by another. Let
us see if we can make out anything of the kind. Take the governmental
development of Rome as being sufficiently long and set down the principal dates.

  B.C.   753, Foundation of Rome
  B.C.   510, Expulsion of the Tarquins
  B.C.   27, Octavius assumes title Augustus
  A.D.   476, End of Western Empire
  A.D.   962, Holy Roman Empire
  A.D.   453, Fall of Constantinople

The last event was one of the most significant in history, especially for
Italy. The intervals are 243, 483, 502, 486, 491 years. All are rather
curiously near equal, except the first which is half the others. Successive
reigns of kings would not commonly be so near equal. Let us set down
a few dates in the history of thought.

  B.C.   585, Eclipse of Thales. Beginnning of Greek philoso-
             phy
  A.D.   30, The crucifixion
  A.D.   529, Closing of Athenian schools. End of Greek philos-
             ophy
  A.D. 1125, (Approximate) Rise of the Universities of Bologna
             and Paris
  A.D. 1543, Publication of the "De Revolutionibus" of Coper-
             nicus. Beginning of Modern Science

The intervals are 615, 499, 596, 418, years. In the history of metaphysics, we may take the following:

B.C.   322, Death of Aristotle
A.D. 1274, Death of Aquinas
A.D. 1804, Death of Kant

The intervals are 1595 and 530 years. The former is about thrice the latter.

From these figures, no conclusion can fairly be drawn. At the same time, they suggest that perhaps there may be a rough natural era of about 500 years. Should there be any independent evidence of this, the intervals noticed may gain some significance.

The agapastic development of thought should, if it exists, be distinguished by its purposive character, this purpose being the development of an idea. We should have a direct agapic or sympathetic comprehension and recognition of it, by virtue of the continuity of thought. I here take it for granted that such continuity of thought has been sufficiently proved by the arguments used in my paper on the "Law of Mind" in *The Monist* of last July. Even if those arguments are not quite convincing in themselves, yet if they are reinforced by an apparent agapasm in the history of thought, the two propositions will lend one another mutual aid. The reader will, I trust, be too well grounded in logic to mistake such mutual support for a vicious circle in reasoning. If it could be shown directly that there is such an entity as the "spirit of an age" or of a people, and that mere individual intelligence will not account for all the phenomena, this would be proof enough at once of agapasticism and of synechism. I must acknowledge that I am unable to produce a cogent demonstration of this; but I am, I believe, able to adduce such arguments as will serve to confirm those that have been drawn from other facts. I believe that all the greatest achievements of mind have been beyond the powers of unaided individuals; and I find, apart from the support this opinion receives from synechistic considerations, and from the purposive character of many great movements, direct reason for so thinking in the sublimity of the ideas and in their occurring simultaneously and independently to a number of individuals of no extraordinary general powers. The pointed Gothic architecture in several of its developments appears to me to be of such a character. All attempts to imitate it by modern architects of the greatest learning and genius appear flat and tame, and are felt by their authors to be so. Yet at the time the style was living, there was quite an abundance of men capable of producing works of this kind of gigantic sublimity and power. In more than one case extant documents show that the cathedral chapters, in the selection of architects, treated high artistic genius as a secondary consideration, as if there were no lack of persons able to supply that; and the results justify their confidence. Were individuals in general, then, in those ages possessed of such lofty natures and high intellect? Such an opinion would break down under the first examination.

How many times have men now in middle life seen great discoveries made independently and almost simultaneously! The first instance I remember was the prediction of a planet exterior to Uranus by Urbain Jean Joseph Leverrier and John Couch Adams. One hardly knows to whom the principle of the conservation of energy ought to be attributed, although it may reasonably be considered as the greatest discovery science has ever made. The mechanical theory of heat was set forth by Rankine and by Clausius during the same month of February, 1850; and there are eminent men who attribute this great step to Thomson.* The kinetical theory of gases, after being started by John Bernoulli and long buried in oblivion, was reinvented and applied to the explanation not merely of the laws of Boyle, Charles, and Avogadro, but also of diffusion and viscosity, by at least three modern physicists separately. It is well known that the doctrine of natural selection was presented by Alfred Russel Wallace and by Darwin at the same meeting of the British Association; and Darwin in his "Historical Sketch" prefixed to the later editions of his book shows that both were anticipated by obscure forerunners. The method of spectrum analysis was claimed for Swan as well as for Kirchhoff, and there were others who perhaps had still better

*Thomson, himself, in his article *Heat* in the *Encyclopedia Britannica*, never once mentions the name of Clausius.

claims. The authorship of the Periodical Law of the Chemical Elements is disputed between a Russian, a German, and an Englishman; although there is no room for doubt that the principal merit belongs to the first. These are nearly all the greatest discoveries of our times. It is the same with the inventions. It may not be surprising that the telegraph should have been independently made by several inventors, because it was an easy corollary from scientific facts well made out before. But it was not so with the telephone and other inventions. Ether, the first anaesthetic, was introduced independently by three different New England physicians. Now ether had been a common article for a century. It had been in one of the pharmacopeias three centuries before. It is quite incredible that its anaesthetic property should not have been known; it was known. It had probably passed from mouth to ear as a secret from the days of Basil Valentine; but for long it had been a secret of the Punchinello kind. In New England, for many years, boys had used it for amusement. Why then had it not been put to its serious use? No reason can be given, except that the motive to do so was not strong enough. The motives to doing so could only have been desire for gain and philanthropy. About 1846, the date of its introduction, philanthropy was undoubtedly in an unusually active condition. That sensibility, or sentimentalism, which had been introduced in the previous century, had undergone a ripening process, in consequence of which, though now less intense than it had previously been, it was more likely to influence unreflecting people than it had ever been. All three of the ether-claimants had probably been influenced by the desire for gain; but nevertheless they were certainly not insensible to the agapic influences.

I doubt if any of the great discoveries ought, properly, to be considered as altogether individual achievements; and I think many will share this doubt. Yet, if not, what an argument for the continuity of mind, and for agapasticism is here! I do not wish to be very strenuous. If thinkers will only be persuaded to lay aside their prejudices and apply themselves to studying the evidences of this doctrine, I shall be fully content to await the final decision.

VI. Pragmatism and Pragmaticism

PEIRCE ANNOUNCED THE pragmatic maxim in 1878 in the essay "How to Make Our Ideas Clear." The doctrine received but little attention until William James used it in 1898. Although James gave Peirce full credit for originating the view, the brunt of a heavy attack on the doctrine fell on James, who replied in two books, *Pragmatism* in 1907 and *The Meaning of Truth* in 1909. Peirce undertook to state his own views in a series of three papers in *The Monist* in 1905–06.[1] The first two papers are reproduced here.

Peirce begins the first paper by describing himself as an "experimentalist." He says that the pragmatic doctrine is simply the doctrine accepted by all experimental scientists that the meaning of a concept is contained in a description of a certain experiment (action) to be performed and of the consequences (experiences) to be expected as a result of performing that action. This leads Peirce to describe thinking not as something passive, a kind of Lockean reflection, but as an activity of the sort that an experimenter engages in—a view that leads to Dewey's instrumentalism where thinking is something done physically by using the body and its extension in scientific apparatus.

Peirce goes on to deny that pragmaticism is basically a phenomenalistic view. He insists that what the pragmatic maxim does is not to describe the sensuous quality of the experience (which, in his view is indescribable), but to describe the *relation* between conduct and experience. To this relation he gives the name "rational purport," i.e., the relation describes the experience that will be had, the purport (the result, the upshot) of the action, and a rational man will keep the relation between this conduct and this experience in mind in selecting his modes of conduct. By keeping these relations in mind he will be able to produce

---

[1] Reprinted in *Collected Papers*, 4.530ff., 5.411 ff., 5.438 ff.

the experiences he seeks and to avoid those he does not wish. When one has described the rational purport, that is the elements in an idea that a rational man will keep in mind in selecting his modes of action, he has described all there is in the idea. Since these rational purports are real, i.e., the relation between the action and the experience is real (it really is true that if one performs the action, he will have the experience), and since these relations are general (if I perform any action of the type A, then I will have an experience of the type B) these relations are real generals. Therefore, generals are real and efficacious, since they influence conduct.

In the second paper of the series Peirce discusses a variety of "Issues of Pragmaticism." The variety of items discussed show the kind of doctrine pragmatism was for Peirce and may help to give the reader a more useful sense of Peirce's pragmaticism than can be obtained from his formal expositions of it.

1.   What Pragmatism Is

The writer of this article has been led by much experience to believe that every physicist, and every chemist, and, in short, every master in any department of experimental science, has had his mind molded by his life in the laboratory to a degree that is little suspected. The experimentalist himself can hardly be fully aware of it, for the reason that the men whose intellects he really knows about are much like himself in this respect. With intellects of widely different training from his own, whose education has largely been a thing learned out of books, he will never become inwardly intimate, be he on ever so familiar terms with them; for he and they are as oil and water, and though they be shaken up together, it is remarkable how quickly they will go their several mental ways, without having gained more than a faint flavor from the association. Were those other men only to take skillful soundings of the experimentalist's mind—which is just what they are unqualified to do, for the most part—they would soon discover that, excepting perhaps upon topics where his mind is trammeled by personal feeling or by his bringing up, his disposition is to think of everything just as everything is thought of in the laboratory, that is, as a question of experimentation. Of course, no living man possesses in their fullness all the attributes characteristic of his type: it is not the typical doctor whom you will see every day driven in buggy or coupé nor is it the typical pedagogue that will be met with in the first school room you enter. But when you have found, or ideally constructed upon a basis of observation, the typical experimentalist, you will find that whatever assertion you may make to him, he will either understand as meaning that if a given prescription for an experiment ever can be and ever is carried out in act, an experience of a given description will result, or else he will see no sense at all in what you say. If you talk to him as Mr. Arthur Balfour talked not long ago to the British Association, saying that "the physicist seeks for something deeper than the laws connecting possible objects of experience," that "his object is a physical reality" unrevealed in experiments, and that the existence of such nonexperimental reality "is the unalterable faith of science," to all such ontological meaning you will find the experimentalist mind to be colorblind. What adds to that confidence in this which the writer owes to his conversations with experimentalists is that he himself may almost be said to have inhabited a laboratory from the age of six until long past maturity; and having all his life associated mostly with experimentalists, it has always been with a confident sense of understanding them and of being understood by them.

That laboratory life did not prevent the writer (who here and in what follows simply exemplifies the experimentalist type) from becoming interested in methods of thinking; and when he came to read metaphysics, although much of it seemed to him loosely reasoned and determined by accidental prepossessions, yet in the writings of some philosophers, especially Kant, Berkeley, and Spinoza, he sometimes came upon strains of thought that recalled the ways of thinking of the laboratory, so that he felt he might trust to them; all of which has been true of other laboratory-men.

Endeavoring, as a man of that type naturally would, to formulate what he so appproved, he framed the theory that a *conception*, that is, the rational purport of a word or other expression, lies exclusively in its conceivable bearing upon the conduct of life; so that, since obviously nothing that might not result from experiment can have any direct bearing upon conduct, if one can define accurately all the conceivable experimental phenomena that the affirmation or denial of a concept could imply, one will have therein a complete definition of the concept, and *there is absolutely nothing more in it.* For this doctrine he invented the name *pragmatism.* Some of his friends wished him to call it *practicism* or *practicalism* (perhaps on the ground that πρακτικός is better Greek than πραγματικός). But for one who had learned philosophy out of Kant, as the writer, along with nineteen out of every twenty experimentalists who have turned to philosophy, had done, and who still thought in Kantian terms most readily, *praktisch* and *pragmatisch* were as far apart as the two poles, the former belonging to a region of thought where no mind of the experimentalist type can ever make sure of solid ground under his feet, the latter expressing relation to some definite human purpose. Now quite the most striking feature of the new theory was its recognition of an inseparable connection between rational cognition and rational purpose; and that consideration it was that determined the preference for the name *pragmatism.*

Concerning the matter of philosophical nomenclature, there are a few plain considerations, which the writer has for many years longed to submit to the deliberate judgment of those few fellow-students of philosophy, who deplore the present state of that study, and who are intent upon rescuing it therefrom and bringing it to a condition like that of the natural sciences, where investigators, instead of condemning each the work of most of the others as misdirected from beginning to end, cooperate, stand upon one another's shoulders, and multiply incontestable results; where every observation is repeated, and isolated observations go for little; where every hypothesis that merits attention is subjected to severe but fair examination, and only after the predictions to which it leads have been remarkably borne out by experience is trusted at all, and even then only provisionally; where a radically false step is rarely taken, even the most faulty of those theories that gain wide credence being true in their main experiential predictions. To those students, it is submitted that no study can become scientific in the sense described, until it provides itself with a suitable technical nomenclature, whose every term has a single definite meaning universally accepted among students of the subject, and whose vocables have no such sweetness or charms as might tempt loose writers to abuse them—which is a virtue of scientific nomenclatures too little appreciated. It is submitted that the experience of those sciences that have conquered the greatest difficulties of terminology, that are unquestionably the taxonomic sciences, chemistry, mineralogy, botany, zoology, has conclusively shown that the one only way in which the requisite unanimity and requisite ruptures with individual habits and preferences can be brought about is so to shape the canons of terminology that they shall gain the support of *moral principle* and of every man.'s sense of decency and that, in particular (under defined restrictions), the general feeling shall be that he who introduces a new conception into philosophy is under an obligation to invent acceptable terms to express it, and that when he has done so, the duty of his fellow-students is to accept those terms, and to resent any wresting of them from their original meanings, as not only a gross discourtesy to him to whom philosophy was indebted for each conception, but also as an injury to philosophy itself; and furthermore, that once a conception has been supplied with suitable and sufficient words for its expression, no other *technical* terms denoting the same things considered in the same relations, should be countenanced. Should this suggestion find favor, it might be deemed needful that the philosophians in congress assembled should adopt, after due deliberation, convenient canons to limit the application of the principle. Thus, just as is done in chemistry, it might be wise to assign fixed meanings to certain prefixes and suffixes. For example, it might be agreed, perhaps, that the prefix *prope-* should mark a broad and rather indefinite extension of the meaning of the term to which it was prefixed—the name of a doctrine would naturally end in *-ism*, while *-icism* might mark a more strictly defined acception of that doctrine, etc. Then again, just as in biology no account is taken of terms antedating Linnaeus, so in philosophy it might be found best not to go back of the scholastic terminology. To illustrate another sort of limitation, it has probably never happened that any philosopher has attempted to give a general name to his own doctrine without that name's soon acquiring in common philosophical usage a signification much broader than was originally intended. Thus, special systems go by the names Kantianism, Benthamism, Comtianism, Spencerianism, etc., while transcendentalism, utilitarianism, positivism, evolutionism, synthetic philosophy, etc., have irrevocably and very conveniently been elevated to broader governments.

After awaiting in vain, for a good many years, some particularly opportune conjuncture of circumstances that might serve to recommend his notions of the ethics of terminology, the writer has now, at last, dragged them in over head and shoulders, on an occasion when he has no specific proposal to offer nor any feeling but satisfaction at the course usage has run without any canons or resolutions of a congress. His word "pragmatism" has gained general recognition in a generalized sense that seems to argue power of growth and vitality. The famed psychologist, James, first took it up, seeing that his "radical empiricism" substantially answered to the writer's definition of pragmatism, albeit with a certain difference in the point of view. Next, the admirably clear and brilliant thinker, Ferdinand C. W. Schiller, casting about for a more attractive name for the "anthropomorphism" of his *Riddle of the Sphinx*, lit, in that most remarkable paper of his on *Axioms as Postulates*, upon the same designation "pragmatism," which in its original sense was in generic agreement with his own doctrine, for which he has since found the more appropriate specification "humanism," while he still retains "pragmatism" in a somewhat wider sense. So far all went happily. But at present, the word begins to be met with occasionally in the literary journals, where it gets abused in the merciless way that words have to expect when they fall into literary clutches. Sometimes the manners of the British have effloresced in scolding at the word as ill-chosen,— ill-chosen, that is, to express some meaning that it was rather designed to exclude. So then, the writer, finding his bantling "pragmatism" so promoted, feels that it is time to kiss his child good by and relinquish it to its higher destiny; while to serve the precise purpose of expressing the original definition, he begs to announce the birth of the word "pragmaticism," which is ugly enough to be safe from kidnappers.*

---

*To show how recent the general use of the word "pragmatism" is, the writer may mention that, to the best of his belief, he never used it in copy for the press before today, except by particular request, in *Baldwin's Dictionary*. Toward the end of 1890, when this part of the *Century Dictionary* appeared, he did not deem that the word had sufficient status to appear in that work. But he has used it continually in philosophical conversation since, perhaps, the mid-seventies.

Much as the writer has gained from the perusal of what other pragmatists have written, he still thinks there is a decisive advantage in his original conception of the doctrine. From this original form every truth that follows from any of the other forms can be deduced, while some errors can be avoided into which other pragmatists have fallen. The original view appears, too, to be a more compact and unitary conception than the others. But its capital merit, in the writer's eyes, is that it more readily connects itself with a critical proof of its truth. Quite in accord with the logical order of investigation, it usually happens that one first forms an hypothesis that seems more and more reasonable the further one examines into it, but that only a good deal later gets crowned with an adequate proof. The present writer having had the pragmatist theory under consideration for many years longer than most of its adherents, would naturally have given more attention to the proof of it. At any rate, in endeavoring to explain pragmatism, he may be excused for confining himself to that form of it that he knows best. In the present article there will be space only to explain just what this doctrine (which, in such hands as it has now fallen into, may probably play a pretty prominent part in the philosophical discussions of the next coming years), really consists in. Should the exposition be found to interest readers of *The Monist*, they would certainly be much more interested in a second article which would give some samples of the manifold applications of pragmaticism (assuming it to be true) to the solution of problems of different kinds. After that, readers might be prepared to take an interest in a proof that the doctrine is true—a proof that seems to the writer to leave no reasonable doubt on the subject, and to be the one contribution of value that he has to make to philosophy. For it would essentially involve the establishment of the truth of synechism.

The bare definition of pragmaticism could convey no satisfactory comprehension of it to the most apprehensive of minds, but requires the commentary to be given below. Moreover, this definition takes no notice of one or two other doctrines without the previous acceptance (or virtual acceptance) of which pragmaticism itself would be a nullity. They are included as a part of the pragmatism of Schiller, but the present writer prefers not to mingle different propositions. The preliminary propositions had better be stated forthwith.

The difficulty in doing this is that no formal list of them has ever been made. They might all be included under the vague maxim, "Dismiss make-believes." Philosophers of very diverse stripes propose that philosophy shall take its start from one or another state of mind in which no man, least of all a beginner in philosophy, actually is. One proposes that you shall begin by doubting everything, and says that there is one thing that you cannot doubt, as if doubting were "as easy as lying." Another proposes that we should begin by observing "the first impressions of sense," forgetting that our very percepts are the results of cognitive elaboration. But in truth, there is but one state of mind from which you can "set out," namely, the very state of mind in which you actually find yourself at the time you do "set out"—a state in which you are laden with an immense mass of cognition already formed, of which you cannot divest yourself if you would and who knows whether, if you could, you would not have made all knowledge impossible to yourself? Do you call it *doubting* to write down on a piece of paper that you doubt? If so, doubt has nothing to do with any serious business. But do not make believe; if pedantry has not eaten all the reality out of you, recognize, as you must, that there is much that you do not doubt, in the least. Now that which you do not at all doubt, you must and do regard as infallible, absolute truth. Here breaks in Mr. Make Believe: "What! Do you mean to say that one is to believe what is not true, or that what a man does not doubt is *ipso facto* true?" No, but unless he can make a thing white and black at once, *he* has to regard what he does not doubt as absolutely true. Now you, *per hypothesiu*, are that man. "But you tell me there are scores of things I do not doubt. I really cannot persuade myself that there is not some one of them about which I am mistaken." You are adducing one of your make-believe facts, which, even if it were established, would only go to show that doubt has a *limen*, that is, is only called into being by a certain finite stimulus. You only puzzle yourself by talking of this metaphysical "truth" and metaphysical "falsity," that you know nothing about. All you have any dealings with are your doubts and beliefs,* with the course of life that forces new beliefs upon you and

*It is necessary to say that "belief" is throughout used merely as the name of the contrary to doubt, without regard to grades of certainty nor to the nature of the proposition held for true, i.e., "believed."

gives you power to doubt old beliefs. If your terms "truth" and "falsity" are taken in such senses as to be definable in terms of doubt and belief and the course of experience (as for example they would be, if you were to define the "truth" as that to a belief in which belief would tend if it were to tend indefinitely toward absolute fixity), well and good: in that case, you are only talking about doubt and belief. But if by truth and falsity you mean something not definable in terms of doubt and belief in any way, then you are talking of entities of whose existence you can know nothing, and which Ockham's razor would clean shave off. Your problems would be greatly simplified, if, instead of saying that you want to know the "Truth," you were simply to say that you want to attain a state of belief unassailable by doubt.

Belief is not a momentary mode of consciousness; it is a habit of mind essentially enduring for some time, and mostly (at least) unconscious; and like other habits, it is (until it meets with some surprise that begins its dissolution), perfectly self-satisfied. Doubt is of an altogether contrary genus. It is not a habit, but the privation of a habit. Now a privation of a habit, in order to be anything at all, must be a condition of erratic activity that in some way must get superseded by a habit.

Among the things that the reader, as a rational person, does not doubt, is that he not merely has habits, but also can exert a measure of self-control over his future actions; which means, however, *not* that he can impart to them any arbitrarily assignable character, but, on the contrary, that a process of self-preparation will tend to impart to action (when the occasion for it shall arise), one fixed character, which is indicated and perhaps roughly measured by the absence (or slightness) of the feeling of self-reproach, which subsequent reflection will induce. Now, this subsequent reflection is part of the self-preparation for action for the next occasion. Consequently, there is a tendency, as action is repeated again and again, for the action to approximate indefinitely toward the perfection of that fixed character, which would be marked by entire absence of self-reproach. The more closely this is approached, the less room for self-control there will be; and where no self-control is possible there will be no self-reproach.

These phenomena seem to be the fundamental characteristics that distinguish a rational being. Blame, in every case, appears to be a modification, often accomplished by a transference, or "projection," of the primary feeling of self-reproach. Accordingly, we never blame anybody for what had been beyond his power of previous self-control. Now, thinking is a species of conduct that is largely subject to self-control. In all their features (which there is no room to describe here), logical self-control is a perfect mirror of ethical self-control—unless it be rather a species under that genus. In accordance with this, what you cannot in the least help believing is not, justly speaking, wrong belief. In other words, for you it is the absolute truth. True, it is conceivable that what you cannot help believing today, you might find you thoroughly disbelieve tomorrow. But then there is a certain distinction between things you "cannot" do, merely in the sense that nothing stimulates you to the great effort and endeavors that would be required, and things you cannot do because in their own nature they are insusceptible of being put into practice. In every stage of your excogitations, there is something of which you can only say, "I cannot think otherwise," and your experientially based hypothesis is that the impossibility is of the second kind.

There is no reason why "thought," in what has just been said, should be taken in that narrow sense in which silence and darkness are favorable to thought. It should rather be understood as covering all rational life, so that an experiment shall be an operation of thought. Of course, that ultimate state of habit to which the action of self-control ultimately tends, where no room is left for further self-control, is, in the case of thought, the state of fixed belief, or perfect knowledge.

Two things here are all-important to assure oneself of and to remember. The first is that a person is not absolutely an individual. His thoughts are what he is "saying to himself," that is, is saying to that other self that is just coming into life in the flow of time. When one reasons, it is that critical self that one is trying to persuade; and all thought whatsoever is a sign, and is mostly of the nature of language. The second thing to remember is that the man's circle of society (however widely or narrowly this phrase may be understood), is a sort of loosely compacted person, in some respects of higher rank than the person of an individual organism. It is these two things alone that render it possible for you—but only in the abstract, and in a Pickwickian sense —to distinguish between absolute truth and what you do not doubt.

Let us now hasten to the exposition of pragmaticism itself. Here it will be convenient to imagine that somebody to whom the doctrine is new, but of rather preternatural perspicacity, asks questions of a pragmaticist. Everything that might give a dramatic illusion must be stripped off, so that the result will be a sort of cross between a dialogue and a catechism, but a good deal more like the latter—something rather painfully reminiscent of *Mangnall's Historical Questions.*

Questioner: I am astounded at your definition of your pragmatism, because only last year I was assured by a person above all suspicion of warping the truth—himself a pragmatist—that your doctrine precisely was "that a conception is to be tested by its practical effects." You must surely, then, have entirely changed your definition very recently.

Pragmaticist: If you will turn to Vols. VI and VII of the *Revue Philosophique,* or to the *Popular Science Monthly* for November, 1877, and January, 1878, you will be able to judge for yourself whether the interpretation you mention was not then clearly excluded. The exact wording of the English enunciation (changing only the first person into the second), was: "Consider what effects that might conceivably have practical bearings you conceive the object of your conception to have. Then your conception of those effects is the WHOLE of your conception of the object."

Questioner: Well, what reason have you for asserting that this is so?

Pragmaticist: That is what I specially desire to tell you. But the question had better be postponed until you clearly understand what those reasons profess to prove.

Questioner: What, then, is the *raison d'être* of the doctrine? What advantage is expected from it?

Pragmaticist: It will serve to show that almost every proposition of ontological metaphysics is either meaningless gibberish—one word being defined by other words, and they by still others, without any real conception ever being reached—or else is downright absurd; so that all such rubbish being swept away, what will remain of philosophy will be a series of problems capable of investigation by the observational methods of the true sciences—the truth about which can be reached without those interminable misunderstandings and disputes which have made the highest of the positive sciences a mere amusement for idle intellects, a sort of chess—idle pleasure its purpose, and reading out of a book its method. In this regard, pragmaticism is a species of prope-positivism. But what distinguishes it from other species is, first, its retention of a purified philosophy; secondly, its full acceptance of the main body of our instinctive beliefs; and thirdly, its strenuous insistence upon the truth of scholastic realism (or a close approximation to that, well-stated by the late Dr. Francis Ellingwood Abbot in the Introduction to his *Scientific Theism*). So, instead of merely jeering at metaphysics, like other prope-positivists, whether by long drawn-out parodies or otherwise, the pragmaticist extracts from it a precious essence, that will serve to give life and light to cosmology and physics. At the same time, the moral applications of the doctrine are positive and potent; and there are many other uses of it not easily classed. On another occasion, instances may be given to show that it really has these effects.

Questioner: I hardly need to be convinced that your doctrine would wipe out metaphysics. Is it not as obvious that it must wipe out every proposition of science and everything that bears on the conduct of life? For you say that the only meaning that, for you, any assertion bears is that a certain experiment has resulted in a certain way: Nothing else but an experiment enters into the meaning. Tell me, then, how can an experiment, in itself, reveal anything more than that something once happened to an individual object and that subsequently some other individual event occured?

Pragmaticist: That question is, indeed, to the purpose—the purpose being to correct any misapprehensions of pragmaticism. You speak of an experiment in itself, emphasizing *"in itself."* You evidently think of each experiment as isolated from every other. It has not, for example, occurred to you, one might venture to surmise, that every connected series of experiments constitutes a single collective experiment. What are the essential ingredients of an experiment? First, of course, an experimenter of flesh and blood. Secondly, a verifiable hypothesis. This is a proposition* relating to the universe environing the experimenter, or to some well-known part of it and affirming or denying of this only some experimental possibility or impossibility. The third indispensable ingredient is a sincere doubt in the experimenter's mind as to the truth of that hypothesis. Passing over several ingredients on which we need not dwell, the purpose, the plan, and the resolve, we come to the act of choice by which the experimenter singles out certain identifiable objects to be operated upon. The next is the external (or quasi-external) ACT by which he modifies those objects. Next, comes the subsequent *reaction* of the world upon the experimenter in a perception; and finally, his recognition of the teaching of the experiment. While the two chief parts of the event itself are the action and the reaction, yet the unity of essence of the experiment lies in its purpose and plan, the ingredients passed over in the enumeration.

Another thing: In representing the pragmaticist as making rational meaning to consist in an experiment (which you speak of as an event in the past), you strikingly fail to catch his attitude of mind. Indeed, it is not in an experiment, but in *experimental phenomena*, that rational meaning is said to consist. When an experimentalist speaks of a *phenomenon*, such as "Hall's phenomenon," "Zeeman's phenomenon" and its modification, "Michelson's phenomenon," or "the chess-board phenomenon," he does not mean any particular event that did happen to somebody in the dead past, but what *surely will* happen to everybody in the living future who shall fulfill certain conditions. The phenomenon consists in the fact that when an experimentalist shall come to *act* according to a certain scheme that he has in mind, then will something else happen, and shatter the doubts of sceptics, like the celestial fire upon the altar of Elijah.

And do not overlook the fact that the pragmaticist maxim says noth-

---

*The writer, like most English logicians, invariably uses the word *proposition*, not as the Germans define their equivalent, *Satz*, as the language-expression of a judgment *(Urtheil)*, but as that which is related to any assertion, whether mental and self-addressed or outwardly expressed, just as any possibility is related to its actualization. The difficulty of the, at best, difficult problem of the essential nature of a proposition has been increased, by the Germans, by their *Urtheil*, confounding, under one designation, the mental *assertion* with the *assertible*.

ing of single experiments or of single experimental phenomena (for what is conditionally true *in futuro* can hardly be singular), but only speaks of *general kinds* of experimental phenomena. Its adherent does not shrink from speaking of general objects as real, since whatever is true represents a real. Now the laws of nature are true.

The rational meaning of every proposition lies in the future. How so? The meaning of a proposition is itself a proposition. Indeed, it is no other than the very proposition of which it is the meaning: It is a translation of it. But of the myriads of forms into which a proposition may be translated, what is that one which is to be called its very meaning? It is, according to the pragmaticist, that form in which the proposition becomes applicable to human conduct, not in these or those special circumstances, nor when one entertains this or that special design, but that form that is most directly applicable to self-control under every situation, and to every purpose. This is why he locates the meaning in future time; for future conduct is the only conduct that is subject to self-control. But in order that that form of the proposition that is to be taken as its meaning should be applicable to every situation and to every purpose upon which the proposition has any bearing, it must be simply the general description of all the experimental phenomena that the assertion of the proposition virtually predicts. For an experimental phenomenon is the fact asserted by the proposition that action of a certain description will have a certain kind of experimental result; and experimental results are the only results that can affect human conduct. No doubt, some unchanging idea may come to influence a man more than it had done; but only because some experience equivalent to an experiment has brought its truth home to him more intimately than before. Whenever a man acts purposively, he acts under a belief in some experimental phenomenon. Consequently, the sum of the experimental phenomena that a proposition implies makes up its entire bearing upon human conduct. Your question, then, of how a pragmaticist can attribute any meaning to any assertion other than that of a single occurrence is substantially answered.

Questioner: I see that pragmaticism is a thorough-going phenomenalism. Only why should you limit yourself to the phenomena of experimental science rather than embrace all observational science? Experiment, after all, is an uncommunicative informant. It never expiates: it only answers "yes" or "no"; or rather it usually snaps out "No!" or, at best, only utters an inarticulate grunt for the negation of its "no." The typical experimentalist is not much of an observer. It is the student of natural history to whom nature opens the treasury of her confidence, while she treats the cross-examining experimentalist with the reserve he merits. Why should your phenomenalism sound the meager jews-harp of experiment rather than the glorious organ of observation?

Pragmaticist: Because pragmaticism is not definable as "thorough-going phenomenalism," although the latter doctrine may be a kind of pragmatism. The *richness* of phenomena lies in their sensuous quality. Pragmaticism does not intend to define the phenomenal equivalents of words and general ideas, but, on the contrary, eliminates their sential element, and endeavors to define the rational purport, and this it finds in the purposive bearing of the word or proposition in question.

Questioner: Well, if you choose so to make Doing the Be-all and the End-all of human life, why do you not make meaning to consist simply in doing? Doing has to be done at a certain time upon a certain object. Individual objects and single events cover all reality, as everybody knows, and as a practicalist ought to be the first to insist. Yet, your meaning, as you have described it, is *general.* Thus, it is of the nature of a mere word and not a reality. You say yourself that your meaning of a proposition is only the same proposition in another dress. But a practical man's meaning is the very thing he means. What do you make to be the meaning of "George Washington"?

Pragmaticist: Forcibly put! A good half dozen of your points must certainly be admitted. It must be admitted, in the first place, that if pragmaticism really made Doing the Be-all and the End-all of life, that would be its death. For to say that we live for the mere sake of action, as action, regardless of the thought it carries out, would be to say that there is no such thing as rational purport. Secondly, it must be admitted that every proposition professes to be true of a certain real individual object, often the environing universe. Thirdly, it must be admitted that pragmaticism fails to furnish any translation or meaning of a proper name, or other designation of an individual object. Fourthly, the pragmaticistic meaning is undoubtedly general; and it is equally indisputable that the general is of the nature of a word or sign. Fifthly, it must be admitted that individuals alone exist; and sixthly, it may be admitted that the very meaning of a word or significant object ought to be the very essence of reality of what it signifies. But when, those admissions having been unreservedly made, you find the pragmaticist still constrained most earnestly to deny the force of your objection, you ought to infer that there is some consideration that has escaped you. Putting the admissions together, you will perceive that the pragmaticist grants that a proper name (although it is not customary to say that it has a *meaning*), has a certain denotative function peculiar, in each case, to that name and its equivalents; and that he grants that every assertion contains such a denotative or pointing-out function. In its peculiar individuality, the pragmaticist excludes this from the rational purport of the assertion, although *the like* of it, being common to all assertions, and so, being general and not individual, may enter into the pragmaticistic purport. Whatever exists, *ex-sists*, that is, really acts upon other existents, so obtains a self-identity, and is definitely individual. As to the general, it will be a help to thought to notice that there are two ways of being general. A statue of a soldier on some village monument, in his overcoat and with his musket, is for each of a hundred families the image of its uncle, its sacrifice to the union. That statue, then, though it is itself single, represents any one man of whom a certain predicate may be true. It is *objectively* general. The word "soldier," whether spoken or written, is general in the same say; while the name, "George Washington," is not so. But each of these two terms remains one and the same noun, whether it be spoken or written, and whenever and wherever it be spoken or written. This noun is not an existent thing: it is a *type*, or *form*, to which objects, both those that are externally existent and those which are imagined, may *conform*, but which none of them can exactly be. This is subjective generality. The pragmaticistic purport is general in both ways.

As to reality, one finds it defined in various ways; but if that principle of terminological ethics that was proposed be accepted, the equivocal language will soon disappear. For *realis* and *realitas* are not ancient words. They were invented to be terms of philosophy in the thirteenth century, and the meaning they were intended to express is perfectly clear. That is *real* which has such and such characters, whether anybody thinks it to have those characters or not. At any rate, that is the sense in which the pragmaticist uses the word. Now, just as conduct controlled by ethical reason tends toward fixing certain habits of conduct, the nature of which (as to illustrate the meaning, peaceable habits and not quarrelsome habits), does not depend upon any accidental circumstances, and *in that sense*, may be said to be *destined;* so, thought, controlled by a rational experimental logic, tends to the fixation of certain opinions, equally destined, the nature of which will be the same in the end, however the perversity of thought of whole generations may cause the postponement of the ultimate fixation. If this be so, as every man of us virtually assumes that it is, in regard to each matter the truth of which he seriously discusses, then, according to the adopted definition of "real," the state of things that will be believed in that ultimate opinion is real. But, for the most part, such opinions will be general. Consequently, *some* general objects are real. (Of course, nobody ever thought that *all* generals were real; but the scholastics used to assume that generals were real when they had hardly any, or quite no, experiential evidence to support their assumption; and their fault lay just there, and not in holding that generals could be real.) One is struck with the inexactitude of thought even of analysts of power, when they touch upon modes of being. One will meet, for example, the virtual assumption that what is relative to thought cannot be real. But why not, exactly? *Red* is relative to sight, but the fact that this or that is in that relation to vision that we call being red is not *itself* relative to sight; it is a real fact.

Not only may generals be real, but they may also be *physically efficient*, not in every metaphysical sense, but in the common-sense acception in which human purposes are physically efficient. Aside from metaphysical nonsense, no sane man doubts that if I feel the air in my study to be stuffy, that thought may cause the window to be opened. My thought, be it granted, was an individual event. But what determined it to take the particular determination it did, was in part the general fact that stuffy air is unwholesome, and in part other *Forms*, concerning which Dr. Carus has caused so many men to reflect to advantage—or rather, *by* which, and the general truth concerning which Dr. Carus's mind was determined to the forcible enunciation of so much truth. For truths, on the average, have a greater tendency to get believed than falsities have. Were it otherwise, considering that there are myriads of false hypotheses to account for any given phenomenon, against one sole true one (or if you will have it so, against every true one), the first step toward genuine knowledge must have been next door to a miracle. So, then, when my window was opened, because of the truth that stuffy air is malsain, a physical effort was brought into existence by the efficiency of a general and nonexistent truth. This has a droll sound because it is unfamiliar; but exact analysis is with it and not against it; and it has besides, the immense advantage of not blinding us to great facts—such as that the ideas "justice" and "truth" are, notwithstanding the iniquity of the world, the mightiest of the forces that move it. Generality is, indeed, an indispensable ingredient of reality; for mere individual existence or actuality without any regularity whatever is a nullity. Chaos is pure nothing.

That which any true proposition asserts is *real*, in the sense of being as it is regardless of what you or I may think about it. Let this proposition be a general conditional proposition as to the future, and it is a real general such as is calculated really to influence human conduct; and such the pragmaticist holds to be the rational purport of every concept.

Accordingly, the pragmaticist does not make the *summum bonum* to consist in action, but makes it to consist in the process of evolution whereby the existent comes more and more to embody those generals which were just now said to be *destined*, which is what we strive to express in calling them *reasonable*. In its higher stages, evolution takes place more and more largely through self-control, and this gives the pragmaticist a sort of justification for making the rational purport to be general.

There is much more in elucidation of pragmaticism that might be said to advantage, were it not for the dread of fatiguing the reader. It might, for example, have been well to show clearly that the pragmaticist does not attribute any different essential mode of being to an event in the future from that which he would attribute to a similar event in the past, but only that the practical attitude of the thinker toward the two is different. It would also have been well to show that the pragmaticist does not make Forms to be the *only* realities in the world, any more than he makes the reasonable purport of a word to be the only kind of meaning there is. These things are, however, implicitly involved in what has been said. There is only one remark concerning the pragmaticist's conception of the relation of his formula to the first principles of logic that need detain the reader.

Aristotle's definition of universal predication, which is usually designated (like a papal bull or writ of court, from its opening words), as the *Dictum de omni,* may be translated as follows: "We call a predication (be it affirmative or negative), *universal,* when, and only when, there is nothing among the existent individuals to which the subject affirmatively belongs, but to which the predicate will not likewise be referred (affirmatively or negatively, according as the universal predication is affirmative or negative)." The Greek is: λέγομεν τὸ κατὰ παντὸς κατηγορεῖσθαι ὅταν μηδὲν ἢ λαβεῖν τῶν τοῦ ὑποκειμένου καθ' οὗ θάτερου οὐ λεχθήσεται· καὶ τὸ κατὰ μηδενὸς ὡσαύτως. The important words "existent individuals" have been introduced into the translation (which English idiom would not here permit to be literal): but it is plain that existent individuals were what Aristotle meant. The other departures from literalness only serve to give modern English forms of expression. Now, it is well known that propositions in formal logic go in pairs, the two of one pair being convertible into another by the interchange of the ideas of antecedent and consequent, subject and predicate, etc. The parallelism extends so far that it is often assumed to be perfect; but it is not quite so. The proper mate of this sort to the *Dictum de omni* is the following definition of affirmative predication: We call a predication *affirmative* (be it universal or particular), when, and only when, there is nothing among the sensational effects that belong universally to the predicate that will not be (universally or particularly, according as the affirmative predication is universal or particular), said to belong to the subject. Now, this is substantially the essential proposition of pragmaticism. Of course, its parallelism to the *Dictum de omni* will only be admitted by a person who admits the truth of pragmaticism.

Suffer me to add one word more on this point. For if one cares at all to know what the pragmaticist theory consists in, one must understand that there is no other part of it to which the pragmaticist attaches quite as much importance as he does to the recognition in his doctrine of the utter inadequacy of action or volition or even of resolve or actual purpose, as materials out of which to construct a conditional purpose or the concept of conditional purpose. Had a purposed article concerning the principle of continuity and synthetizing the ideas of the other articles of a series in the early volumes of *The Monist* ever been written, it would have appeared how, with thorough consistency, that theory involved the recognition that continuity is simply what generality becomes in the logic of relatives, and thus, like generality, and more than generality, is an affair of thought, and is the essence of thought. Yet even in its truncated condition, an extra-intelligent reader might discern that the theory of those cosmological articles made reality to consist in something more than feeling and action could supply, inasmuch as the primeval chaos, where those two elements were present, was explicitly shown to be pure nothing. Now, the motive for alluding to that theory just here is, that in this way one can put in a strong light a position that the pragmaticist holds and must hold, whether that cosmological theory be ultimately sustained or exploded, namely, that the third category—the category of thought, representation, triadic relation, mediation, genuine thirdness, thirdness as such—is an essential ingredient of reality, yet does not by itself constitute reality, since this category (which in that cosmology appears as the element of habit), can have no concrete being without action, as a separate object on which to work its government, just as action cannot exist without the immediate being of feeling on which to act. The truth is that pragmaticism is closely allied to the Hegelian absolute idealism, from which, however, it is sundered by its vigorous denial that the third category (which Hegel degrades to a mere stage of thinking), suffices to make the world, or is even so much as self-sufficient. Had Hegel, instead of regarding the first two stages with his smile of contempt, held on to them as independent or distinct elements of the triune Reality, pragmaticists might have looked up to him as the great vindicator of the truth. (Of course, the external trappings of his doctrine are only here and there of much significance.) For pragmaticism belongs essentially to the triadic class of philosophical doctrines, and is much more essentially so than Hegelianism is. (Indeed, in one passage, at least, Hegel alludes to the triadic form of his exposition as to a mere fashion of dress.)

MILFORD, PA.

September, 1904.

POSTSCRIPT.

During the last five months I have met with references to several objections to the above opinions, but not having been able to obtain the text of these objections, I do not think I ought to attempt to answer them. If gentlemen who attack either pragmatism in general or the variety of it which I entertain would only send me copies of what they write, more important readers they could easily find, but they could find none who would examine their arguments with a more grateful avidity for truth not yet apprehended, nor any who would be more sensible of their courtesy.

February 9, 1905.

2. Issues of Pragmaticism

Pragmaticism was originally enounced* in the form of a maxim, as follows: Consider what effects that might *conceivably* have practical bearings you *conceive* the objects of your *conception* to have. Then,

---

*Popular Science Monthly, XII, 293; for Jan., 1878. An introductory article opens the volume, in the number for Nov., 1877.

your *conception* of those effects is the whole of your *conception* of the object.

I will restate this in other words, since often one can thus eliminate some unsuspected source of perplexity to the reader. This time it shall be in the indicative mood, as follows: The entire intellectual purport of any symbol consists in the total of all general modes of rational conduct that, conditionally upon all the possible different circumstances and desires, would ensue upon the acceptance of the symbol.

Two doctrines that were defended by the writer about nine years before the formulation of pragmaticism may be treated as consequences of the latter belief. One of these may be called Critical Common-Sensism. It is a variety of the Philosophy of Common Sense, but is marked by six distinctive characters, which had better be enumerated at once.

Character I. Critical Common-Sensism admits that there not only are indubitable propositions but also that there are indubitable inferences. In one sense, anything evident is indubitable; but the propositions and inferences that Critical Common-Sensism holds to be original, in the sense one cannot "go behind" them (as the lawyers say) are indubitable in the sense of being acritical. The term "reasoning" ought to be confined to such fixation of one belief by another as is reasonable, deliberate, self-controlled. A reasoning must be conscious; and this consciousness is not mere "immediate consciousness," which (as I argued in 1868, *J. Spec. Phil.*, Vol. II) is simple Feeling viewed from another side, but is in its ultimate nature (meaning in that characteristic element of it that is not reducible to anything simpler), a sense of taking a habit, or disposition to respond to a given kind of stimulus in a given kind of way. As to the nature of that, some *éclaircissements* will appear below and again in my third paper, on the Basis of Pragmaticism. But the secret of rational consciousness is not so much to be sought in the study of this one peculiar nucleolus, as in the review of the process of self-control in its entirety. The machinery of logical self-control works on the same plan as does moral self-control, in multiform detail. The greatest difference, perhaps, is that the latter serves to inhibit mad puttings forth of energy, while the former most characteristically insures us against the quandary of Buridan's ass. The formation of habits under imaginary action (see the paper of Jan., 1878, [this volume, p. 137]) is one of the most esential ingredients of both; but in the logical process the imagination takes far wider flights, proportioned to the generality of the field of inquiry, being bounded in pure mathematics solely by the limits of its own powers, while in the moral process we consider only situations that may be apprehended or anticipated. For in moral life we are chiefly solicitous about our conduct and its inner springs, and the approval of conscience, while in intellectual life there is a tendency to value existence as the vehicle of forms. Certain obvious features of the phenomena of self-control (and especially of habit), can be expressed compactly and without any hypothetical addition, except what we distinctly rate as imagery, by saying that we have an occult nature of which and of its contents we can only judge by the conduct that it determines, and by phenomena of that conduct. All will assent to that (or all but the extreme nominalist), but antisynechistic thinkers wind themselves up in a facticious snarl by falsifying the phenomena in representing consciousness to be, as it were, a skin, a separate tissue, overlying an unconscious region of the occult nature, mind, soul, or physiological basis. It appears to me that in the present state of our knowledge a sound methodeutic prescribes that, in adhesion to the appearances, the difference is only relative and the demarcation not precise.

According to the maxim of pragmaticism, to say that determination affects our occult nature is to say that it is capable of affecting deliberate conduct; and since we are conscious of what we do deliberately, we are conscious *habitualiter* of whatever hides in the depths of our nature; and it is presumable (and *only* presumable,* although curious instances are on record), that a sufficiently energetic effort of attention would bring it out. Consequently, to say that an operation of the mind is controlled is to say that it is, in a special sense, a conscious operation; and this no doubt is the consciousness of reasoning. For this theory requires that in reasoning we should be conscious, not only of the conclusion, and of our deliberate approval of it, but also of its being the result of the premise

---

*But see the experiments of J. Jastrow and me "On Slight Differences of Sensation" in the *Memoirs of the National Academy of Sciences.* Vol. III.

from which it does result, and furthermore that the inference is one of a possible class of inferences that conform to one guiding principle. Now in fact we find a well-marked class of mental operations, clearly of a different nature from any others that do possess just these properties. They alone deserve to be called *reasonings;* and if the reasoner is conscious, even vaguely, of what his guiding principle is, his reasoning should be called a *logical argumentation.* There are, however, cases in which we are conscious that a belief has been determined by another given belief, but are not conscious that it proceeds on any general principle. Such is St. Augustine's *"cogito, ergo sum."* Such a process should be called, not a reasoning but an *acritical inference.* Again, there are cases in which one belief is determined by another, without our being at all aware of it. These should be called *associational suggestions of belief.*

Now the theory of pragmaticism was originally based, as anybody will see who examines the papers of Nov., 1877, and Jan., 1878, upon a study of that experience of the phenomena of self-control that is common to all grown men and women; and it seems evident that to some extent, at least, it must always be so based. For it is to conceptions of deliberate conduct that pragmaticism would trace the intellectual purport of symbols; and deliberate conduct is self-controlled conduct. Now control may itself be controlled, criticism itself subjected to criticism; and ideally there is no obvious definite limit to the sequence. But if one seriously inquires whether it is possible that a completed series of actual efforts should have been endless or beginningless (I will spare the reader the discussion), I think he can only conclude that (with some vagueness as to what constitutes an effort) this must be regarded as impossible. It will be found to follow that there are, besides perceptual judgments, original (i.e., indubitable because uncriticized) beliefs of a general and recurrent kind, as well as indubitable acritical inferences.

It is important for the reader to satisfy himself that genuine doubt always has an external origin, usually from surprise; and that it is as impossible for a man to create in himself a genuine doubt by such an act of the will as would suffice to imagine the condition of a mathematical theorem, as it would be for him to give himself a genuine surprise by a simple act of the will.

I beg my reader also to believe that it would be impossible for me to put into these articles over two per cent. of the pertinent thought that would be necessary in order to present the subject as I have worked it out. I can only make a small selection of what it seems most desirable to submit to his judgment. Not only must all steps be omitted that he can be expected to supply for himself, but unfortunately much more that may cause him difficulty.

Character II. I do not remember that any of the old Scotch philoso-
ь. rs ever undertook to draw up a complete list of the original beliefs, but they certainly thought it a feasible thing, and that the list would hold good for the minds of all men from Adam down. For in those days Adam was an undoubted historical personage. Before any waft of the air of evolution had reached those coasts how could they think otherwise? When I first wrote, we were hardly orientated in the new ideas, and my impression was that the indubitable propositions changed with a thinking man from year to year. I made some studies preparatory to an investigation of the rapidity of these changes, but the matter was neglected, and it has been only during the last two years that I have completed a provisional inquiry that shows me that the changes are so slight from generation to generation, though not imperceptible even in that short period, that I thought to own my adhesion, under inevitable modification, to the opinion of that subtle but well-balanced intellect, Thomas Reid, in the matter of Common Sense (as well as in regard to immediate perception, along with Kant).*

Character III. The Scotch philosophers recognized that the original beliefs, and the same thing is at least equally true of the acritical inferences, were of the general nature of instincts. But little as we know about instincts, even now, we are much better acquainted with them than were the men of the eighteenth century. We know, for example, that they

---

*I wish I might hope, after finishing some more difficult work, to be able to resume this study and to go to the bottom of the subject, which needs the qualities of age and does not call upon the powers of youth. A great range of reading is necessary; for it is the belief men *betray* and not that which they *parade* that has to be studied.

can be somewhat modified in a very short time. The great facts have always been known; such as that instinct seldom errs, while reason goes wrong nearly half the time, if not more frequently. But one thing the Scotch failed to recognize is that the original beliefs only remain indubitable in their application to affairs that resemble those of a primitive mode of life. It is, for example, quite open to reasonable doubt whether the motions of electrons are confined to three dimensions, although it is good methodeutic to presume that they are until some evidence to the contrary is forthcoming. On the other hand, as soon as we find that a belief shows symptoms of being instinctive, although it may seem to be dubitable, we must suspect that experiment would show that it is not really so; for in our artificial life, especially in that of a student, no mistake is more likely than that of taking a paper-doubt for the genuine metal. Take, for example, the belief in the criminality of incest. Biology will doubtless testify that the practice is unadvisable; but surely nothing that it has to say could warrant the intensity of our sentiment about it. When, however, we consider the thrill of horror that the idea excites in us, we find reason in that to consider it to be an instinct; and from that we may infer that if some rationalistic brother and sister were to marry, they would find that the conviction of horrible guilt could not be shaken off.

In contrast to this may be placed the belief that suicide is to be classed as murder. There are two pretty sure signs that this is not an instinctive belief. One is that it is substantially confined to the Christian world. The other is that when it comes to the point of actual self-debate, this belief seems to be completely expunged and ex-sponged from the mind. In reply to these powerful arguments, the main points urged are the authority of the fathers of the church and the undoubtedly intense instinctive clinging to life. The latter phenomenon is, however, entirely irrelevant. For though it is a wrench to part with life, which has its charms at the very worst, just as it is to part with a tooth, yet there is no *moral* element in it whatever. As to the Christian tradition, it may be explained by the circumstances of the early Church. For Christianity, the most terribly earnest and most intolerant of religions—[See *The Book of Revelations of St. John the Divine*]—and it remained so until diluted with civilization—recognized no morality as worthy of an instant's consideration except Christian morality. Now the early Church had need of martyrs, i.e., witnesses, and if any man had done with life, it was abominable infidelity to leave it otherwise than as a witness to its power. This belief, then, should be set down as dubitable; and it will no sooner have been pronounced dubitable, than reason will stamp it as false.

The Scotch School appear to have no such distinction, concerning the limitations of indubitability and the consequent limitations of the jurisdiction of original belief.

Character IV. By all odds, the most distinctive character of the Critical Common-Sensist, in contrast to the old Scotch philosopher, lies in his insistence that the acritically indubitable is invariably vague.

Logicians have been at fault in giving vagueness the go-by, so far as not even to analyze it. The present writer has done his best to work out the Stechiology (or Stoicheiology), Critic, and Methodeutic of the subject, but can here only give a definition or two with some proposals respecting terminology.

Accurate writers have apparently made a distinction between the *definite* and the *determinate*. A subject is *determinate* in respect to any character that inheres in it or is (universally and affirmatively) predicated of it, as well as in respect to the negative of such character, these being the very same respect. In all other respects it is *indeterminate*. The *finite* shall be defined presently. A sign (under which designation I place every kind of thought, and not alone external signs) that is in any respect objectively indeterminate (i.e., whose object is undetermined by the sign itself) is objectively *general* in so far as it extends to the interpreter the privilege of carrying its determination further.* *Example:* "Man is mor-

---

*Hamilton and a few other logicians understood the subject of a universal proposition in the collective sense; but every person who is well-read in logic is familiar with many passages in which the leading logicians explain with an iteration that would be superfluous if all readers were intelligent, that such a subject is distributively not collectively general. A term denoting a collection is singular, and such a term is an "abstraction" or product of the operation of hypostatic abstraction as truly as is the name of the essence. "Mankind" is quite as much an abstraction and *ens rationis* as is "humanity." Indeed, every object of a conception is either a signate individual or some kind of indeterminate individual. Nouns in the plural are usually distributive and general; common nouns in the singular are usually indefinite.

tal." To the question, What man? the reply is that the proposition explicitly leaves it to you to apply its assertion to what man or men you will. A sign that is objectively indeterminate in any respect is objectively *vague* in so far as it reserves further determination to be made in some other conceivable sign, or at least does not appoint the interpreter as its deputy in this office. *Example:* "A man whom I could mention seems to be a little conceited." The *suggestion* here is that the man in view is the person addressed; but the utterer does not authorize such an interpretation or *any* other application of what she says. She can still say, if she likes, that she does *not* mean the person addressed. Every utterance naturally leaves the right of further exposition in the utterer; and therefore, in so far as a sign is indeterminate, it is vague, unless it is expressly or by a well-understood convention rendered general. Usually, an affirmative predication covers *generally* every essential character of the predicate, while a negative predication *vaguely* denies some essential character. In another sense, honest people, when not joking, intend to make the meaning of their words determinate, so that there shall be no latitude of interpretation at all. That is to say, the character of their meaning consists in the implications and nonimplications of their words; and they intend to fix what is implied and what is not implied. They believe that they succeed in doing so, and if their chat is about the theory of numbers, perhaps they may. But the further their topics are from such precise, or "abstract," subjects, the less possibility is there of such precision of speech. In so far as the implication is not determinate, it is usually left vague; but there are cases where an unwillingness to dwell on disagreeable subjects causes the utterer to leave the determination of the implication to the interpreter; as if one says, "That creature is filthy, in every sense of the term."

Perhaps a more scientific pair of definitions would be that anything is *general* in so far as the principle of excluded middle does not apply to it and is *vague* in so far as the principle of contradiction does not apply to it. Thus, although it is true that "Any proposition you please, *once you have determined its identity,* is either true or false"; yet *so long as it remains indeterminate and so without identity,* it need neither be true that any proposition you please is true, nor that any proposition you please is false. So likewise, while it is false that "A proposition *whose identity I have determined* is both true and false," yet until it is determinate, it may be true that a proposition is true and that a proposition is false.

In those respects in which a sign is not vague, it is said to be *definite*, and also with a slightly different mode of application, to be *precise*, a meaning probably due to *praecisus* having been applied to curt denials and refusals. It has been the well-established, ordinary sense of *precise* since the Plantagenets; and it were much to be desired that this word, with its derivatives *precision, precisive*, etc., should, in the dialect of philosophy, be restricted to this sense. To express the act of *rendering precise* (though usually only in reference to numbers, dates, and the like), the French have the verb *préciser*, which, after the analogy of *décider*, should have been *précider*. Would it not be a useful addition to our English terminology of logic, to adopt the verb *to precide*, to express the general sense, to render precise? Our older logicians with salutary boldness seem to have created for their service the verb *to prescind*, the corresponding Latin word meaning only to "cut off at the end," while the English word means to suppose without supposing some more or less determinately indicated accompaniment. In geometry, for example, we "prescind" shape from color, which is precisely the same thing as to "abstract" color from shape, although very many writers employ the verb "to abstract" so as to make it the equivalent of "prescind." But whether it was the invention or the courage of our philosophical ancestors that exhausted itself in the manufacture of the verb "prescind," the curious fact is that instead of forming from it the noun *prescission*, they took pattern from the French logicians in putting the word *precision* to his second use. About the same time* [See Watts, *Logick*, 1725, I, vi, 9 *ad fin.*] the adjective *precisive* was introduced to signify what *precissive* would have more unmistakably conveyed. If we desire to rescue the good ship Philosophy for the service of Science from the hands of lawless rovers of the sea of literature, we shall do well to

---

*But unfortunately it has not been in the writer's power to consult the *Oxford Dictionary* concerning these words; so that probably some of the statements in the text might be corrected with the aid of that work.

keep prescind, presciss, precission, and precissive on the one hand, to refer to dissection in hypothesis, while precide, precise, precision, and precisive are used so as to refer exclusively to an expression of determination which is made either full or free for the interpreter. We shall thus do much to relieve the stem "abstract" from staggering under the double burden of conveying the idea of prescission as well as the unrelated and very important idea of the creation of *ens rationis* out of an ἔπος πτερόεν, —to filch the phrase to furnish a name for an expression of nonsubstantive thought—an operation that has been treated as a subject of ridicule—this hypostatic abstraction—but which gives mathematics half its power.

The purely formal conception that the three affections of terms, *determination, generality,* and *vagueness* form a group dividing a category of what Kant calls "functions of judgment" will be passed by as unimportant by those who have yet to learn how important a part purely formal conceptions may play in philosophy. Without stopping to discuss this, it may be pointed out that the "quantity" of propositions in logic, that is, the distribution of the first subject,* is either *singular* (that is, determinate, which renders it substantially negligible in formal logic), or *universal* (that is, general), or *particular* (as the medieval logicians say, that is, vague or *indefinite*). It is a curious fact that in the logic of relations it is the first and last quantifiers of a proposition that are of chief importance. To affirm of anything that it is a horse is to yield to it *every* essential character of a horse: To deny of anything that it is a horse is vaguely to refuse to it *some* one or more of those essential characters of the horse. There are, however, predicates that are unanalyzable in a given state of intelligence and experience. These are, therefore, determinately affirmed or denied. Thus, this same group of concepts reappears. Affirmation and denial are in themselves unaffected by these concepts, but it is to be remarked that there are cases in which

*Thus returning to the writer's original nomenclature, in despite of *Monist* VII, 209, where an obviously defective argument was regarded as sufficient to determine a mere matter of terminology. But the quality of propositions is there regarded from a point of view that seems extrinsic. I have not had time, however, to re-explore all the ramifications of this difficult question by the aid of existential graphs, and the statement in the text about the last quantifier may need modification.

we can have an apparently definite idea of a border line between affirmation and negation. Thus, a point of a surface may be in a region of that surface, or out of it, or on its boundary. This gives us an indirect and vague conception of an intermediary between affirmation and denial in general, and consequently of an intermediate, or nascent state, between determination and indetermination. There must be a similar intermediacy between generality and vagueness. Indeed, in an article in the seventh volume of *The Monist*, pp. 205–217, there lies just beneath the surface of what is explicitly said, the idea of an endless series of such *intermediacies*. We shall find below some application for these reflections.

Character V. The Critical Common-Sensist will be further distinguished from the old Scotch philosopher by the great value he attaches to doubt, provided only that it be the weighty and noble metal itself, and no counterfeit nor paper substitute. He is not content to ask himself whether he does doubt, but he invents a plan for attaining to doubt, elaborates it in detail, and then puts it into practice, although this may involve a solid month of hard work; and it is only after having gone through such an examination that he will pronounce a belief to be indubitable. Moreover, he fully acknowledges that even then it may be that some of his indubitable beliefs may be proved false.

The Critical Common-Sensist holds that there is less danger to heuretic science in believing too little than in believing too much. Yet for all that, the consequences to heuretics of believing too little may be no less than disaster.

Character VI. Critical Common-Sensism may fairly lay claim to this title for two sorts of reasons; namely, that on the one hand it subjects four opinions to rigid criticism: its own; that of the Scotch school; that of those who would base logic or metaphysics on psychology or any other special science, the least tenable of all the philosophical opinions that have any vogue; and that of Kant; while on the other hand it has besides some claim to be called Critical from the fact that it is but a modification of Kantism. The present writer was a pure Kantist until he was forced by successive steps into Pragmaticism. The Kantist has only to abjure from the bottom of his heart the proposition that a thing-in-itself can, however indirectly, be conceived; and then correct the details of Kant's doctrine accordingly, and he will find himself to have become a Critical Common-Sensist.

Another doctrine that is involved in pragmaticism as an essential consequence of it, but which the writer defended (*J. Spec. Phil.*, Vol. II, p. 155 *ad fin.* 1868, and *N. Am. Rev.*, Vol. CXIII, pp. 449–472, 1871), before he had formulated, even in his own mind, the principle of pragmaticism, is the scholastic doctrine of realism. This is usually defined as the opinion that there are real objects that are general, among the number being the modes of determination of existent singulars, if, indeed, these be not the only such objects. But the belief in this can hardly escape being accompanied by the acknowledgment that there are, besides, real *vagues*, and especially real possibilities. For possibility being the denial of a necessity, which is a kind of generality, is vague like any other contradiction of a general. Indeed, it is the reality of some possibilities that pragmaticism is most concerned to insist upon. The article of Jan., 1878, endeavored to [gloss] over this point as unsuited to the esoteric public addressed; or perhaps the writer wavered in his own mind. He said that if a diamond were to be formed in a bed of cotton-wool, and were to be consumed there without ever having been pressed upon by any hard edge or point, it would be merely a question of nomenclature whether that diamond should be said to have been hard or not. No doubt, this is true, except for the abominable falsehood in the word MERELY, implying that symbols are unreal. Nomenclature involves classification; and classification is true or false, and the generals to which it refers are either reals in the one case, or figments in the other. For if the reader will turn to the original maxim of pragmaticism at the beginning of this article, he will see that the question is, not what *did* happen, but whether it would have been well to engage in any line of conduct whose successful issue depended upon whether that diamond *would* resist an attempt to scratch it, or whether all other logical means of determining how it ought to be classed *would* lead to the conclusion which, to quote the very words of that article, would be "the belief which alone could be the result of investigation carried *sufficiently far.*" Pragmaticism makes the ultimate intellectual purport of what you please to consist in conceived conditional resolutions, or their substance; and therefore, the conditional propositions, with their hypothetical antecedents, in which such resolutions consist, being of the ultimate nature of meaning, must be capable of being true, that is, of expressing whatever there be that is such as the proposition expresses, independently of being thought to be so in any judgment, or being represented to be so in any other symbol of any man or men. But that amounts to saying that possibility is sometimes of a real kind.

Fully to understand this, it will be needful to analyze modality, and ascertain in what it consists. In the simplest case, the most subjective meaning, if a person does not know that a proposition is false, he calls it *possible*. If, however, he knows that it is *true*, it is much more than possible. Restricting the word to its characteristic applicability, a state of things has the modality of the possible—that is, of the merely possible —only in case the contradictory state of things is likewise possible, which proves possibility to be the vague modality. One who knows that Harvard University has an office in State Street, Boston, and has the impression that it is at No. 30, but yet suspects that 50 is the number, would say "I think it is at No. 30, but it *may* be at No. 50," or "it *is possibly* at No. 50." Thereupon, another, who does not doubt his recollection, might chime in, "It *actually is* at No. 50," or simply "it *is* at No. 50," or "it *is* at No. 50, *de inesse.*" Thereupon, the person who had first asked, what the number was might say, "Since you are so positive, it *must be* at No. 50," for "I know the first figure is 5. So, since you are both certain the second is a 0, why 50 it *necessarily is.*" That is to say, in this most subjective kind of modality, that which is known by direct recollection is in the mode of *actuality*, the determinate mode. But when knowledge is indeterminate among alternatives, either there is one state of things that alone accords with them all, when this is the mode of *necessity*, or there is more than one state of things that no knowledge excludes, when each of these is in the mode of *possibility*.

Other kinds of subjective modality refer to a sign or representamen which is assumed to be true, but which does not include the utterer's (i.e., the speaker's, writer's, thinker's or other symbolizer's) total knowledge, the different modes being distinguished very much as above.

There are other cases, however, in which, justifiably or not, we certainly think of modality as objective. A man says, "I *can go* to the seashore if I like." Here is implied, to be sure, his ignorance of how he will decide to act. But this is not the point of the assertion. It is that the complete determination of conduct in the *act* not yet having taken place, the further determination of it belongs to the subject of the action regardless of external circumstances. If he had said, "I *must* go where my employers may send me," it would imply that the function of such further determination lay elsewhere. In "You *may* do so and so," and "You *must* do so," the "may" has the same force as "can," except that in the one case freedom from particular circumstances is in question, and in the other freedom from a law or edict. Hence the phrase, "You *may* if you *can.*" I must say that it is difficult for me to preserve my respect for the competence of a philosopher whose dull logic, not penetrating beneath the surface, leaves him to regard such phrases as misrepresentations of the truth. So an act of hypostatic abstraction that in itself is no violation of logic, however it may lend itself to a dress of superstition, may regard the collective tendencies to variableness in the world, under the name of chance, as at one time having their way, and at another time overcome by the element of order; so that, for example, a superstitious cashier, impressed by a bad dream, may say to himself of a Monday morning, "*May be*, the bank has been robbed." No doubt, he recognizes his total ignorance in the matter. But besides that, he has in mind the absence of any particular cause that should protect his bank more than others that are robbed from time to time. He thinks of the variety in the universe as vaguely analogous to the indecision of a person, and borrows from that analogy the garb of his thought. At the other extreme stand those who declare as inspired (for they have no rational proof of what they allege), that an actuary's advice to an insurance company is based on nothing at all but ignorance.

There is another example of objective possibility: "A pair of intersecting rays, i.e., unlimited straight lines conceived as movable objects, *can* (or *may*) move, without ceasing to intersect, so that one and the same hyperboloid shall be completely covered by the track of each of them." How shall we interpret this, remembering that the object spoken of, the pair of rays, is a pure creation of the utterer's imagination, although it is required (and, indeed, forced) to conform to the laws of space? Some minds will be better satisfied with a more subjective or nominalistic interpretation, others with a more objective or realistic interpretation. But it must be confessed on all hands that whatever degree or kind of reality belongs to pure space belongs to the substance of that proposition, which merely expresses a property of space.

Let us now take up the case of that diamond which, having been crystallized upon a cushion of jeweler's cotton, was accidentally consumed by fire before the crystal of corundum that had been sent for had had time to arrive, and indeed without being subjected to any other pressure than that of the atmosphere and its own weight. The question is, was that diamond *really* hard? It is certain that no discernible *actual* fact determined it to be so. But is its hardness not, nevertheless, a *real fact?* To say, as the article of January, 1878, seems to intend, that it is just as an arbitrary "usage of speech" chooses to arrange its thoughts, is as much as to decide against the reality of the property, since the real is that which is such as it is regardless of how it is, at any time, thought to be. Remember that this diamond's condition is not an isolated fact. There is no such thing; and an isolated fact could hardly be real. It is an unsevered, though prescis part of the unitary fact of nature. Being a diamond, it was a mass of pure carbon, in the form of a more or less transparent crystal (brittle, and of facile octahedral cleavage, unless it was of an unheard of variety), which, if not trimmed after one of the fashions in which diamonds may be trimmed, took the shape of an octahedron, apparently regular (I need not go into minutiae), with grooved edges, and probably with some curved faces. Without being subjected to any considerable pressure, it could be found to be insoluble, very highly refractive, showing under radium rays (and perhaps under "dark light" and X-rays) a peculiar bluish phosphorescence, having as high a specific gravity as realgar or orpiment, and giving off during its combustion less heat than any other form of carbon would have done. From some of these properties hardness is believed to be inseparable. For like it they bespeak the high polymerization of the molecule. But however this may be, how can the hardness of all other diamonds fail to bespeak *some* real relation among the diamonds without which a piece of carbon would not be a diamond? Is it not a monstrous perversion of the word and concept *real* to say that the accident of the nonarrival of the corundum prevented the hardness of the diamond from having the *reality* that it otherwise, with little doubt, would have had?

At the same time, we must dismiss the idea that the occult state of things (be it a relation among atoms or something else), that constitutes the reality of a diamond's hardness can possibly consist in anything but in the truth of a general conditional proposition. For to what else does the entire teaching of chemistry relate except to the "behavior" of different possible kinds of material substance? And in what does that behavior consist except that if a substance of a certain kind should be exposed to an agency of a certain kind, a certain kind of sensible result *would* ensue, according to our experiences hitherto. As for the pragmaticist, it is precisely his position that nothing else than this can be so much as *meant* by saying that an object possesses a character. He is therefore obliged to subscribe to the doctrine of a real modality, including real necessity and real possibility.

A good question, for the purpose of illustrating the nature of pragmaticism, is, What is time? It is not proposed to attack those most difficult problems connected with the psychology, the epistemology, or the metaphysics of time, although it will be taken for granted, as it must be according to what has been said, that time is real. The reader is only invited to the humbler question of what we mean by time, and not of every kind of meaning attached to past, present, and future either. Certain peculiar feelings are associated with the three general determinations of time, but those are to be sedulously put out of view. That the reference of events to time is irresistible will be recognized; but as to how it may differ from other kinds of irresistibility is a question not here to be considered. The question to be considered is simply, What is the intellectual purport of the past, present, and future? It can only be treated with the utmost brevity.

That time is a particular variety of objective modality is too obvious for argumentation. The past consists of the sum of *faits accomplis* and this accomplishment is the existential mode of time. For the past really acts upon us, and *that* it does, not at all in the way in which a law or principle influences us, but precisely as an existent object acts. For instance, when a *Nova Stella* bursts out in the heavens, it acts upon one's eyes just as a light struck in the dark by one's own hands would; and yet it is an event that happened before the pyramids were built. A neophyte may remark that its reaching the eyes, which is all we know, happens but a fraction of a second before we know it. But a moment's considera- tion will show him that he is losing sight of the question, which is not whether the distant past can act upon us *immediately*, but whether it acts upon us just as any existent does. The instance adduced (certainly a commonplace enough fact), proves conclusively that the mode of the past is that of actuality. Nothing of the sort is true of the future, to compass the understanding of which it is indispensable that the reader should divest himself of his necessitarianism—at best, but a scientific theory—and return to the Common-Sense state of nature. Do you never say to yourself, "I *can* do this or that as well tomorrow as today"? Your necessitarianism is a theoretical pseudo-belief—a make-believe belief— that such a sentence does not express the real truth. That is only to stick to proclaiming the unreality of that time, of which you are invited, be it reality or figment, to consider the meaning. You need not fear to compromise your darling theory by looking out at its windows. Be it true in theory or not, the unsophisticated conception is that everything in the future is either *destined*, i.e., necessitated already, or is *undecided*, the contingent future of Aristotle. In other words, it is not actual, since it does not act except through the idea of it, that is, as a law acts; but is either necessary or possible, which are of the same mode since (as remarked above) negation being outside the category of modality cannot produce a variation in modality. As for the present instant, it is so inscrutable that I wonder whether no skeptic has ever attacked its reality. I can fancy one of them dipping his pen in his blackest ink to commence the assault, and then suddenly reflecting that his entire life is in the present—the "living present," as we say, this instant when all hopes and fears concerning it come to their end, this living death in which we are born anew. It is plainly that nascent state between the determinate and the indeterminate that was noticed above.

Pragmaticism consists in holding that the purport of any concept is its conceived bearing upon our conduct. How, then, does the past bear upon conduct? The answer is self-evident: Whenever we set out to do anything, we "go upon," we base our conduct on facts already known, and for these we can only draw upon our memory. It is true that we may institute a new investigation for the purpose; but its discoveries will only become applicable to conduct after they have been made and reduced to a memorial maxim. In short, the past is the storehouse of all our knowledge.

When we say that we know that some state of things exists, we mean that it used to exist, whether just long enough for the news to reach the brain and be retransmitted to tongue or pen, or longer ago. Thus, from whatever point of view we contemplate the past, it appears as the existential mode of time.

How does the future bear upon conduct? The answer is that future facts are the only facts that we can, in a measure, control; and whatever there may be in the future that is not amenable to control are the things that we *shall* be able to infer, or *should* be able to infer under favorable circumstances. There may be questions concerning which the pendulum of opinion never would cease to oscillate, however favorable circumstances may be. But if so, those questions are *ipso facto* not *real* questions, that is to say, are questions to which there is no true answer to be given. It is natural to use the future tense (and the conditional mood is but a mollified future) in drawing a conclusion or in stating a consequence. "If two unlimited straight lines in one plane and crossed by a third making the sum . . . then these straight lines *will* meet on the side, etc." It cannot be denied that acritical inferences may refer to the past in its capacity as past; but according to pragmaticism, the conclusion of a reasoning power must refer to the future. For its meaning refers to conduct, and since it is a reasoned conclusion must refer to deliberate conduct, which is controllable conduct. But the only controllable conduct is future conduct. As for that part of the past that lies beyond memory, the pragmaticist doctrine is that the meaning of its being believed to be in connection with the past consists in the acceptance as truth of the conception that we ought to conduct ourselves according to it (like the meaning of any other belief). Thus, a belief that Christopher Columbus discovered America really refers to the future. It is more difficult, it must be confessed, to account for beliefs that rest upon the double evidence of feeble but direct memory and upon rational inference. The difficulty does not seem insuperable; but it must be passed by.

What is the bearing of the present instant upon conduct?

Introspection is wholly a matter of inference. One is immediately conscious of his feelings, no doubt; but not that they are feelings of an *ego*. The *self* is only inferred. There is no time in the present for any inference at all, least of all for inference concerning that very instant. Consequently the present object must be an external object, if there be any objective reference in it. The attitude of the present is either conative or perceptive. Supposing it to be perceptive, the perception must be immediately known as external—not indeed in the sense in which a hallucination is *not* external, but in the sense of being present regardless of the perceiver's will or wish. Now this kind of externality is conative externality. Consequently, the attitude of the present instant (according to the testimony of common sense, which is plainly adopted throughout) can only be a conative attitude. The consciousness of the present is then that of a struggle over what shall be; and thus we emerge from the study with a confirmed belief that it is the nascent state of the actual.

But how is temporal modality distinguished from other objective modality? Not by any general character since time is unique and *sui generis*. In other words there is only one time. Sufficient attention has hardly been called to the surpassing truth of this for time as compared with its truth for space. Time, therefore, can only be identified by brute compulsion. But we must not go further.

Milford. Pa.

VII. Some Contributions to Baldwin's Dictionary

PEIRCE WROTE A number of definitions for James Baldwin's *Dictionary of Philosophy and Psychology*, which was published in 1902. Reproduced here are three of them, "pragmatism," "uniformity," and "synechism," which may serve to give a summary of the main doctrines of Peirce's thought.

In the definition of pragmatism there is a paragraph marked "W. J.," which was contributed by William James and gives his definition of that doctrine.

1. Pragmatism

. . . (2) The opinion that metaphysics is to be largely cleared up by the application of the following maxim for attaining clearness of apprehension: " Consider what effects, that might conceivably have practical bearings, we conceive the object of our conception to have. Then, our conception of these effects is the whole of our conception of the object." (C. S. P.)

The doctrine that the whole "meaning" of a conception expresses itself in practical consequences, consequences either in the shape of conduct to be recommended, or in that of experiences to be expected, if the conception be true; which consequences would be different if it were untrue, and must be different from the consequences by which the meaning of other conceptions is in turn expressed. If a second conception should not appear to have other consequences, then it must really be only the first conception under a different name. In methodology it is certain that to trace and compare their respective consequences is an admirable way of establishing the differing meanings of different conceptions.   (w. j.)

This maxim was first proposed by Charles S. Peirce in the *Popular Science Monthly* for January, 1878 (xii. 287); and he explained how it was to be applied to the doctrine of reality. The writer was led to the maxim by reflection upon Kant's *Critic of the Pure Reason*. Substantially the same way of dealing with ontology seems to have been practiced by the Stoics. The writer subsequently saw that the principle might easily be misapplied, so as to sweep away the whole doctrine of incommensurables, and, in fact, the whole Weierstrassian way of regarding the calculus. In 1896 William James published his *Will to Believe*, and later his *Philosophical Conceptions and Practical Results*, which pushed this method to such extremes as must tend to give us pause. The doctrine appears to assume that the end of man is action—a stoical axiom which, to the present writer at the age of sixty, does not recommend itself so forcibly as it did at thirty. If it be admitted, on the contrary, that action wants an end, and that that end must be something of a general description, then the spirit of the maxim itself, which is that we must look to the upshot of our concepts in order rightly to apprehend them, would direct us towards something different from practical facts, namely, to general ideas, as the true interpreters of our thought. Nevertheless, the maxim has approved itself to the writer, after many years of trial, as of great utility in leading to a relatively high grade of clearness of thought. He would venture to suggest that it should always be put into practice with conscientious thoroughness, but that, when that has been done, and not before, a still higher grade of clearness of thought can be attained by remembering that the only ultimate good that the practical facts to which it directs attention can subserve is to further the development of concrete reasonableness; so that the meaning of the concept does not lie in any individual reactions at all, but in the manner in which those reactions contribute to that development. Indeed, in the article of 1878, above referred to, the writer practiced better than he preached;

for he applied the stoical maxim most unstoically, in such a sense as to insist upon the reality of the objects of general ideas in their generality.

A widely current opinion during the last quarter of a century has been that reasonableness is not a good in itself, but only for the sake of something else. Whether it be so or not seems to be a synthetical question, not to be settled by an appeal to the principle of contradiction —as if a reason for reasonableness were absurd. Almost everybody will now agree that the ultimate good lies in the evolutionary process in some way. If so, it is not in individual reactions in their segregation, but in something general or continuous. Synechism is founded on the notion that the coalescence, the becoming continuous, the becoming governed by laws, the becoming instinct with general ideas, are but phases of one and the same process of the growth of reasonableness. This is first shown to be true with mathematical exactitude in the field of logic, and is thence inferred to hold good metaphysically. It is not opposed to pragmatism in the manner in which Peirce applied it, but includes that procedure as a step. . . .　　　　　　　　　　　　　　　(c. s. p.)

2.　Uniformity

. . . (1) A fact consisting in this: that, of a certain genus of facts, a proportion approaching unity (the whole) belong, in the course of experience, to a certain species; so that, though of itself the knowledge of this uniformity gives no information concerning a certain thing or character, yet it will strengthen any inductive conclusion of a certain kind.

It is, therefore, a high objective probability concerning an objective probability. There are, in particular, four classes of uniformities, the knowledge of any of which, or of its falsity, may deductively strengthen or weaken an inductive conclusion. These four kinds of uniformity are as follows:

i.　The members of a class may present an extraordinary resemblance to one another in regard to a certain line of characters. Thus, the Icelanders are said to resemble one another most strikingly in their opinions about general subjects. Knowing this, we should not need to question many Icelanders, if we found that the first few whom we met all shared a common superstition, in order to conclude with considerable confidence that nearly all Icelanders were of the same way of thinking. Philodemus insists strongly upon this kind of uniformity as a support of induction.

ii. A character may be said that, in whatever genus it occurs at all, it almost always belongs to all the species of that genus; or this uniformity may be lacking. Thus, when only white swans were known, it would have been hazardous to assert that all swans were white, because whiteness is not usually a generic character. It is considerably more safe to assert that all crows are black, because blackness is oftener a generic character. This kind of uniformity is especially emphasized by Mill as important in inductive inquiries.

iii. A certain set of characters may be intimately connected so as to be usually all present or all absent from certain kinds of objects. Thus, the different chemical reactions of gold are so inseparable that a chemist need only to succeed in getting, say, the purple of Cassius, to be confident that the body under examination will show every reaction of gold.

iv. Of a certain object it may be known that its characteristic is that when it possesses one of a set of characters within a certain group of such sets, it possesses the rest. Thus, it may be known of a certain man that to whatever party he belongs, he is apt to embrace without reserve the entire creed of that party. We shall not, then, need to know many of his opinions, say in regard to politics, in order to infer with great confidence his position upon other political questions.

(2) The word "uniformity" plays such a singular and prominent *rôle* in the logic of Mill that it is proper to note it. He was apt to be greatly influenced by Ockham's razor in forming theories that he defended with great logical acumen; but he differed from other men of that way of thinking in that his natural candor led to his making many admissions without perceiving how fatal they were to his negative theories. In addition to that, perhaps more than other philosophers, in endeavoring to embrace several ideas under a common term, he often leaves us at a loss to find any other character common and peculiar to those notions

except that of their having received from him that common designation. In one passage of his *System of Logic* (1842), he declares, in reference to the difference in strength between two inductive conclusions, that whoever shall discover the cause of that difference will have discovered the secret of inductive reasoning. When, therefore, he shortly afterwards points out that the distinction between those two inductions is that one of them is supported by a uniformity of the second of the above four classes, while the other is met by a distinct diversity of the same kind, and when he himself gives to that uniformity this designation when he afterwards declares that the validity of induction depends upon uniformity, his reader naturally supposes he means uniformity in that sense. But we find that he employs the word for quite another purpose. Namely, he does not like the word *law*, as applied to an inductive generalization of natural facts—such as the "law" of gravitation—because it implies an element in nature, the reality of a general, which no nominalist can admit. He, therefore, desires to call the reality to which a true universal proposition about natural phenomena corresponds, a "uniformity." The implication of the word, thus used, is that the facts are, in themselves, entirely disconnected, and that it is the mind alone which unites them. One stone dropping to the earth has no real connection with another stone dropping to the earth. It is, surely, not difficult to see that this theory of uniformities, far from helping to establish the validity of induction, would be, if consistently admitted, an insuperable objection to such validity. For if two facts, *A* and *B*, are entirely independent in their real nature, then the truth of *B* cannot follow, either necessarily or probably, from the truth of *A*. If I have tried the experiment with a million stones and have found that every one of them fell when allowed to drop, it may be very natural for me to believe that almost any stone will act in the same way. But if it can be proved that there is no real connection between the behavior of different stones, then there is nothing for it but to say that it was a chance coincidence that those million stones all behaved in the same way; for if there was any *reason* for it, and they *really* dropped, there was a *real reason*, that is, a real general. Now, if it is mere chance that they all dropped, that affords no more reason for supposing that the next will drop, than my throwing three double-sixes successively with a pair of dice is a reason for thinking that the next throw will be double-sixes.

(3)   But now we find that Mill's good sense and candor will not allow him to take the course that a Hobbes would have taken, and utterly deny the validity of induction; and this leads to a new use of the word *uniformity*, in which he speaks of the "uniformity of nature." Before asking exactly what this phrase means, it may be noted that, whatever it means, the assertion of it is an assent to scholastic realism, except for a difference of emphasis. For to say that throughout the whole course of experience, events always, or even only usually, happen alike under the same conditions (what is usually called the "invariability" of nature), is to assert an agreement (complete or partial) that could not be ascribed to chance without self-contradiction. For chance is merely the possible discrepancy between the character of the limited experience to which it belongs and the whole course of experience. Hence, to say that of the *real*, objective facts some *general* character can be predicated, is to assert the reality of a general. It only differs from scholastic realism in that Mill and his followers treat this aspect of the matter lightly—that is to say, the objective reality of the general—while the Scholastics regarded it as a great and vital feature of the universe. Instead of "uniformity" now importing that what others call "laws" are fabrications of the human mind, this "uniformity of nature" is erected by Mill into the greatest of laws and absolutely objective and real.

Let us now inquire what the "uniformity of nature," with its synonymous expressions that "the future resembles the past," and so forth, can mean. Mill says that it means that if all the circumstances attending two phenomena are the same, they will be alike. But taken strictly this means absolutely nothing, since no two phenomena ever can happen in circumstances precisely alike, nor are two phenomena precisely alike. It is, therefore, necessary to modify the statement in order to give it any meaning at all; and it will be found that, however it may be so modified, the moment it begins to carry a definite meaning, one of three things results: it becomes either, first, grossly false, or, second, an assertion that there is really no good reason to believe even approximately true, or thirdly, it becomes a quasi-subjective truth, not lending any color of validity to induction proper. If, for example, we were to say that under any given species of circumstances presenting any similarity, phenomena of any given genus would be found to have a specific general resemblance in contrast with the specific character of phenomena of the same genus occurring under a different species of circumstances of the same genus, this would be monstrously false, whether intended as an absolutely universal proposition or merely as one approximately true. Let, for example, the genus of phenomena be the values of the throws of a pair of dice in a given series of successive throws indefinitely continued. Let the first species of circumstances be that the ordinal number of a throw in the series is *prime*. It is pretty certain that there would be no general character in the corresponding values of throws to distinguish them from those that would result when the ordinal number is divisible by 2, or by 3, or by any other prime. It thus appears that when we take *any* genus of circumstances, the law turns out false. Suppose, then, that we modify it by saying that, taking any genus of phenomena and separating this into two species, there will be found in the discoverable circumstances *some* general resemblance for all those attending phenomena of the same species in contrast to those attending phenomena of the other species. This is a proposition that there is not the slightest reason to believe. Take, for example, as the genus of phenomena, the many thousands of Latin descriptions of American species of plants by Asa Gray and his scholars. Now consider the species of this genus of phenomena that agree in this respect, that the two first words of the description have their first vowels the same. There is no reason to suppose that there was any general respect in which the circumstances of that species of the genus of phenomena agree with one another and differ from others, either universally or usually. It is a mere chance result. It is true that some persons will not be inclined to assent to this judgment; but they cannot prove it otherwise. It can afford no adequate basis for induction. We see, then, that when we consider *all* phenomena, there is no way of making the statement sufficiently definite and certain. Suppose, then, that we attempt still another modification of the law, that, of *interesting* resemblances and differences between phenomena, some considerable proportion are accompanied by corresponding resemblances and differences between those of the circumstances that appear to us to be *pertinent*. The proposition is now rather psychological than metaphysical. It would be impossible, with any evidentiary basis, to strengthen the expression "some considerable proportion"; and in other respects the statement is vague enough. Still, there is sufficient truth in it, perhaps, to warrant the presumptive adoption of hypotheses, provided this adoption merely means that they are taken as sufficiently reasonable to justify some expense in experimentation to test their truth by induction; but it gives no warrant at all to induction itself. For, in the first place, induction needs no such dubious support, since it is mathematically certain that the general character of a limited experience will, as that experience is prolonged, approximate to the character of what will be true in the long run, if anything is true in the long run. Now all that induction infers is what would be found true in the usual course of experience, if it were indefinitely prolonged. Since the method of induction must generally approximate to that truth, that is a sufficient justification for the use of that method, although no definite probability attaches to the inductive conclusion. In the second place, the law, as now formulated, neither helps nor hinders the validity of induction proper; for induction proper consists in judging of the relative frequency of a character among all the individuals of a class by the relative frequency of that character among the individuals of a random sample of that class. Now the law, as thus formulated, may tend to make our hypothesis approximately true; but that advantage has been gained before the operation of induction, which merely tests the hypothesis, begins. This inductive operation is just as valid when the hypothesis is bad as when it is good, when the character dealt with is trivial as when it is interesting. The ratio that induction ascertains may be nearer ½, and more remote from 1 or 0, when the characters are uninteresting; and in that case a larger number of instances will usually be requisite for obtaining the ratio with any given degree of precision (for if the ratio is really 1 or 0, it will be almost a miracle if in the sample it is far from that ratio, although this will not be impossible, if the whole class is infinite), but the essential validity of the process of induction remains unaffected by that circumstance.

What is usually meant by the uniformity of nature probably is that in proportion as the circumstances are alike or unlike, so are any phenomena connected with them alike or unlike. It may be asked to what degree nature is uniform in that sense. The only tenable answer is that it is as little uniform as it possibly could be imagined to be; for were any considerable proportion of existing uniformities, or laws, of nature destroyed, others would necessarily thereby result.

In fact, the great characteristic of nature is its diversity. For every uniformity known, there would be no difficulty in pointing out thousands of nonuniformities; but the diversities are usually of small use to us, and attract the attention of poets mainly, while the uniformities are the very staff of life. Hence, the higher and wider are our desires, the greater will be the general impression of uniformity produced upon us by the contemplation of nature as it interests us.

(4)   There are senses in which nature may not irrationally be held to be uniform; but opinions differ very widely as to the extent and nature of this uniformity. The chief of these are as follows:

(a)   The majority of physicists, at least of the older generation, hold, with regard to the physical universe, that its elements are masses, their positions, and the variations of these positions with time. It is believed that every motion exactly obeys certain laws of attraction and repulsion; and there is no other kind of law, except that each atom or corpuscle is a center of energy arranged in equipotential surfaces about it, which follow a regular law; and that this is a permanency. But the equations of motion are differential equations of the second order, involving, therefore, two arbitrary constants for each moving atom or corpuscle, and there is no uniformity connected with these constants. At least, no such uniformity is, with the least probability, discoverable. As for the distribution of potential about an atom or corpuscle, it is regular; but there is no ulterior reason for that regularity, or, at least, none is probably discoverable. What is absolutely beyond discovery, whether direct and specific or indirect and general, may be considered to be nonexistent.

From this usual and in some sense standard opinion there are many divergences in both directions. First, in the direction of greater uniformity.

(b) Some hold that there is some exact uniformity in the arbitrary constants of the motion of the atoms, so that, for example, perhaps at some initial instant they all had some symmetrical or regular arrangement, like a pack of cards unshuffled; and that the velocities at that instant were regular also. But this regularity being of a purely aesthetic or formal kind, and the laws of motion equally formal and unrelated to any purpose, it follows that all kinds of arrangements will be produced, ungoverned by any uniformity, but mere effects of chance. Three stars may, for example, at some instant form an equilateral triangle; but there would be no particular reason for this: It would be merely a casual coincidence.

(c) Others go further and maintain that the constants of position and velocity are subject to a law not merely formal, but are governed by final causes in such a way that there is no arrangement or coincidence whatever that was not specially intended by the Creator. To this theory, such words as *pro*-vidence and *fore*-knowledge are ill adapted; because the two constants that each atom or corpuscle has, remain constant throughout all time, and ought not to be considered as having been fixed at any particular epoch. The very idea is that the arrangement is determined by what would be the result of different arrangements at each period of time. If, for example, a given prayer effects rain, it must be supposed that in view of that prayer, and as its consequence, the different atoms had the appropriate constants; but that these were not given to the atoms at any particular epoch, being permanent values. Any intentional action on the part of a free agent is to be explained in the same way. If an agent is to be supposed really free, it is difficult to see what other physical explanation is compatible with the exactitude of law. This seems to be substantially the notion of most of those who have supported free will.

On the other hand, many philosophers suppose a less degree of uniformity in nature than is supposed in opinion *(a)*. Of these the following have come to the present writer's notice as being actually defended.

(d) Some suppose that while law is absolute, yet there are constantly arising cases analogous to unstable equilibrium in which, owing to a passage of a velocity through infinity or otherwise, the law does not

determine what the motion shall be. Thus if one Boscovichian point attracts another inversely as the square of the distance, and they move in one straight line, then when they come together they may move through one another, or move backwards on the same line, or may separate along any other line, without violating the differential equation. Such "singularities," as the mathematicians say, are theoretically possible; and may be supposed to occur very often. But to suppose that free action becomes possible in such a way is very illogical. In the first place it supposes a direct interaction between "mind" and matter; infinitesimal, no doubt, but none the less real. Why not better suppose a slight but finite action of this kind and so avoid the following objections? Namely, in the second place, this is to put faith, not scientific credence, in the inductive laws of matter infinitely beyond what induction can ever warrant. We know very well that mind, in some sense, acts on matter, and matter on mind: the question is *how*. It is not in speculations of this fanciful kind that the true answer is likely to be found. In the third place, although this speculation wanders so far beyond all present knowledge, it nevertheless comes into conflict with a legitimate induction, namely, the supposition of any real "singularity" or breach of continuity in nature is in as distinct conflict with all our knowledge as is a miracle.

(e) Sundry far less tenable hypotheses of lacunae between inviolable laws have often been proposed. One opinion frequently met with is that the law of energy does not prescribe the direction of velocity; but only its amount; so that the mind can cause atoms to "swerve," in regular Lucretian fashion. This singular notion has even been embraced by mathematicians, who are thinking of a projectile shot into a curved tube, or other case of an equation of condition. Of course, if mind can construct absolute constraints, it can much easier exert force that is finite. Other writers suppose lacunae, without telling us of what particular description they are; they seem to think law is absolute as far as it goes, but that its jurisdiction is limited.

(f) Much more philosophical and less logically objectionable is the notion of St. Augustine and others (it is near to the opinion of Aristotle) that the only fundamental kind of causation is the action of final causes; and that efficient causation is, in all cases, secondary. Accordingly, when

a miracle occurs there is no violation of the real *cursus naturae*, but only of the apparent course of things.

(g)   The hypothesis suggested by the present writer is that all laws are results of evolution; that underlying all other laws is the only tendency that can grow by its own virtue, the tendency of all things to take habits. Now since this same tendency is the one sole fundamental law of mind, it follows that the physical evolution works towards ends in the same way that mental action works towards ends, and thus in one aspect of the matter it would be perfectly true to say that final causation is alone primary. Yet, on the other hand, the law of habit is a simple formal law, a law of efficient causation; so that either way of regarding the matter is equally true, although the former is more fully intelligent. Meantime, if law is a result of evolution, which is a process lasting through all time, it follows that no law is absolute. That is, we must suppose that the phenomena themselves involve departures from law analogous to errors of observation. But the writer has not supposed that this phenomenon had any connection with free will. In so far as evolution follows a law, the law of habit, instead of being a movement from homogeneity to heterogeneity, is growth from difformity to uniformity. But the chance divergences from law are perpetually acting to increase the variety of the world, and are checked by a sort of natural selection and otherwise (for the writer does not think the selective principle sufficient), so that the general result may be described as "organized heterogeneity," or better rationalized variety. In view of the principle of continuity, the supreme guide in framing philosophical hypotheses, we must, under this theory, regard matter as mind whose habits have become fixed so as to lose the powers of forming them and losing them, while mind is to be regarded as a chemical genus of extreme complexity and instability. It has acquired in a remarkable degree a habit of taking and laying aside habits. The fundamental divergences from law must here be most extraordinarily high, although probably very far indeed from attaining any directly observable magnitude. But their effect is to cause the laws of mind to be themselves of so fluid a character as to simulate divergences from law. All this, according to the writer, constitutes a hypothesis capable of being tested by experiment.

Literature: besides most treatises on LOGIC (q.v., especially inductive) see Renouvier and Prat, *La nouvelle Monadologie* (1899). . . .

(C. S. P.)

3. Synechism

Synechism [Gr. συνεχης, continuous holding together, from συν + εχειν, to hold]: not in use in the other languages. That tendency of philosophical thought that insists upon the idea of continuity as of prime importance in philisophy, and in particular, upon the necessity of hypotheses involving true continuity.

A true CONTINUUM (q.v.) is something whose possibilities of determination no multitude of individuals can exhaust. Thus, no collection of points placed upon a truly continuous line can fill the line so as to leave no room for others, although that collection had a point for every value towards which numbers endlessly continued into the decimal places could approximate; nor if it contained a point for every possible permutation of all such values. It would be in the general spirit of synechism to hold that time ought to be supposed truly continuous in that sense. The term was suggested and used by Charles S. Peirce in *The Monist*, ii. 534 (July, 1892). Cf. PRAGMATISM, passim.

The general motive is to avoid the hypothesis that this or that is inexplicable. For the synechist maintains that the only possible justification for so much as entertaining a hypothesis, is that it affords an explanation of the phenomena. Now, to suppose a thing inexplicable is not only to fail to explain it, and so to make an unjustifiable hypothesis, but much worse—it is to set up a barrier across the road of science, and to forbid all attempts to understand the phenomenon.

To be sure, the synechist cannot deny that there is an element of the inexplicable and ultimate, because it is directly forced upon him; nor does he abstain from generalizing from this experience. True generality is, in fact, nothing but a rudimentary form of true continuity. Continuity is nothing but perfect generality of a law of relationship.

It would, therefore, be most contrary to his own principle for the synechist not to generalize from that which experience forces upon him, especially since it is only so far as facts can be generalized that they can be understood; and the very reality, in his way of looking at the matter, is nothing else than the way in which facts must ultimately come to be understood. There would be a contradiction here, if this ultimacy were looked upon as something to be absolutely realized; but the synechist cannot consistently so regard it. Synechism is not an ultimate and absolute metaphysical doctrine; it is a regulative principle of logic, prescribing what sort of hypotheses are fit to be entertained and examined. The synechist, for example, would never be satisfied with the hypothesis that matter is composed of atoms, all spherical and exactly alike. If this is the only hypothesis that the mathematicians are as yet in condition to handle, it may be supposed that it may have features of resemblance with the truth. But neither the eternity of the atoms nor their precise resemblance is, in the synechist's view, an element of the hypothesis that is even admissible hypothetically. For that would be to attempt to explain the phenomena by means of an absolute inexplicability. In like manner, it is not a hypothesis fit to be entertained that any given law is absolutely accurate. It is not, upon synechist principles, a question to be asked, whether the three angles of a triangle amount precisely to two right angles, but only whether the sum is greater or less. So the synechist will not believe that some things are conscious and some unconscious, unless by consciousness be meant a certain grade of feeling. He will rather ask what are the circumstances that raise this grade; nor will he consider that a chemical formula for protoplasm would be a sufficient answer. In short, synechism amounts to the principle that inexplicabilities are not to be considered as possible explanations; that whatever is supposed to be ultimate is supposed to be inexplicable; that continuity is the absence of ultimate parts in that which is divisible; and that the form under which alone anything can be understood is the form of generality, which is the same thing as continuity. . . .   (C.S.P.)

Suggestions for Further Reading

The Collected Papers of Charles Sanders Peirce, 8 Vols., Volumes I–VI edited by Charles Hartshorne and Paul Weiss, (Cambridge: Harvard University Press, 1931–35). Volumes VII and VIII edited by Arthur W. Burks (Cambridge: Harvard University Press, 1958).

The Papers of Charles S. Peirce: Microfilm Edition. The Harvard University Library Microreproduction Service, Houghton Library, Cambridge, Massachusetts, 1967. Reels 1–30.

Robin, Richard S., *Annotated Catalogue of the Papers of Charles S. Peirce* (Amherst: The University of Massachusetts Press, 1967).

Bernstein, Richard J., ed., *Perspectives on Peirce* (New Haven: Yale University Press, 1966). Five essays discussing Peirce's place in American thought, and analyzing his logic of discovery, his concept of action, and his notion of community.

Boler, John F., *Charles Peirce and Scholastic Realism* (Seattle: The University of Washington Press, 1963). A careful discussion of Peirce's realistic position and its relation to his logic, pragmatism, and idealism.

Buchler, Justus, *Charles Peirce's Empiricism* (New York: Harcourt, Brace, 1939). An exposition of the methodological side of Peirce's thought. A discussion of his empiricism, his critical common-sensism, pragmatism, and his theory of the formal sciences.

Feiblelman, James, *An Introduction to Peirce's Philosophy* (New York: Harper, 1946). One of the earliest introductions to the general philosophy of Peirce with an effort to interpret his work as a philosophical system.

Gallie, W. B., *Peirce and Pragmatism* (Harmondsworth, Middlesex: Penguin, 1952). An introduction to Peirce for the general reader of philosophy with chapters on his relation to Cartesianism, his critical common-sensism and his theory of signs.

Goudge, Thomas A., *The Thought of C. S. Peirce* (Toronto: University of Toronto Press, 1950). An interpretation of Peirce that sees him as having two basic views, which the author describes as "naturalism" and "transcendentalism." The major discrepancies in Peirce's philosophy are considered as effects of the antagonism of these two views.

Leib, Irwin C., ed., *Charles S. Peirce's Letters to Lady Welby* (New Haven: Whitlock, 1953). An interesting set of letters containing correspondence in the years 1903–1911 between Peirce and Lady (Victoria) Welby. A primary emphasis is on Peirce's theory of signs.

Moore, Edward C., *American Pragmatism: Peirce, James and Dewey* (New York: Columbia University Press, 1961). An elaboration of a number of the ideas discussed in the introduction to the present set of selections. Particular attention is given to pragmatism as a theory of meaning and its uses by Peirce, James, and Dewey.

Moore, Edward C. and Richard S. Robin, eds., *Studies in the Philosophy of Charles Sanders Peirce: Second Series* (Amherst: The University of Massachusetts Press, 1964). A collection of twenty-six essays by various scholars concluding with an extensive bibliography by Max H. Fisch. The book begins with a section of biographical material, followed by sections on logic, pragmatism, normative science, and metaphysics.

Murphey, Murray G., *The Development of Peirce's Philosophy* (Cambridge: Harvard University Press, 1961). The classic effort to establish the basic principles upon which Peirce's philosophy rests. A serious effort to interpret the chronology of Peirce's thought.

Potter, Vincent G., S. J., *Charles S. Peirce on Norms and Ideals* (Amherst: The University of Massachusetts Press, 1967). An analysis of Peirce's views on the normative sciences and their relations to his pragmatism and metaphysics.

Thompson, Manley, *The Pragmatic Philosophy of C. S. Peirce* (Chicago: University of Chicago Press, 1953). A treatment of the chronological development of Peirce's pragmatism with its relations to his early epistemology and his later metaphysics.

Wiener, Philip P., *Evolution and the Founders of Pragmatism* (Cambridge, Harvard University Press, 1949). A study of the varieties and origins of pragmatism. Emphasis on the influence of evolution on such philosophers as Peirce, Chauncey Wright, and William James.

Wiener, Philip P. and Frederick H. Young, eds., *Studies in the Philosophy of Charles Sanders Peirce* (Cambridge: Harvard University Press, 1952). A collection of twenty-four essays on various aspects of Peirce's philosophy by an early (1952) group of Peirce scholars.

Suggestions for Future Reading (Post 1972)

WRITINGS BY PEIRCE

Contributions to the Nation. 3 vols. Compiled and annotated by K.L. Ketner and J.E. Cook. Lubbock: Texas Tech Press, 1975–79.

The New Elements of Mathematics. 4 vols. Edited by Carolyn Eisele. The Hague: Mouton Publishers, 1976.

Reasoning and the Nature of Things: The Cambridge Conferences Lectures of 1898. Edited by K. L. Ketner. Cambridge: Harvard University Press, 1992. Hilary Putnam's commentary is noteworthy.

Semiotic and Significs: The Correspondence between Charles S. Peirce and Victoria Lady Welby. Edited by Charles Hardwick. Bloomington: Indiana University Press, 1977. This is an expanded version of Irwin Leib's Charles S. Peirce's Letters to Lady Welby.

Writings of Charles S. Peirce: A Chronological Edition. 5 vols. (30 projected). Edited by Max Fisch, E. C. Moore, Christian J.W. Kloesel, and Nathan Houser. Bloomington: Indiana University Press, 1982–.

WRITINGS ABOUT PEIRCE

Anderson, D. *The Strands of System: The Philosophy of Charles Peirce.* Lafayette: Purdue University Press, 1995.

Apel, K.-O. *Charles S. Peirce: From Pragmatism to Pragmaticism.* Amherst: University of Massachusetts Press, 1981.

Brent, J. *Charles Sanders Peirce: A Life.* Bloomington: Indiana University Press, 1993, revised 1998.

Brunning, J. and Forster, P. eds. *The Rule of Reason: The Philosophy of Charles Sanders Peirce.* Toronto: University of Toronto Press, 1997.

Colapietro, V. *Peirce's Approach to the Self: A Semiotic Perspective on Human Subjectivity.* Albany: State University of New York Press, 1989.

Corrington, R. *An Introduction to C. S. Peirce: Philosopher, Semiotician, and Ecstatic Naturalist.* Lanham: Rowman and Littlefield, 1993.

Delaney, C. *Science, Knowledge, and Mind.* Notre Dame: University of Notre Dame Press, 1993.

Eisele, C. *Studies in the Scientific and Mathematical Philosophy of Charles S. Peirce.* The Hague: Mouton Publishers, 1979.

Esposito, J. *Evolutionary Metaphysics: The Development of Peirce's Theory of Categories.* Athens: Ohio University Press, 1980.

Fisch, Matt. *Peirce, Semeiotic, and Pragmaticism.* Bloomington: Indiana University Press, 1986.

Hausman, C. *Charles S. Peirce's Evolutionary Philosophy.* New York: Cambridge University Press, 1993.

Hookway, C. *Peirce.* London: Routledge & Kegan Paul, 1985.

Kent, B. *Charles S. Peirce: Logic and the Classification of the*

Sciences. Montreal: McGill - Queen's University Press, 1987.

Liszka, J. *A General Introduction to the Semeiotic of Charles Sanders Peirce.* Bloomington: Indiana University Press, 1996.

Misak, C. *Truth and the End of Inquiry: A Peircean Account of Truth.* Oxford: Clarendon Press, 1991.

Parker, K. *The Continuity of Peirce's Thought.* Nashville and London: Vanderbilt University Press, 1998.

Potter, V. *Peirce's Philosophical Perspectives.* Edited by V. Colapietro. New York: Fordham University Press, 1996.

Raposa, M. *Peirce's Philosophy of Religion.* Bloomington: Indiana University Press, 1989.

Rescher, N. *Peirce's Philosophy of Science.* Notre Dame: University of Notre Dame Press, 1978.

Rosenthal, S. *Charles Peirce's Pragmatic Pluralism.* Albany: State University of New York Press, 1994.

Sesquicentennial Congress Papers. 6 vols. See Preface for details.

Skagestad, P. *The Road of Inquiry: Charles S. Peirce's Pragmatic Realism.* New York: Columbia University Press, 1981.

Smyth, R. *Reading Peirce Reading.* Lanham, Boulder, New York, Oxford: Rowman & Littlefield Publishers, 1997.

The Transactions of the Charles S. Peirce Society: A Quarterly Journal in American Philosophy regularly carries articles on Peirce of a scholarly interest and has done so throughout the thirty-four years of its existence. *The Journal of Speculative Philosophy,* with its interest in American philosophy, might profitably be consulted as well. *The Peirce Seminar Papers* 3 vols. has carved out a niche for itself by its focus upon the interdisciplinary potential of semiotic. *The American Journal of Semiotics and Semiotica*

deserve special mention as places where articles on Peirce
are occasionally found.

GREAT BOOKS IN PHILOSOPHY PAPERBACK SERIES

ETHICS

Aristotle—*The Nicomachean Ethics* $8.95
Marcus Aurelius—*Meditations*   5.95
Jeremy Bentham—*The Principles of Morals and Legislation*   8.95
John Dewey—*The Moral Writings of John Dewey, Revised Edition*
    (edited by James Gouinlock)   10.95
Epictetus—*Enchiridion*   4.95
Immanuel Kant—*Fundamental Principles of the Metaphysic of Morals*   5.95
John Stuart Mill—*Utilitarianism*   5.95
George Edward Moore—*Principia Ethica*   8.95
Friedrich Nietzsche—*Beyond Good and Evil*   8.95
Plato—*Protagoras, Philebus,* and *Gorgias*   7.95
Bertrand Russell—*Bertrand Russell On Ethics, Sex, and Marriage*
    (edited by Al Seckel)   19.95
Arthur Schopenhauer—*The Wisdom of Life* and *Counsels and Maxims*   6.95
Benedict de Spinoza—*Ethics* and *The Improvement of the Understanding*   9.95

SOCIAL AND POLITICAL PHILOSOPHY

Aristotle—*The Politics*   7.95
Francis Bacon—*Essays*   6.95
Mikhail Bakunin—*The Basic Bakunin: Writings, 1869–1871*
    (translated and edited by Robert M. Cutler)   11.95
Edmund Burke—*Reflections on the Revolution in France*   7.95
John Dewey—*Freedom and Culture*   10.95
G. W. F. Hegel—*The Philosophy of History*   9.95
G. W. F. Hegel—*Philosophy of Right*   9.95
Thomas Hobbes—*The Leviathan*   7.95
Sidney Hook—*Paradoxes of Freedom*   9.95
Sidney Hook—*Reason, Social Myths, and Democracy*   11.95
John Locke—*Second Treatise on Civil Government*   5.95
Niccolo Machiavelli—*The Prince*   5.95
Karl Marx (with Friedrich Engels)—*The German Ideology,*
    including *Theses on Feuerbach and Introduction to the*
    Critique of Political Economy   10.95
Karl Marx—*The Poverty of Philosophy*   7.95
Karl Marx/Friedrich Engels—*The Economic and Philosophic Manuscripts of 1844*
    and *The Communist Manifesto*   6.95
John Stuart Mill—*Considerations on Representative Government*   6.95
John Stuart Mill—*On Liberty*   5.95
John Stuart Mill—*On Socialism*   7.95
John Stuart Mill—*The Subjection of Women*   5.95
Friedrich Nietzsche—*Thus Spake Zarathustra*   9.95
Thomas Paine—*Common Sense*   5.95
Thomas Paine—*Rights of Man*   7.95
Plato—*Lysis, Phaedrus,* and *Symposium*   6.95
Plato—*The Republic*   9.95
Jean-Jacques Rousseau—*The Social Contract*   5.95
Mary Wollstonecraft—*A Vindication of the Rights of Men*   5.95
Mary Wollstonecraft—*A Vindication of the Rights of Women*   6.95

METAPHYSICS/EPISTEMOLOGY

Aristotle—*De Anima*	6.95
Aristotle—*The Metaphysics*	9.95
George Berkeley—*Three Dialogues Between Hylas and Philonous*	5.95
René Descartes—*Discourse on Method* and *The Meditations*	6.95
John Dewey—*How We Think*	10.95
John Dewey—*The Influence of Darwin on Philosophy and Other Essays*	11.95
Epicurus—*The Essential Epicurus: Letters, Principal Doctrines,*	
Vatican Sayings, and Fragments	
(translated, and with an introduction, by Eugene O'Connor)	5.95
Sidney Hook—*The Quest for Being*	11.95
David Hume—*An Enquiry Concerning Human Understanding*	6.95
David Hume—*Treatise of Human Nature*	9.95
William James—*The Meaning of Truth*	11.95
William James—*Pragmatism*	7.95
Immanuel Kant—*Critique of Practical Reason*	7.95
Immanuel Kant—*Critique of Pure Reason*	9.95
Gottfried Wilhelm Leibniz—*Discourse on Method* and the *Monadology*	6.95
John Locke—*An Essay Concerning Human Understanding*	9.95
Charles S. Peirce—*The Essential Writings*	
(edited by Edward C. Moore, preface by Richard Robin)	10.95
Plato—*The Euthyphro, Apology, Crito,* and *Phaedo*	5.95
Bertrand Russell—*The Problems of Philosophy*	8.95
George Santayana—*The Life of Reason*	9.95
Sextus Empiricus—*Outlines of Pyrrhonism*	8.95

PHILOSOPHY OF RELIGION

Marcus Tullius Cicero—*The Nature of the Gods* and *On Divination*	6.95
Ludwig Feuerbach—*The Essence of Christianity*	8.95
David Hume—*Dialogues Concerning Natural Religion*	5.95
John Locke—*A Letter Concerning Toleration*	5.95
Lucretius—*On the Nature of Things*	7.95
John Stuart Mill—*Three Essays on Religion*	7.95
Thomas Paine—*The Age of Reason*	13.95
Bertrand Russell—*Bertrand Russell On God and Religion* (edited by Al Seckel)	19.95

ESTHETICS

Aristotle—*The Poetics*	5.95
Aristotle—*Treatise on Rhetoric*	7.95

GREAT MINDS PAPERBACK SERIES

ECONOMICS

Charlotte Perkins Gilman—*Women and Economics: A Study of the*	
Economic Relation between Women and Men	11.95
John Maynard Keynes—*The General Theory of Employment, Interest, and Money*	11.95
Thomas R. Malthus—*An Essay on the Principle of Population*	14.95
Alfred Marshall—*Principles of Economics*	11.95
David Ricardo—*Principles of Political Economy and Taxation*	10.95
Adam Smith—*Wealth of Nations*	9.95
Thorstein Veblen—*Theory of the Leisure Class*	11.95

RELIGION

Thomas Henry Huxley—*Agnosticism and Christianity and Other Essays*	10.95
Ernest Renan—*The Life of Jesus*	11.95
Voltaire—*A Treatise on Toleration and Other Essays*	8.95

SCIENCE

Nicolaus Copernicus—*On the Revolutions of Heavenly Spheres*	8.95
Charles Darwin—*The Descent of Man*	18.95
Charles Darwin—*The Origin of Species*	10.95
Albert Einstein—*Relativity*	8.95
Michael Faraday—*The Forces of Matter*	8.95
Galileo Galilei—*Dialogues Concerning Two New Sciences*	9.95
Ernst Haeckel—*The Riddle of the Universe*	11.95
William Harvey—*On the Motion of the Heart and Blood in Animals*	9.95
Julian Huxley—*Evolutionary Humanism*	10.95
Edward Jenner—*Vaccination against Smallpox*	5.95
Johannes Kepler—*Epitome of Copernican Astronomy* and *Harmonies of the World*	8.95
Isaac Newton—*The Principia*	14.95
Louis Pasteur and Joseph Lister—*Germ Theory and Its Application to Medicine* and *On the Antiseptic Principle of the Practice of Surgery*	7.95
Alfred Russel Wallace—*Island Life*	16.95

HISTORY

Edward Gibbon—*On Christianity*	9.95
Herodotus—*The History*	13.95
Thucydides—*History of the Peloponnesian War*	15.95
Andrew D. White—*A History of the Warfare of Science with Theology in Christendom*	19.95

SOCIOLOGY

Emile Durkheim—*Ethics and the Sociology of Morals* (translated with an introduction by Robert T. Hall)	8.95

CRITICAL ESSAYS

Desiderius Erasmus—*The Praise of Folly*	9.95
Jonathan Swift—*A Modest Proposal and Other Satires* (with an introduction by George R. Levine)	8.95
H. G. Wells—*The Conquest of Tme* (with an introduction by Martin Gardner)	8.95

(Prices subject to change without notice.)

ORDER FORM

Prometheus Books
59 John Glenn Drive • Amherst, New York 14228–2197
Telephone: (716) 691–0133

Phone Orders (24 hours):
Toll free (800) 421–0351 • FAX (716) 691–0137
Email: PBooks6205@aol.com

Ship to: _____

Address _____

_____

City _____

County (*N.Y. State Only*) _____

Telephone _____

Prometheus Acct. # _____

❑ Payment enclosed (or)

Charge to ❑ VISA ❑ MasterCard

A/C: ☐☐☐☐☐☐☐☐☐☐☐☐☐☐☐☐☐☐☐☐☐☐☐☐☐

Exp. Date _____ / _____

Signature _____